Beyond the adoption
order

Beyond the adoption order

Challenges, interventions and adoption disruption

Julie Selwyn, Sarah Meakings
and Dinithi Wijedasa

Published by British Association
for Adoption & Fostering
(BAAF)
Saffron House
3rd Floor, 6–10 Kirby Street
London EC1N 8TS
www.baaf.org.uk

Charity registration 275689 (England and Wales)
and SC039337 (Scotland)

British Library Cataloguing in Publication Data
A catalogue record for this book is available
from the British Library

ISBN 978 1 910039 23 6

Project management by Jo Francis, Publications,
BAAF
Designed by Helen Joubert Associates
Typeset by Avon DataSet Ltd, Bidford on Avon
Printed in Great Britain by TJ International
Trade distribution by Turnaround Publisher Services,
Unit 3, Olympia Trading Estate, Coburg Road,
London N22 6TZ

BAAF is the leading UK-wide membership
organisation for all those concerned with
adoption, fostering and child care issues.

Contents

List of figures

List of tables

List of acronyms

ACA-SF   Assessment Checklist for Adolescents short form
ADD   Attention Deficit Disorder
ADHD   Attention Deficit Hyperactivity Disorder
AFCARS   Adoption and Foster Care Reporting System
ANOVA   Analysis of variance
ASD   Autistic Spectrum Disorder
ASFA   Adoption and Safe Families Act
AUK   Adoption UK
BAAF   British Association for Adoption & Fostering
BESD   Behavioural, Emotional and Social Difficulties
CAMHS   Child and Adolescent Mental Health Service
CLG   Communities and Local Government
CPR   Child Permanence Report
CPV   Child to Parent Violence
CVAA   Consortium of Voluntary Adoption Agencies
DfE   Department for Education
DCSF   Department for Children, Schools and Families
DDP   Dyadic Developmental Psychotherapy
DLA   Disability Living Allowance
DSM   Diagnostic and Statistical Manual (of Mental Disorder)
EBD   Emotional and Behavioural Difficulties
EDT   Emergency Duty Team
EHA   Event History Analysis
FASD   Foetal Alcohol Spectrum Disorder
GCSE   General Certificate of Secondary Education
GP   General Practitioner
HADS   Hospital Anxiety and Depression Scale
ID   Identifying number
LA   Local Authority
LAC   Looked After Children
LEA   Local Education Authority
MP   Member of Parliament
MTFC   Multi Treatment Foster Care
NEET   Not in Education, Employment, or Training
NHS   National Health Service
NSPCC   National Society for the Prevention of Cruelty to Children
OCD   Obsessive Compulsive Disorder

OFSTED	Office for Standards in Education, Children's Services and Skills
PALS	Post-Adoption Linking Scheme
PTSD	Post-Traumatic Stress Disorder
RAD	Reactive Attachment Disorder
RO	Residence Order
SD	Standard Deviation
SDQ	Strengths and Difficulties Questionnaire
SGO	Special Guardianship Order
SPSS	Statistical Package for the Social Sciences
SSD	Social Services Department
UK	United Kingdom
US	United States
VAA	Voluntary Adoption Agency

Acknowledgements

This study would not have been possible without funding from the Department for Education (DfE), the managers who responded to requests for information on adoption disruptions, and support in the second phase from the 13 sample local authorities. We are most grateful to the adoptive parents and adopted young people who were prepared to talk about subjects that were extremely distressing, in the hope that services might be improved for others.

We would also like to thank the members of the study's advisory group, who gave their time and were willing to comment on drafts:

Gail Peachey   Department for Education
Richard White   Department for Education

Members of the Adoption Policy Team, Department for Education
Shelagh Beckett   Independent childcare consultant
Mary Blanchard   Hampshire County Council
Barry Luckock   University of Sussex
Florence Mo   London Borough of Greenwich
Jonathan Pearce   former Chief Executive of Adoption UK
Nigel Priestley   Ridley and Hall Solicitors
Rosemarie Roberts   Programme Director for the National Implementation Team for Multidimensional Treatment Foster Care in England
Chris Smith   Consortium of Voluntary Adoption Agencies
John Simmonds   BAAF
Caroline Thomas   University of Stirling
Jim Wade   University of York

We are also very grateful to Emeritus Professor David Quinton, who undertook the analysis of the children's well-being measures, and to Paul Bassett (paul@statsconsultancy.co.uk) for statistical advice.

Notes about the authors

Professor Julie Selwyn is Director of the Hadley Centre for Adoption and Foster Care Studies, School for Policy Studies, at the University of Bristol. Before joining the university, Julie worked as a children's social worker and residential worker for 15 years. She has published widely on substitute care, including: the placement of minority ethnic children; studies of young people's views of foster care and informal kinship care; outcomes for older children placed for adoption; and letterbox contact. Research findings can be accessed at www.bristol. ac.uk/hadley. Julie is a member of the national Adoption Leadership Board, and is currently working on a study of looked after children and young people's views of how their well-being should be measured.

Dr Sarah Meakings is a Research Associate at the Hadley Centre for Adoption and Foster Care Studies, School for Policy Studies, at the University of Bristol. With an early career in mental health nursing, her doctoral thesis examined the service provision for young people with serious emotional and behavioural difficulties. Sarah has been involved in a range of research activity at the university, including work on a large study of informal kinship care, and the national adoption disruption studies in England and Wales. She has recently joined a multi-disciplinary research team at Cardiff University, to work on the Wales Adoption Cohort Study.

Dinithi Wijedasa is a Research Associate at the Hadley Centre for Adoption and Foster Care Studies, School for Policy Studies, at the University of Bristol. Dinithi has been involved in numerous research studies, which include looking at pathways to permanence in the care system for minority ethnic children; educational support services provided by independent foster care providers; an evaluation of a new model for providing adoption services; adoption and the inter-agency fee; reunification of looked after children with their parents; and transition to adulthood for adopted young people. She is currently leading an ESRC-funded study to explore the extent of kinship care in the UK through analysis of census data.

1　Background to the study

Introduction

Adoption offers tremendous advantages for maltreated children, and the Government's adoption reform agenda in England has rightly encouraged the use of adoption for children who cannot return home. There is a strong evidence base for the benefits of adoption (see, for example, Quinton and Selwyn, 2007; Biehal *et al*, 2010; Donaldson Adoption Institute, 2013). Adoptive family life can help foster developmental recovery and many adopted children do make significant progress. However, for a minority of families, the adoption journey can, at times, be fraught with difficulty and, in some instances, results in the child moving out of their adoptive home prematurely (referred to as adoption disruption).

At the time this study began, there was some debate about the prevalence of adoption disruption. There was a view that adoptions disrupted frequently, with various commentators citing disruption rates ranging from five per cent to 50 per cent. However, there was little evidence to support these claims.

There has been no national study on adoption disruption in the UK or US. Most of the research to date has focused on narrowly defined populations, of children placed before 1990, and on disruptions that occurred before the adoption order was made. In the UK, adoption disruption has been considered as just one of the outcomes in studies that have examined adoption outcomes more generally; disruption has rarely received specific attention. This is partly because it has been impossible to use available administrative data to link a child's pre- and post-care histories, as the child's social care, National Health Service and pupil numbers change after the adoption order is made. There are similar issues in linking administrative data in the US (Child Welfare Information Gateway, 2012). Furthermore, after the making of an adoption order, agencies are under no obligation to keep in touch with adoptive families and some adoptive parents want to cut ties with children's services.

Three key issues relate to the published research on adoption disruption: lack of agreed definitions, assumptions that findings from the US apply to the UK, and limited analysis of available data.

Inconsistent use of the term "adoption disruption"

The term "disruption" or "breakdown" has been defined in many different ways. In some studies, adoption disruption refers to the child's return to the agency between placement and legal finalisation; other studies distinguish between disruptions pre- and post-order; while some use a wider definition based on whether the child is living in the adoptive home at the time of the research study. This distinction between pre- and post-order has not been made consistently in the UK literature and so, by conflating new placements with those that have been stable for some time, the relative risks have been difficult to ascertain. There is more movement in all types of "new" placements.

In the US, distinctions are usually made between breakdowns that occur before the adoption order (disruption) and those that break down post-order (dissolution). In more recent years, "dissolution" has started to be replaced in the US by the term "displacement" (e.g. Goerge *et al*, 1997; Howard *et al*, 2006). Displacement has been used in the US to indicate three possible outcomes after a disruption:

- the adoption is legally dissolved;
- the child remains adopted but stays in care; and
- the child returns to their adoptive home after spending some time in care.

It should be noted that in the UK there is no statutory basis for revocation of an adoption order except by the making of another adoption order (Masson *et al*, 2008). The adoptive parents remain the legal parents of the child whether or not the placement disrupts. The UK does not have terms that differentiate between pre- and post-order disruptions, and UK studies often use disruption and breakdown interchangeably.

Comparing US and UK adoption breakdown rates

There are important differences in the US and UK adoption populations that mean that comparisons of research findings should be viewed with caution. US data (AFCARS, 2013) show that in 2012, 52,039 children were adopted with child welfare services involvement and 101,719 were waiting to be adopted. Aside from the large numbers of adopted children in the US compared with the UK, a greater proportion (55%) of US adoptions were of minority ethnic children compared with England, where 18 per cent of children adopted were of minority ethnicity (Department for Education (DfE), 2013a). Importantly, in the US, the majority of children (56%) were adopted by their foster carers with stranger/matched adoptions accounting for only 14 per cent of adoptions (AFCARS, 2013). In the UK, the reverse is true, with only about 15 per cent of the 3,800 children adopted by previous foster carers and 85 per cent by strangers (DfE, 2013a).

Most US children live with their foster carers for some time before an agreement is signed that converts the foster placement to that of an adoptive placement. US disruption studies consider disruption from the point that the adoption agreement was signed and not when the child was first placed. This administrative decision is likely to explain why US research (e.g. Barth *et al*, 1988) has found that foster care adoptions have lower disruption rates than stranger adoptions, as problematic placements are likely to have already ended.

Limited analysis

Particularly in the UK, and because of small sample sizes, analysis has been generally limited to examining statistical associations between factors thought to be associated with breakdown. However, these analyses have failed to take into account those adoptions that are continuing and may therefore find statistical associations where none exist. Few UK studies (an exception is Fratter *et al*, 1991) have used more sophisticated regression techniques, and none, to our knowledge, have taken into account the length of time between order and disruption.

Research on disruption rates pre-order

The vast majority of studies in the US and UK have examined disruptions before the placement was legalised (Appendix A). In the US, disruption rates pre-order range from 10–25 per cent, depending on the population studied, the duration of the study, geographic and other factors (e.g. Festinger, 1986, 1990, 2002; Goerge *et al*, 1997). In the US, efforts to reduce delay in adoption have been ongoing since the mid-1990s. Shortened legal timeframes and decreased time to adoption led to fears that this might lead to inadequate selection and preparation of adoptive homes and therefore an increase in disruptions. These fears have not been realised. Since the introduction of the Adoption and Safe Families Act (ASFA, 1997), which brought reduced timescales and a greater focus on adoption, there is evidence that the disruption rate has, in fact, reduced (Festinger, 2014). Reviewing data in Illinois, Smith *et al* (2006) found that there was a 12 per cent greater risk of disruption before ASFA than after.

In the UK, Rushton's (2003) review of four UK and eight US studies estimated a general breakdown rate of 20 per cent (range 10–50 per cent depending on age at placement). However, it should be noted that most of the UK studies combined pre- and post-order and included adoptions that had broken down within a few weeks of the child being placed. UK studies that have separated out pre- and post-order generally indicate a disruption rate of 3–10 per cent pre-order, depending on the sample of children studied (Appendix A).

Research on disruption rates post-order

In the UK and US, there has been very little research on adoption breakdowns post-order. In the US, Festinger (2002) reported a 3.3 per cent rate of adoption dissolution four years after the legal order. A similar rate (3%) was reported by McDonald and colleagues (2001) in a study of children 18–24 months after legal finalisation. Earlier studies reported higher rates (Groze, 1996; Goerge *et al*, 1997). It should be noted that these studies had a very short follow-up period, and none have tracked a population up to 18 years of age.

In the UK, it has been estimated that four per cent of children return to care every year after an adoption order is granted (Triseliotis, 2002). In a study of late-placed children, all of whom had many behavioural difficulties, six per cent of adoptions had ended, on average, seven years after the making of the order (Selwyn *et al*, 2006a). Rushton and Dance's study (2004) of late-placed children described a higher rate (19%), but highlighted how a return to care did not necessarily mean a breakdown of relationships. Shared care between the local authority and the adoptive parents could be used as a way of supporting the family. However, both these studies had samples of older and harder-to-place children and were not representative of adopted children generally. The few studies that have separated out pre- and post-order disruptions quote a breakdown rate of four–six per cent (Appendix A).

Factors associated with disruption

Since 1998, the UK Government has promoted the use of adoption for children unable to live with members of their family (Department of Health, 1998). New legislation (Children and Families Act 2014; Adoption and Children Act 2002), regulations, and guidance have been introduced to minimise delay, and to improve the support given to adoptive families. These interventions may have helped reduce disruptions. There have been a number of substantial reviews of the adoption disruption literature (Rosenthal, 1993; Sellick and Thoburn, 1996; Rushton, 2004; Evan B Donaldson Institute, 2004; Coakley and Berrick, 2008; Child Welfare Information Gateway, 2012) and specific reviews and research on the process of matching in adoption (Dance *et al*, 2010; Evan B Donaldson Institute, 2010; Quinton, 2012). The research evidence is consistent on factors that are associated with disruptions. These include child-related factors, such as older age at placement and behaviour difficulties; birth family factors, such as child maltreatment and domestic violence; and system-related factors, such as delay and lack of support to adoptive families. Some studies have also identified multiple previous placements and inaccurate assessments of the child's difficulties as increasing the risk of disruption. Placements of children with physical or learning disabilities are not at higher risk of disruption (Fratter *et al*, 1991); indeed, some studies show that the risks of disruption decrease for children with physical disability (Boyne *et al*, 1984; Glidden, 2000).

There have been mixed findings on the impact of separation from siblings. Early research suggested that separation from siblings increased the risk of disruption (Fratter *et al*, 1991), but as Rushton (1999) noted, separated siblings were more likely to have challenging behaviour and to have more special needs than children placed together.

There has been a focus, in research, on understanding outcomes for older children, because research has consistently found that age at placement is a strong predictor of disruption (see the research reviews by Coakley and Berrick (2008) and the Evan B Donaldson Institute (2008)). Consequently, we know very little about the infants who have been placed over the last 20 years, although the developmental risks they carry, such as maternal misuse of alcohol and drugs, are much greater than the risks carried by infants placed before 1980.

Clinicians' accounts (e.g. Hopkins, 2006; Rustin, 2006; Wright, 2009) of working with adopted children highlight the importance of the internal world of the child and, in particular, the child's search for a coherent account of their life and origins. Lack of attention to the child's grief and loss, and incomplete or misunderstood histories are thought to play an important part in the child's inability to develop an integrated sense of self and are associated with disruption.

Most of the studies have a short follow-up, and few include late adolescence and young adulthood. Howe's (1996) research suggested that some of the disruptions that occurred during teenage years were not permanent and that many young people returned to their adoptive families in adulthood. This chimes with the findings in recent research from the US (Festinger and Maza, 2009), but we have no published longitudinal studies in the UK of children adopted from care, or studies that have examined the transition to adulthood for adopted children.

Most studies examine the family situation at a point in time. All those working in the adoption field know that family life changes rapidly, often from day to day. Parents who appear to be coping well can suddenly call an agency, in crisis. Conversely, families whose relationships are thought to be fractured can report that relationships are improving. The dynamic nature of family life is important in any consideration of disruption and raises questions about the language used. The terms "disruption", "displacement" or "breakdown" can evoke undesirable negative images and a sense of finality.

It has been argued that labels can trigger changes in the behaviour of the "labelled" and in those who apply the label (e.g. Stager *et al*, 1983). For example, the bleak connotations attached to "breakdown" might influence adoptive parents' willingness to seek support and affect social work judgements and behaviours towards the child and the family. It has been suggested that adoptive parents feel that they are more harshly treated than birth parents by social workers if their child returns to care. As Treacher and Katz (2000) point out, 'social workers too are bound by the same narratives and myths, subject to the same emotional need to rescue and to blame, and buffeted by the same powerful media and political forces as the other points in the triangle' (p. 216).

The number of adoption disruptions tells us only something about where the child or young person is living. They reveal nothing about the quality of family relationships. Some young people may move out of home, but retain meaningful relationships with family members, albeit from a distance. On the other hand, children living in their adoptive home may have unfulfilled relationships, with little family cohesion.

There is much to learn about the mechanisms of adoption disruption – how they disrupt and what might make a difference to those who live through crises and disruptions. In the next chapter, we set out the aims of the study, the research questions, and the design.

Please note, the names of all survey respondents in this study have been changed.

Summary

- The UK research literature on adoption disruption is very limited. Most of the research to date has focused on narrowly defined populations, of children placed before 1990, and on disruptions that occurred before the adoption order was made. In the UK, adoption disruption has been considered as just one of the outcomes in studies that have examined adoption outcomes more generally. Disruption has rarely received specific attention.

- Disruption has been defined in many different ways, pre- and post-order disruption numbers combined and there is little evidence on the stability of adoption over time. In the UK, "disruption" and "breakdown" are used interchangeably. In the US literature, "disruption" applies to placements that end pre-order and "dissolution" is used for placements that end post-order.

- The available evidence from UK studies suggests that pre-order disruptions range from 3–10 per cent and post-order from 4–6 per cent, depending on the characteristics of the children studied.

- There are important differences between the US and UK adoption populations and therefore it is not possible to assume that US findings apply to the UK. In the US, the majority of looked after children are adopted by their foster carer, whereas the majority of these children in the UK are adopted by strangers. Furthermore, in the UK it is not possible, except in exceptional circumstances, to revoke an adoption order. Despite the differences in the populations, research from the UK and US has found similar factors to be associated with adoption disruption.

2 Study design and methods

Introduction

The aims of this study were to understand why adoptions disrupted post-order and to compare the stability of adoption with that of special guardianship and residence orders.[1] The study was funded by the Department for Education (DfE) and approved by the Ethics Committee of the School for Policy Studies at the University of Bristol. Before exploring the method, we briefly summarise the differences between the three legal orders that are available to the parents/carers of children who are looked after. Whilst all three orders change the status of the child, who no longer remains in the care of the local authority (LA), they vary in the extent of parental responsibility transferred to the parents/carers.

Adoption orders

Adoptive parents hold *all* parental responsibility and make all decisions about the child's upbringing. The adopters become the legal parents of the child and they remain so for the rest of the child's life, irrespective of whether or not the placement disrupts. The order can only be discharged by the making of another adoption order.

Special guardianship orders

These are relatively new and were introduced in England and Wales in December 2005. Unlike adoption orders, special guardianship orders (SGOs) end when a child reaches 18 years of age. The carers hold parental responsibility for most day-to-day matters, although birth parents retain some residual responsibilities and the LA named in the care order has the right to apply to the court to vary or end the order if circumstances change. Unlike adoption orders, there are no restrictions on parents or other relatives applying for contact,

---

1 Residence orders were replaced by child arrangements orders in s.12 of the Children and Families Act 2014.

prohibited steps or specific issues orders once the SGO is made, unless their right to do so is restricted by the court. In comparison with an adoption order, carers have a more limited legal relationship with the child; the legal relationship with the birth parents is not severed; and there is less protection against further litigation.

Residence orders

Carers/parents with residence orders (ROs) have the least legal protection and share parental responsibility with anyone else who holds this (usually the birth parent/s) for as long as the order is in force – possibly until the child is 18 years of age. There is an expectation that agreements will be reached between the carer and those with parental responsibility in the making of major decisions (e.g. school to be attended, religion). Those with parental responsibility have a right to apply to the court to revoke a residence order at any time.

Aims of the study

Using a mixed method design, the four specific objectives of the study were:

- to establish the *rate* of adoption disruption post-order and to explore:
  a) how long after the order had been made the disruption occurred; and
  b) how the adoption disruption rate compared with the disruption rates of special guardianship orders and residence orders;
- to investigate the factors associated with disruption;
- to explore the experiences of adopters, children and social workers;
- to provide recommendations on how disruptions might be prevented.

Definitions

In this study, an adoption was considered to have disrupted when a previously looked after child, who had been the subject of an adoption order, left their adoptive home under the age of 18, because of difficulties in family life. They may have become looked after again, be living independently or living with extended family or friends. Most of the young people in this study who had experienced a disruption had become looked after. Intercountry and step-parent adoptions were excluded.

Phase 1: Establishing the rate of disruption

To identify looked after children in England who left care on an adoption order, SGO or RO, the DfE supplied national data on all adopted children (1 April 2000–31 March 2011) and on all looked after children (1 April 2002–31 March 2011). The national datasets are known as the SSDA903 and comprise information provided annually by every LA to the DfE on all looked after children. Information is at child level (i.e. available for each child), and includes the child's gender, ethnicity, date of birth, dates of entry to care and dates of movement, legal changes and number and types of placements. Each child has a unique identifying number (ID) and a care history for each child can be assembled. Information on every child has been collected since 2002; before 2002, data were collected on only a one-third sample.

In the dataset, there were 37,335 children who, between 2000 and 2011, had been the subject of an adoption order; 5,921 with a SGO (available from December 2005); and 5,771 with a RO (recorded since April 2005). We would have liked to have made comparisons with the stability of long-term foster care placements, but national datasets do not identify these.

Children who return to care after a SGO or RO disrupts retain the same unique ID as the one used before they left care. It was therefore possible to identify SGO and RO disruptions in the national data. Of course, if the children had become looked after by a different LA from the one that had placed them, a new ID would have been allocated and these cases could not be identified in the dataset. However, previous research (Wade *et al*, 2011; Selwyn *et al*, 2013) would suggest that many families who take out these orders remain in the same local authority area.

Adopted children who re-enter care should always be given a new

ID, as required by regulations, and therefore adoption disruptions could not be identified in the dataset. Every adoption manager in England was contacted by the research team and asked to provide basic demographic information on adopted children who had returned to care and to provide the child's original ID, so that they could be identified in the SSDA903 and their care history subsequently assembled. Data were returned by 87 per cent of LAs. In addition, a few other adoption disruptions were identified from information supplied by Welsh adoption managers on English children placed with Welsh families, voluntary adoption agencies, published court judgements, and by identifying in the SSDA903 dataset a few adopted children where the placing LA had failed to change the child's ID as required. We were concerned that some adoption managers were unsure that they had been able to identify all the adoption disruptions. They tended to be managers in LAs that placed most of their children out of area, or where boundary and staff changes had resulted in a loss of the collective team memory of cases. So, to examine disruption using a different method, a survey was sent out to adoptive parents, as described below.

Surveys of adoptive parents

To try to ensure that as many disruptions as possible were identified, a survey was sent out to adoptive parents who had legally adopted a child between 1 April 2002 and 31 March 2004 in 13 LAs. The local authorities were selected to reflect geographical diversity (a London borough, northern and southern authorities, and urban and rural authorities) and practice variations (some LAs that placed children mainly "in-house" and others that placed all their children outside the LA area). Trying to contact a complete sample of adopters who had legally adopted 10 years ago was not straightforward, as LAs were no longer in touch with many of the parents. The last known home addresses were checked with publicly available records – seven per cent could not be traced. The LA survey return rate was modest (34%), although typical for such approaches when trying to trace families who adopted more than a decade ago.

The same survey was placed on the Adoption UK[2] (AUK) website on a disruption thread, for completion by anyone who had legally adopted a looked after child over any time period. The study was widely publicised and adoptive parents made good use of Twitter to circulate the message that we wanted to hear from parents about how adoptive family life was faring.

In total, surveys were returned by 390 adoptive parents caring for 689 children who had been placed by 77 different LAs. There were some key differences between the survey respondents. The LA survey was completed by those who had adopted a child within a two-year timeframe and consequently most adopted young people were adolescents. The AUK survey respondents were parenting children with a wider age range and more variablility in the length of time as an adoptive family.

Information was received on 60 post-order adoption disruptions but all of these had already been identified by the local authority involved.

Creating a new database

A database was created for this study that merged information from the various files held in the SSDA903 dataset and the new information on adoption disruptions. The database contained details of:

- **37,335 adoption orders**, of which 565 were known to have disrupted;
- **5,921 special guardianship orders**, of which 121 were known to have disrupted;
- **5,771 residence orders**, of which 415 were known to have disrupted.

Strengths of the dataset

The dataset was substantial. Achieving a sample size this large through other research methods would be very difficult to achieve due to time

---

2 Adoption UK is a registered adoption support agency run by adopters for adopters and offering peer-to-peer support, training, and publications, including *Children who Wait* [www.adoptionuk.org].

and cost constraints. The number of cases allowed more sophisticated statistical analyses to be conducted, which examined precise research questions and enabled specific sub-groups to be examined in more detail. It also allowed the testing of some of the widely held beliefs about the factors that increase the risk of disruption. A further strength was the longitudinal nature of the dataset, with the capacity to track children over time using their unique ID number.

Limitations of the dataset

All data have limitations and this was also the case here. First, analyses were limited to the variables in the national datasets. For example, we would have liked to examine whether different types of abuse influenced outcomes, but abuse and neglect were merged into one category. Neither were data collected on prebirth risks, such as infant exposure to alcohol/drugs or on whether the child was placed as part of a sibling group, or placed with a LA-approved or voluntary adoption agency-approved adopter. We were also limited in only being able to analyse disruptions that resulted in children returning to care (some placements may disrupt and the family might find other ways to manage the situation), and of course some disruptions on all three types of order are likely to have not been reported. We were also limited in some of the analysis because the information collected had changed over time or new questions had been added. For example, the marital status of adopters has only been collected since 2006 and therefore we could not test whether single adopters were more at risk of a disruption than couple adopters.

Analysis of the dataset

The characteristics of the children on the three types of legal orders were initially explored using tests such as the Chi-square test and Mann-Whitney U. We then took an in-depth look within each group to explore whether children on the three types of order who experienced disruptions were different from those children whose placements were intact. Event history analysis (EHA) (also known as survival or hazards models) was used to estimate and explore disruption rates. A Kaplan-Meier analysis was used to establish the overall disruption rate, followed by Cox proportional hazards models to explore the predictors of disruption. There were several advantages of using this type of analysis. First, a simple reporting of the disruption rates as proportions would have inadvertently underestimated the rates as, given the longitudinal nature of the dataset, some children would *not have had the time* to experience a disruption. The database contained information on children of *different ages* who had a legal order made at *different points in time*. EHA analysis allows "time to event" to be considered and importantly takes into account those who have experienced the event (disruption) and those who have not. A further advantage is that Cox regression models consider "time to the disruption" in calculations and allow each variable to be controlled against all other variables.

Each of the age and time variables were first explored individually within Cox regression models to see whether they met the proportional hazards assumption. We fitted the original linear term alongside squared and cubed terms in the Cox regression model. A significant result for the squared or cubed term indicated that the relationship between the age/time variable and the time to disruption was not linear. Data that did not meet the assumption were recoded into categorical variables based on the values of the hazard ratio [exp (B)] plots.

Phase 2: Interviews

The work plan was to interview 35 parents whose child had left home prematurely (disruption), and 35 parents who were finding parenting very challenging but whose child was still living at home. The survey sent out by the 13 LAs also helped us to recruit a sample of adoptive parents to interview. The brief survey had asked parents how the adoption was faring, if the child was still living at home and, if not, their whereabouts, and whether the parents would consent to be inter-viewed. All the adoptive parents from the LA survey who reported disruptions and gave consent were selected for interview. However, because so few were reported, 11 families who had experienced a disruption were also selected from the AUK survey responses. Similarly, six of the 35 families where the child was at home but who were finding parenting very challenging came from the AUK survey responses.

Interviews with adoptive parents (n = 70)

Interview questions were developed drawing on previous research findings on disruption (McRoy *et al*, 1988), from advice given by the advisory group, our previous research (Selwyn *et al*, 2006a), the work of Brodzinsky (2006) and Wrobel and colleagues (1998) on communicative openness, and that by Joseph and Butler (2010) on recovery from trauma. The main interview themes were established in advance; these were:

a)   adopters' motivations and the child that they originally had "in mind";
b)   the quality of preparation and assessment;
c)   the experience of matching, introductions and the early days of the placement;
d)   emerging difficulties and the response of services; and
e)   the experience of disruption.

The interview schedule used pre-coded questions (providing numerical data) but also included open questions that allowed adoptive parents to answer freely. Interviews were piloted with two families who had experienced a disruption and one family who were in crisis.

The 70 interviews took place as planned. In the chapters that follow, the 35 families where the child had left home prematurely are referred to as the "Left home" group, whilst those parenting challenging children still living at home are referred to as the "At home" group. It was clear during the interviews that parents did not like the terms "disruption" and "breakdown", as they implied finality. Parents were keen to point out that they remained the child's legal parents and, although the young person was not living in the family, they were often parenting from a distance.

Nearly all of the interviews took place in the adopters' homes and lasted between two to five hours. Adoptive parents gave graphic accounts of the difficulties they had faced and were often distressed and tearful. Some adopters had experienced more than one disruption; in these families, parents were asked to focus on the child who had moved out of home first. Other parents had more than one challenging child living at home; where this was the case, adopters were asked to focus on the most challenging child. A case summary was written up as soon as possible after the interview had been completed. All interviews were transcribed.

Measuring well-being

Prior to the interview, adopters in the "Left home" and "At home" groups were sent a pack containing a number of well-being measures. In addition, the same pack was sent to the 35 adopters who had responded to the LA survey stating that the adoption was going well and there were no or very few difficulties. This group (the "Going well" group) was for comparison and was not interviewed. The measures used are described in Appendix B.

Interviews with young people (n = 12)

Twelve young people who were no longer living with their adoptive families were interviewed about their experience of a disrupted adoption. The young people seemed to enjoy the interview and some said it was the first time that anyone had asked them about their experiences as an adopted child. However, it was difficult to access young people. Interviews with children under 16 years of age needed parental consent, but adoptive parents often refused because they had no faith in services being in place if the young person needed counselling or support, post-interview. Even where consent was given, the social worker often felt that the young person was "not in a good place" to be interviewed and in a few cases no-one knew the whereabouts of the young person. To reach young people we went through parents, then social workers, followed sometimes by Independent Reviewing Officers, residential key workers, and participation workers. Most of those interviewed were over 16 years of age. Five young people had parents who had been interviewed as part of the study. The 13 LAs that had helped with the survey also helped the researchers gain access to seven young people who were currently looked after or had recently left care.

Interviews with adoption managers (n = 12)

Interviews were also undertaken with 12 of the 13 LA adoption team managers (nine face-to-face and three by telephone). One team manager left the LA during the study and was unable to be interviewed. The focus of the interview was on adoption support services and how disruption might be prevented or better managed.

Analyses of the interviews and measures

Quantitative data from the interviews with adoptive parents were analysed in SPSS v19 using bivariate and multivariate statistical methods to compare similarities and differences between the "Left home" and the "At home" groups of families. Completed psychosocial measures were scored and analysed using recommended methods. The qualitative data were entered into NviVo and analysed thematically, initially using the structure of the interviews to guide this process. Analysis used five key stages, comprising:

- familiarisation with the data and the context;
- identification of themes;
- indexing;
- mapping; and
- interpretation.

It was through this process that unanticipated themes emerged.

Summary

- The aims of the study were: a) to establish the rate of disruption post-adoption order and to compare that rate with the disruption rates of SGOs and ROs; and b) to explore the experiences of adoptive parents and adopted young people who had experienced a disruption post-order, and social workers.

- Using national data, a new dataset was created comprising 37,335 children who had left care on adoption orders, 5,921 on SGOs and 5,771 on ROs. Children who had returned to care after a breakdown of a SGO or RO could be identified in the dataset, but information on adoption disruptions was added to the dataset from a survey of all LAs in England (87 per cent response rate) and from other sources.
- There were concerns that some LA adoption managers had not been able to identify all the adoption disruptions and therefore a survey was sent out by 13 LAs to adoptive parents who had adopted a child between 1 April 2002 and 31 March 2004 (post-order). The survey asked adopters how the adoption was faring and if the child was still living at home. The same survey was placed on the AUK website for completion by anyone who had adopted a looked after child. No new cases were identified in the AUK responses from 390 adoptive parents.
- Adoptive parents were selected for in-depth face-to-face interviews from the survey responses: 35 parents who had experienced a disruption (the "Left home" group) and 35 who were finding parenting a child living at home very challenging (the "At home" group). Prior to interview, adoptive parents completed a range of well-being measures. In addition, 35 parents who had stated in their survey response that things were going well were also asked to complete the measures as a comparison group. The "Going well" group was not interviewed. Twelve young people and 12 adoption managers were also interviewed about their experiences of adoption disruption and support.
- Many of the parents and young people stated that they appreciated being asked to reflect on their whole adoption journey and had not had that opportunity before.

3 The characteristics of looked after children who left care on adoption, special guardianship and residence orders

We began the analyses by comparing the number of orders made in England on looked after children between 2001 and 2013. Adoption orders have been available and recorded in the national dataset (SSAD903) for the whole time period, whereas special guardianship orders (SGOs) only became available in December 2005 and, although available, residence orders (ROs) were not recorded until April 2005. Figure 3.1 shows the rapid increase in the use of SGOs since they became available, and the rise in the number of adoption orders. From a low base, even the number of residence orders increased by 50 per cent. These results suggest that permanency planning is improving and that more children are leaving care with legal orders than ever before.

Adoption remains the most used legal order for looked after children in England who are unable to be reunified with their birth families. In the year ending 31 March 2013, 68,110 children were looked after, and during that year about 14 per cent of children who had ceased to be looked after left on an adoption order, 10 per cent on a SGO and six per cent on a RO (DfE, 2013a).

In the next sections, we explore the similarities and differences in the characteristics of the children on the three different types of order.

The characteristics of the children on the three legal orders

In the dataset created for this study, there were 37,335 adopted children, 5,921 children on a SGO and 5,771 on a RO. In the analyses that follow, the numbers differ because before 2002 the Government did not collect information on every child in care, only on a one-third sample.

Figure 3.1
Number of children leaving care on adoption orders, SGOs and ROs, 2001–2013

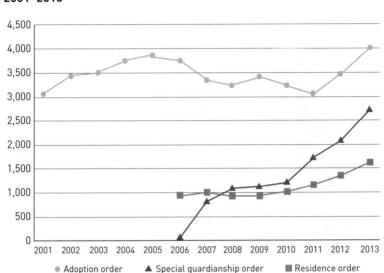

Adoption order   ▲ Special guardianship order   ■ Residence order

Gender

The gender distribution was similar across the three types of order, with the percentage of males on adoption orders, SGOs and ROs being 51 per cent, 50 per cent and 52 per cent respectively.

Age at entry to care

Children who were placed with an adoptive family were younger at entry to care compared with the children on SGOs or ROs.[3] Adopted children were on average 14 months old at entry to care while children on SGOs were 3.4 years; children on ROs were the oldest on average, at 4.5 years old (Figure 3.2). Nevertheless, more than half of all the children were under the age of four years when they were first looked after.

---

3   $\chi^2(2) = 4654.62, p<.001$

Figure 3.2

Age at entry to care for children on adoption orders, SGOs and ROs

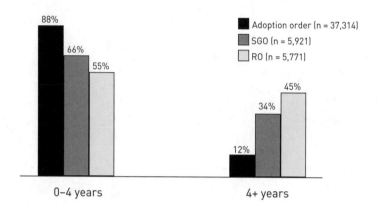

Ethnicity

The majority (about 75%) of looked after children in England are white. Therefore, the majority of children on all three types of order were white (adoption order 85%; SGO 78%; RO 79%). Minority ethnic children were slightly more likely to have a SGO or RO rather than an adoption order. If adopted, minority ethnic children were statistically more likely to have been adopted by their previous foster carers than by a stranger adopter.[4]

Legal status at entry to care

There were also differences in children's legal status as they entered care. Compared with the children on SGOs and ROs, children who went on to have adoption orders were more likely to come into care under Section 20 and less likely to come into care on interim care orders[5] (Figure 3.3). Section 20 of the Children Act (1989) allows the child to be accommodated with parental consent rather than through a court order.

---

4   χ^2 (1) = 427.16, *p<.001*
5   χ^2 (4) = 315.92, *p<.001*

Figure 3.3
Legal status at entry to care for children on adoption orders, SGOs and ROs

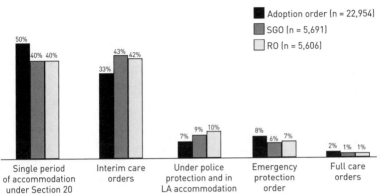

Reason for entry to care

As expected, the majority of the children on adoption orders (72%), SGOs (70%) and ROs (72%) became looked after because of maltreatment. All three groups of children were *more* likely to have been abused and neglected than the care population as a whole, where 65 per cent of children entered care due to abuse and neglect (DfE, 2013a).

First placements

More than one-third (36%) of the children on SGOs and one-quarter (26%) of the children on ROs were first placed with a family or friends carer (Figure 3.4). In comparison, only four per cent of the adopted children were initially placed with kin.

Placements and moves in care

Previous research (e.g. Sinclair *et al*, 2007) has shown that children who have multiple placements in care are at increased risk of disruption compared with those who experience fewer moves. We were interested in knowing where children had been placed, but examining changes of carer was not possible. The national dataset only allows

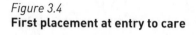

Figure 3.4
First placement at entry to care

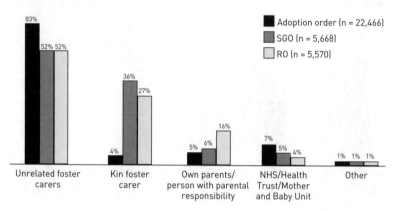

movement to be examined and the number of moves does not necessarily equate with the number of carers. For example, we were concerned to see in the dataset some very young children with up to 58 moves in care: adopted children 0–58 moves; SGO children 0–37 moves; and RO children 0–40 moves. We contacted individual LAs with some of the highest numbers of recorded moves to understand whether the numbers were errors or if the children concerned had really experienced so many moves. The LAs confirmed that the numbers were correct and that most moves were because of respite care arrangements. It is important to recognise that any move, even if it is for planned shared care, can be detrimental to children, as it produces additional stress, instability and discontinuity in children's lives (Rubin *et al*, 2004, 2007).

Surprisingly, adopted children experienced the most moves of all.[6] Thirty-eight per cent of children on SGOs and ROs did not experience any moves in care after their first placement; in contrast, this was the case for only 0.3 per cent (n = 87) of the adopted group. Children who were placed with family or friends as their first placement had the

---

6   χ^2 (4)= 1157.46, *p<.001*

fewest number of moves.[7] The stability of kinship placements partly explains why children who went on to have SGOs and ROs had fewer moves compared with the adopted group.

Reunification attempts

It has been shown that failed attempts at reunification can lead to worse outcomes for children in care (Selwyn *et al*, 2006b; Wade *et al*, 2011). Very few of those adopted (8%) or on SGOs (10%) had experienced attempts to reunify them with their birth parents. However, 39 per cent of children on ROs had experienced one or more failed reunifications and the difference was statistically significant.[8]

Age at final placement and time to placement from entry to care

As expected, nearly three-quarters of the adopted group were younger than four years of age at the time of placement with their adoptive parents (Figure 3.5). Adopted children were more likely to be younger than the children on SGOs and ROs.[9]

Figure 3.5
Child's age at final permanent placement

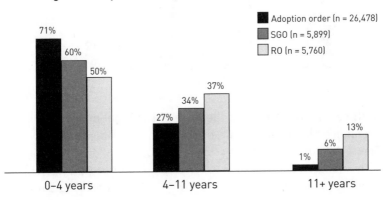

---

7   Mann Whitney U = 45606339, Z = –54.02, $p<.001$
8   χ^2 (4) = 4253.33, $p<.001$
9   χ^2 (4) = 2309.68, $p<.001$

Although adopted children were, on average, the youngest at placement, they waited *longer* from entry to care to placement with their adoptive parents,[10] compared with the children who left care through ROs and SGOs (Figure 3.6). The speed of placement for those on SGOs and ROs is partly attributable to 38 per cent of children having their first placement with carers who went on to take out a legal order. However, the delays for adopted children were also associated with having multiple moves in the care system and the length of time between the decision that adoption was the right plan and the match with their adoptive parents.[11] Delays may have been caused by administrative and legal delays, poor practice or a lack of suitable adopters.

Figure 3.6
Time from entry to care to the "final placement" pre-order

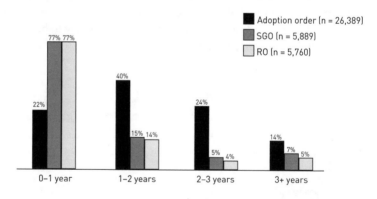

Adoption order (n = 26,389)
SGO (n = 5,889)
RO (n = 5,760)

77% 77%

40%

22%

24%

15% 14%

5% 4%

14%

7% 5%

0–1 year   1–2 years   2–3 years   3+ years

Children's placements at the time of the legal order

Children's placements at the time of the legal order are shown in Figure 3.7. The vast majority (85%) of adopted children were placed with stranger adopters. Few foster carers (15%) became the child's adoptive parents but nearly one-third (31%) of special guardians had

---

10 χ^2 (4) = 9632.74, *p<.001*
11 Pearson's *r* = 0.49, *p<.001*

been the child's foster carers, as were 27 per cent of those who had taken out ROs. Foster carers' choice of order may have been influenced by their lack of knowledge, the different arrangements for support associated with each type of order, or carers feeling under pressure from social workers to take out an order (Hunt and Waterhouse, 2012; Selwyn *et al*, 2013).

Figure 3.7
Children's placements at the time of the legal order

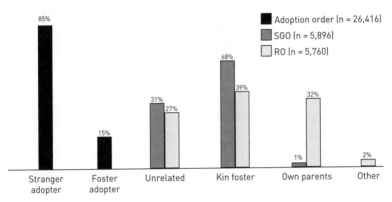

Length of time between final placement and date of the order

Compared with the other two groups of children, the children on ROs were the quickest[12] to have the legal order made after being placed with their carers (Figure 3.8). Nearly three-quarters of the children on ROs had the order made within a year of being placed.

In this chapter, we have explored the characteristics of looked after children on adoption orders, SGOs and ROs. We have shown how the characteristics of the children differed at the point of the order. Adopted children generally had entered care at a young age but many had experienced placement changes and delays whilst in care. In contrast, children on ROs carried different risks: they had entered care generally at older ages and had more failed reunification attempts.

---

12 χ^2 (4) = 1792.30, *p*<.001

Figure 3.8
Length of time between placement and order

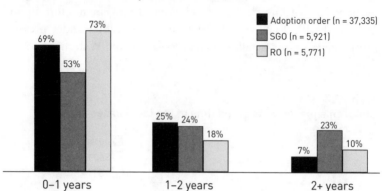

Although cemented by legal orders, some children were unable to remain in these permanent placements, so the placement disrupted. In the next chapter, we take an in-depth look into each of the three types of legal orders to explore whether children who experienced disruptions had different characteristics to those who remained in their placements.

Summary

- Adoption remains the most frequently used legal order for looked after children who need a permanent substitute family. The number of SGOs has increased rapidly since 2005 and the number of ROs has also risen. More children are leaving care on a legal order, suggesting that permanency planning has improved.
- Children who went on to be legally adopted were on average younger at entry to care compared to children on SGOs or ROs. However, the majority of all the children were under the age of four when they first entered care.
- Adopted children were more likely to have entered care under a Section 20 order compared with children on SGOs and ROs.
- Minority ethnic children were more likely to be on SGOs and ROs and, if adopted, for the order to have been made to a previous foster

carer. Foster carers were more likely to apply for SGOs and ROs rather than adoption orders.

- A little more than half (51%) of the children on SGOs and one-third (33%) of the children on ROs were placed with a family or friends carer as their first placement. In contrast, very few (0.3%) adopted children were initially placed with kin.

- Adopted children had experienced more placement moves in foster care compared with children on SGOs or ROs.

- Thirty-nine per cent of children on ROs had one or more failed reunification attempts. Failed reunifications and older age at first entry to care led to children generally being older at the time of the order compared with adopted children or children on SGOs.

- Although nearly three-quarters of the adopted group were under four years of age at the time they were placed for adoption, they waited longer from entry to care to being placed with their adoptive family compared with the waiting time for children on other orders. Some of the difference in timeliness can be explained by 38 per cent of children on SGOs and ROs having only one placement, as their first placement with kin became their final placement. Adopted children also had more moves in care, and delays were also significantly related to the time between the decision to place for adoption and the match taking place.

4   The characteristics of children whose placements disrupted

In this chapter, we focus on the children whose placements disrupted after the legal order had been made. We begin with the children on adoption orders (n = 37,335) and explore the characteristics of children who experienced an adoption disruption (n = 525) compared with those children whose adoptions were intact. The characteristics of the children who experienced SGOs or ROs will be similarly explored. Information on adoption disruptions came from a national survey of adoption managers and from other sources (see Chapter 2 on research method) while information on SGO and RO disruptions was from the national SSDA903 database. In the following analyses, the number of children varies because national data were only collected on a one-third sample of looked after children between 1998 and 2002. Information, particularly on placement history, was missing for some children. The national dataset on adopted and looked after children (SSDA903) is concerned with the children in contact with child welfare services and until recently has had little information on the characteristics of the adults who become adoptive parents. Similarly, there is very little information on the adults who take out SGOs or ROs.

Adoption disruptions

As can be seen in Figure 4.1, nearly two-thirds of the adoption disruptions occurred during the secondary school years. Children were on average 13 years old when they left their families. The majority (57%) of the disruptions occurred more than five years after the adoption order had been made: 29 per cent disrupted between two to five years later and 14 per cent disrupted within two years.

Figure 4.1
Children's age at the time of the adoption disruption

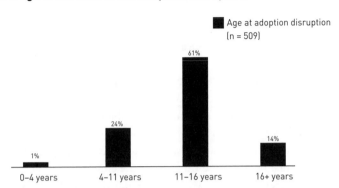

Children and their care careers before adoption

Importantly, the child's gender, ethnicity or the reason they first became looked after was not associated with adoption disruption.

Age at entry to care

Previous research has shown that delayed entry to care and the consequent longer exposure to maltreatment are associated with increased risk of disruption (Howe, 1997; Selwyn *et al*, 2006a). This was supported by the adoption data: the children whose adoptions had disrupted were significantly older at entry to care (average three years old) compared with children who were living with their adoptive families (average one year old).[13]

Placement moves prior to being placed for adoption

In the previous chapter, we highlighted the number of placement moves adopted children had experienced. Moves in care were statistically associated with adoption disruption: 65 per cent of children in the disrupted group had two or more moves prior to their

---

13 Mann Whitney U = 4870891 Z = −24.19 p<.01

adoptive placement, compared with 48 per cent of the intact group.[14] However, caution is needed in relation to the finding, as there was a great deal of missing information on placement moves – missing for 50 per cent of those who had experienced a disruption and for 18 per cent of intact adoptions.

Time from entry to care to adoptive placement

Delays in social work decision-making and in the court process can often lead to children "drifting" in care before being placed for adoption. Nearly three-quarters of the children who experienced an adoption disruption had waited two or more years for an adoptive placement, whilst nearly three-quarters of the children in intact placements had been placed *within* two years of entering care (Figure 4.2).[15]

Figure 4.2
Time from entry to care to the adoptive placement

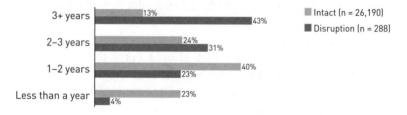

The DfE regularly publishes the time it takes between the various decision-making points in a child's adoption journey. Table 4.1 presents the DfE (2012) national statistics and compares these to the average time for children whose adoptions disrupted and for those whose adoptions were intact.

The children whose adoptions disrupted were significantly more likely to have had lengthier adoption processes compared with those children whose adoptions were intact. This was the case for children

---

14 χ^2 (3) = 114.93, $p<.001$
15 χ^2 (3) = 245.55, $p<.001$

Table 4.1
Average time between adoption milestones (years: months)

Time in years	DfE statistics in 2012 (all ages)	0–4 years at entry to care		4 years and older at entry to care	
		Intact (n = 32,377)	Disruption (n = 302)	Intact (n = 4,297)	Disruption (n = 206)
Entry to care to adoption decision (BI)	0:11	1:2	1:11	1:10	1:9
Adoption decision to matching	0:10	0:7	1:10	0:10	0:11
Matching to being placed for adoption	0:1	0:1	0:2	0:2	0:2
Being placed for adoption to the adoption order	0:9	0:11	1:4	1:2	1:5
Total average time between entry into care and adoption order	2:7	2:9	4:3	4:1	4:3

who entered care under the age of four[16] and those who entered care over the age of four.[17] The delays for young children are particularly concerning. Examining the length of the adoption processes for the disrupted group who entered care under the age of four, it can be seen that the total average time between entry to care and the adoption

16 Mann Whitney U = 2763760, Z = −15.86, $p<.001$
17 Mann Whitney U = 422687, Z =−3.181, $p<.01$

order was 4.3 years – the same length of time it had taken for those who had entered care *over* the age of four and who are generally thought of as much harder to place. The advantage of entering care under the age of four years old had been lost. The evidence from the analysis of this large dataset supports the use of concurrent planning and of ensuring that children get into their permanent placements as quickly as possible.

The child's age at the time of the adoptive placement

The children who experienced an adoption disruption were generally older at entry to care and grew even older as they waited longer in the care system. Three-quarters of the children who experienced a disruption were more than four years old at the time of their adoptive placement, compared with the intact group, where the majority (70%) of children were aged less than four years old. This difference was statistically significant (Figure 4.3).[18]

Figure 4.3
Child's age when placed with their adoptive family[19]

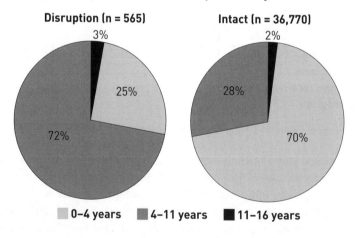

Disruption (n = 565)   Intact (n = 36,770)

■ 0–4 years   ■ 4–11 years   ■ 11–16 years

---

18 $\chi^2(2) = 555.04$, $p<.001$
19 For children adopted by their former foster carers, the child's age was calculated from the point that the foster placement was confirmed as an adoptive placement.

Children adopted by their previous foster carers

Previous research conducted over a decade ago indicated that about 13 per cent of children were adopted by their former foster carers (Ivaldi, 2000). This proportion has barely risen – between 2000 and 2011, only 15 per cent of adoptive parents were the child's previous foster carers. For a long time it has been assumed that foster carer adoptions are more stable than adoptions by strangers. It has been thought that foster carers have well-established relationships with children and therefore have based a decision to adopt on a realistic view of caring for the child. However, we found that foster care adoptions were *not* more stable compared with stranger adoptions.

There may be several explanations for this finding. First, it may be that adoption managers were more likely to report foster carer than stranger adoptive disruptions, because those who had continued to foster other children would still be in touch with the LA. Second, the withdrawal of support post-order from foster carers may increase the risk, especially because many were single parents.[20] Third, foster carers may adopt children with more special needs than children adopted by stranger adopters. However, another factor was that children waited longer to be legally adopted by their foster carers than did children adopted by strangers. Children's and carers' feelings of insecurity may have had a detrimental effect on the stability of the placement.

Children who were adopted by foster carers first entered care under two years old (average 1.5 years) and were on average 2.4 years old when they were placed with the foster carers who went on to adopt them. At entry to care, children adopted by foster carers had a similar age profile to the children adopted by strangers. However, the children waited, on average, two years before their foster placement was con-

---

20 Thirty-four per cent of foster carer adopters were single, compared with 13 per cent of stranger adoptive parents. Although this finding is very similar to that reported in previous research (Ivaldi, 2000), it should be treated with caution, as national data on marital status has only been collected since 2006 and therefore data were missing for 82 per cent of the disruption group and 57 per cent of the intact group.

firmed as an adoptive placement and a quarter waited more than three years. By the time of the order, children adopted by foster carers were on average 5.3 years old, compared with children who were adopted by stranger adopters (average 3.8 years old). Delays may have been because adoptive parents could not be found, so the foster carers stepped in to become adoptive parents; negotiations for acceptable support packages were lengthy; the LA did not support the foster carer's application to adopt; or other delays caused by legal and social work practice.

Calculating the adoption disruption rate

A main aim of this study was to calculate the rate of adoptive placement disruption *after* the order had been made and to compare the adoption disruption rate to that of other types of order.

As the adopted children (n = 37,335) had their adoption orders made over an 11-year period and we had information on 565 disruptions that occurred before July 2012, the length of time in placement differed for each child, as did their age. Therefore, calculating a rate of disruption as a proportion of all adoptions was inadequate, as it would not have allowed for the fact that some children had a shorter period at risk of disruption, i.e. the adoptions had not had time to break down. Statistical methods known as survival modelling allow "time" to be considered in analyses and Kaplan–Meier and Cox proportional hazards modelling were used in the following calculations.

The disruption rate of adoption orders

We found that the national adoption disruption rate was 3.2 per cent, which indicated that three in 100 adoptions would disrupt over a 12-year period. Table 4.2 shows the cumulative proportions of adoption disruptions over time.

Table 4.2
**Time in years since the adoption order and cumulative rate of
adoption disruption**

Time in years since adoption order	Cumulative percentage adoption disruptions over time	Risk of disruption
1	0.10%	1 in 1,000
2	0.19%	2 in 1,000
3	0.41%	4 in 1,000
4	0.58%	6 in 1,000
5	0.72%	7 in 1,000
6	1.07%	10 in 1,000
7	1.33%	13 in 1,000
8	1.87%	19 in 1,000
9	2.25%	23 in 1,000
10	2.54%	25 in 1,000
11	2.91%	29 in 1,000
12	3.24%	32 in 1,000

Modelling the factors that increase the risk of adoption disruption

The overall disruption rate is quite a crude figure and gives no
indication of which factors increase the relative risk of adoption
disruption. Therefore, we explored the factors that predicted adoption
disruption through a Cox proportional hazards model. Based on
previous research, the analysis in the previous chapters and the
information available in the databases, we chose to enter the following
variable, into the statistical model:

- gender (male/female);
- whether the adopters were the child's previous foster carers (yes/
  no);
- child's age at the time of the adoptive placement. For children who
  were adopted by their previous foster carers, the child's age when
  the foster placement became an adoptive placement was used;

- time between entry to care and adoptive placement;
- time between adoptive placement and adoption order;
- age since adoption order as a time varying covariate.

We were able to investigate how a child's age (as it increased over the course of the 12 years) had an effect on the stability of the adoption. We wondered, 'Were the teenage years riskier than other ages?' Statistically, this was achieved by including age as a "time varying covariate" into the model. We would have also liked to have included the "number of placement moves", but there were too many children whose placement histories were incomplete (50 per cent of disrupted and 28 per cent intact were missing). Table 4.3 shows the significant results. Not significant were gender, adopted by foster carer or stranger, and time from entry to care to placement. The latter was probably not significant because it was so closely related to the child's age.

To read and understand a Cox regression table, it is important to know that the hazard is the risk (probability) of reaching the event (disruption), given that the individual has not reached it up to this point. The hazard ratio is understood in relation to the "reference category". For example, we can look in Table 4.3 at the effect of the child's age at the time of their adoptive placement on disruption. A child aged 1–2 years at placement was nearly three times more likely, a child 2–4 years six times more likely, and a child aged four or more years 13 times more likely to disrupt in comparison with a child placed under the age of one and after adjustment for all the other explanatory variables in the model. All the coefficients (B in the table) are positive. This means that the risk is higher. If B were negative, the risk would be lower.

The child's age, age at adoptive placement, and time between placement and order were all independently significant in predicting adoption disruption.

The child's age
The biggest contributor to the model (controlling for all other variables) was the child's age and, in particular, "being a teenager".

Table 4.3
Relative risk of an adoption (n = 37,335) disrupting over a 12-year period

	B	SE	Sig.	Hazard ratio	95.0% CI for hazard ratio	
					Lower	Upper
Age since order			.00			
0–4 years (reference category)						
4–11 years	.80	.49	.100	2.22	.86	5.74
11–16 years	2.26	.51	.000	9.61	3.53	26.17
16 + years	1.54	.55	.05	4.68	1.60	13.69
Age at adoptive placement			.00			
0–1 year (reference category)						
1–2 years	1.08	.48	.026	2.94	1.14	7.55
2–4 years	1.82	.46	.000	6.16	2.49	15.23
4 + years	2.60	.47	.000	13.45	5.38	13.64
Time between adoptive placement and order			.012			
0–1 year (reference category)						
1–2 years	.02	.10	.842	1.02	.84	1.23
2 + years	.35	.12	.005	1.42	1.11	1.81

Teenagers (11–16 years old) were 10 times more likely to have a disruption compared with children younger than four. The risk of disruption for a child who was 16 years or older was about five times higher than if the child was younger than four.

Age at placement
A finding replicated in many studies (e.g. Rushton, 2004) is that age at placement is a major predictor of adoption disruption. Not surprisingly in this national dataset, the child's age at placement was a strong predictor of disruption after controlling for other variables.

Time between adoptive placement and order
Also significant was the time between the placement and the adoption order. The adoptions of children who waited more than two years to

get the order were 1.5 times more likely to disrupt compared to those who had an adoption order within a year of placement. However, the hazard ratio was much smaller compared with age and age at placement, suggesting that this delay was not as significant. The same types of analyses were repeated on the SGO and RO data.

Special guardianship order and residence order disruptions

The database had information on 5,921 SGOs made between 30 December 2005 and 31 March 2011, and 5,771 ROs made between 1 April 2005 and 31 March 2011. The same database indicated that 121 SGOs and 415 ROs had disrupted during the same period.

The child's age at the time of disruption

The majority of SGO disruptions (69%) and RO disruptions (68%) occurred before the child was 11 years old. More than a quarter (27%) of RO disruptions and 22 per cent of SGO disruptions occurred when the child was less than four years old. The average age of the child at the time of disruption was eight years old for children on SGOs and ROs. In comparison, most adoptions had disrupted during the teenage years.

Length of time between the making of the order and disruption

The majority of SGO and RO disruptions occurred just over a year after the order had been made. Eighty-one per cent of RO disruptions and 75 per cent of the SGO disruptions occurred within two years of the order (Figure 4.4). This pattern of disruption is very different to that seen in adoption, where only 14 per cent of adoptions had disrupted within two years. It should be remembered that data were available on only five years of SGOs and six years of ROs and there may be another spike in disruption rates as more children reach the teenage years.

Figure 4.4
Time to disruption from the date of the legal order for children on ROs (n = 5,771) and SGOs (n = 5,921)

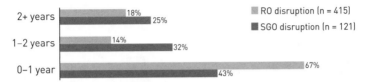

Children and their care careers

Just as we saw with children who were adopted, children's gender and ethnicity had no statistical effect on disruptions.

Reason for entry to care

Although the majority of children came into care due to abuse or neglect, children who experienced a SGO disruption were significantly more likely to have come into care due to acute family stress or family dysfunction rather than because of abuse or neglect.[21] We do not know why these reasons for entry to care should be associated with SGO disruption. We wondered if perhaps the children were not subject to care proceedings, but this was not the case. More than 70 per cent of the children who entered care for reasons other than abuse and neglect were in care proceedings. The reason for entry to care was not associated with disruption for adopted children or those on ROs.

The child's age at entry to care

Just as with the adopted children, older age at entry to care was associated with disruption for those on a SGO or a RO (Figure 4.5).

Attempts at reunification

Very few adopted children (4%) or children on SGOs (6%) had any attempts at reunification. However, 15 per cent of children on ROs had at least one reunification attempt. Nearly one in 10 children (9%)

---

21 χ^2 (2) = 10.09, $p<.01$

Figure 4.5
SGO and RO disruptions: children's age at entry to care

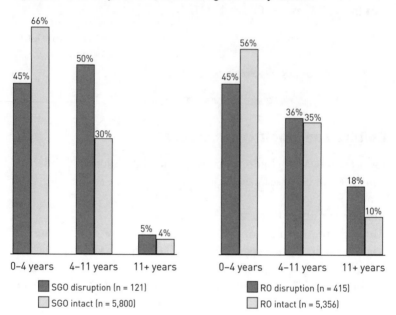

who experienced a RO disruption had two or more failed attempts at reunification, unlike those whose RO placements were intact.[22]

Number of placement moves whilst looked after

Children who had a SGO or a RO disruption had experienced more placement moves (an average of four placements) before being placed with their guardians compared to the children whose placements were intact (an average of two placements). There were far less missing data on the placement histories of children on SGOs and ROs compared to the histories of the adopted children. Therefore, we can be more confident that placement moves were having a very detrimental impact on the stability of permanent placements.

---

22 $\chi^2(2) = 9.12$ $p<.05$

Kinship placements

SGOs[23] and ROs[24] made to family or friends carers were far more stable compared with orders made to unrelated carers.

Timeliness

Unlike the adopted children, the time between entry to care and placement with the adult who became the special guardian or who took out the residence order was not associated with disruption. Delay was not a concern for the SGO and RO children, as the majority of children (about 75%) were placed within a year of entry to care. However, there was a statistical association in the time between placement and the date of the order, but only for children on ROs. Unlike adoptions, where delay between placement and the date of the order was associated with disruption, the placements of children on ROs who had the legal order made very quickly (within a year of placement), were more likely to disrupt.[25]

Age at placement

As expected, in both the SGO and RO groups, children who experienced a disruption were much more likely to have been placed with their guardians/carers at an older age compared with the children whose placements were intact (Figure 4.6).

The child's age at the time of the legal order

Following the same trend of older age at entry to care and at placement being associated with disruption, the child's age at the time of the order was similarly associated with disruption. Children on SGOs[26] and ROs[27] that disrupted were significantly older at the time of the order (Figure 4.7).

The same methods used in the adoption disruption calculations

---

23 χ^2 (2) = 38.35 $p<.001$
24 χ^2 (2) = 6.28 $p<.05$
25 χ^2 (2) = 12.68 $p<.01$
26 χ^2 (2) = 17.72 $p<.001$
27 χ^2 (2) = 25.32 $p<.001$

Figure 4.6
Child's age at placement with guardians: SGOs and ROs

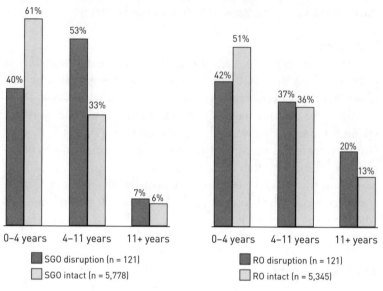

Figure 4.7
Child's age at the time of the legal order: SGOs and ROs

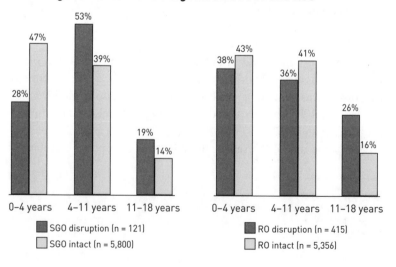

Table 4.4
Time in years since the SGO and cumulative rate of SGO disruption

Time in years since SGO	Cumulative percentage of SGO disruptions over time	Risk of disruption
1	1.0%	10 in 1,000
2	2.1%	21 in 1,000
3	2.8%	30 in 1,000
4	3.6%	36 in 1,000
5	5.7%	57 in 1,000

were used to establish the rates and predictors of disruption of SGOs. The database had information on 5,921 SGOs between 1 December 2005 and 31 March 2011. During the same period, 121 SGOs were known to have disrupted.

The disruption rate of SGOs

Over a five-year period, the national rate of SGO disruption was 5.7 per cent.

Table 4.4 indicates that, in the first year after the SGO, one in 100 SGOs were at risk of breaking down. This risk increases to nearly six in 100 over a five-year period. This is greater than the cumulative adoption disruption rate over a 12-year follow-up period.

Modelling the factors that increase the risk of SGO disruption

The same checks and modelling of individual variables were undertaken with the SGO data as had been undertaken with the adoption data. The variables entered into the Cox model (Table 4.5) were:

- age at placement;
- reason for entry to care;
- number of moves in care before SGO placement;
- whether the children were living with kin at the time of the SGO;

- age since SGO as a time varying covariate (to consider the effect of age).

Age at entry to care and age at SGO were not used in the final model, as both were highly correlated with age at placement.

Table 4.5
Relative risk of a SGO (n = 5,921) disrupting over a five-year period

	B	SE	Sig.	Hazard ratio	95.0% CI for hazard ratio	
					Lower	Upper
Reason for entry to care			.00			
Abuse or neglect (reference category)						
Disability of child or parent	.14	.34	.678	1.15	.60	2.24
Other family reason[28]	.66	.20	.001	1.94	1.31	2.86
Number of moves	.38	.03	.000	1.44	1.3	1.55
SGO placement is not with kin	1.01	.19	.000	2.78	1.91	3.95

Entering care due to acute stress or family dysfunction, more placement moves in care and the SGO being made to a carer who was not a relative or friend were all independently significant in predicting SGO disruptions.

Unlike adoption, being a teenager and the child's age at the time they were placed with their guardians had *no* effect on the likelihood of SGO disruption.

Children who were placed with unrelated guardians were nearly three times more likely to experience a SGO disruption compared with children placed with kin on a SGO. This factor was the biggest contributor to the SGO model. For each move that a child had in care, the risk of disruption increased by nearly 1.5 times. Furthermore,

---

28 Acute stress, family dysfunction, socially unacceptable behaviour, low income, absent parenting.

children entering care for reasons other than abuse or neglect were nearly twice as likely to face a disruption, compared with children who came into care due to abuse or neglect.

The disruption rate of ROs

The database had information on 5,771 ROs made since 1 April 2005. There were 415 known disruptions.

Over a six-year period, the national rate of RO disruption was calculated as 25.3 per cent. This indicates that, nationally, around 25 in 100 ROs would disrupt over a six-year period (Table 4.6).

Table 4.6 indicates that, in the first year after the making of the RO, eight in 1,000 ROs were at risk of breaking down. This risk increased to nearly 15 per 100 over a five-year period.

Modelling the factors that predicted RO disruptions

Based on the results of the previous sections, and the information available in the databases, the variables entered in the Cox model (Table 4.7) were:

- age at entry to care;
- number of moves in care before placement;

Table 4.6
Time in years since the RO and cumulative rate of RO disruption

Time in years since RO	Cumulative percentage of RO disruptions over time	Risk of disruption
1	0.8%	8 in 1,000
2	2.4%	24 in 1,000
3	5.2%	52 in 1,000
4	8.7%	87 in 1,000
5	14.7%	147 in 1,000
6	25.3%	253 in 1,000

- whether the children were living with kin at the time of the RO;
- time between placement and RO;
- previous reunification attempts with parents;
- legal status at entry to care;
- age since RO as a time varying covariate (to consider how age varied over the years since the order).

Age at placement and age at RO were not used in the final model as both were highly correlated with age at entry.

Not statistically significant were the child's age, the legal status at entry to care, previous reunification attempts, and time between placement and order, once the other variables were considered.

The child's age at entry to care

The biggest risk factor for RO disruption was being older at entry to care. The risk for children aged 11 years or older was more than twice that for children who started to be looked after under the age of four.

Type of placement

Children who were living with unrelated carers at the time of the RO were 1.3 times more likely to have a disruption compared with children who had their ROs made to kin.

Table 4.7

Relative risk of a RO (n = 5,771) disrupting over a six-year period

	B	SE	Sig.	Hazard ratio	95.0% CI for hazard ratio	
					Lower	Upper
Age at entry to care			.00			
0–4 years (reference category)						
4–11 years	.39	.15	.008	1.48	1.11	1.98
11+ years	.84	.26	.000	2.32	1.19	1.24
Number of moves	.19	.01	.000	1.21	1.06	1.62
RO placement is not with kin	.27	.11	.014	1.31	1.15	1.62

Number of moves in care before placement
For each move a child on a RO had experienced in care, the risk of disruption increased nearly 1.2 times.

The likelihood of disruption by type of legal order

In the previous sections, we separately explored the rates and the predictors of adoption, special guardianship order and residence order disruptions. A key objective of our study was to compare the adoption disruption rate with the disruption rates of other types of orders. Therefore, here we go on to build a statistical model including all three types of order.

Data were available for the three orders for different time periods: adopted group data for 12 years; SGO data for five years; and RO data for six years. Therefore, to ensure that we were comparing "like with like", all the following analyses are based on a maximum of a five-year follow-up period. The cumulative proportions of disruptions for the three groups over a five-year period are shown in Figure 4.8.

This clearly shows that on a comparison of the three orders using "time in years since the order", adoption was significantly more stable. Two further Kaplan-Meier estimates were run selecting only children who were four years or older at the time of the order, and only orders made to family or friends. Each analysis found adoption to have the lowest risk of disruption.

However, given that age since order (being a teenager) was highly statistically significant in the adoption model, but had less importance in the SGO/RO models, we explored how the impact of the child's age differed by type of orders. A Cox regression model was run with an interaction term on age since order and type of order, controlling for all the variables listed below:

- type of order (adoption/special guardianship/residence);
- gender (male/female);
- age at placement (with adopters/special guardians/carers on residence orders);
- time between entry to care and placement;

Figure 4.8
Kaplan-Meier survival estimates of the cumulative proportion of disruptions after the legal order

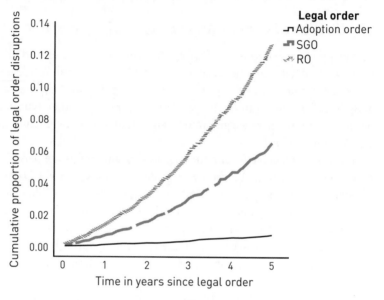

- time between placement and legal order;
- age since order as a time varying covariate (to consider how it varied over the years since the order);
- an interaction term for placement type and age since the order.

As expected, the interaction term for legal order types and age was found to be highly statistically significant in the Cox regression model (p<.001). For children on SGOs and ROs, disruptions were not much affected by the child's age since the making of the order: RO and SGO disruptions occurred irrespective of the child's age since the legal order. On the other hand, adoption disruptions *were* affected by the child's age since the order, with most occurring in the teenage years. There could be various explanations for this difference; perhaps adoptive parents found the teenage years more difficult to manage compared with guardians or carers. More likely, given the overall patterns of disruption, is that adoptive parents persevered and remained committed to children for longer.

Variation in disruption rates by local authority

As with many other studies (e.g. Sinclair *et al*, 2007), we too noticed local authority variation in the proportion of intact and disrupted placements. For adoption, the percentage of disruptions (as a proportion of all the adoptions in the LA) varied between 0 per cent and 7.4 per cent. For SGOs, the proportion that disrupted between 1 December 2005 and 31 March 2011 varied between 0 per cent and 16.7 per cent and for ROs between 0 per cent and 33.3 per cent.

We explored whether local authorities that had a high proportion of adoption disruptions were more likely to also have a higher proportion of disrupted SGOs and ROs. This was not the case. There was no correlation between the proportions of disruptions of the three types of orders within each of the local authorities. Much more research is needed to understand LA variation, as it may be that some LAs have much better practice and we need to understand what works well. It may also be that LAs with the highest disruption rates may not have the poorest practice, but may be placing older children and/or those with more special needs.

Administrative data, whilst very useful for establishing rates and key predictive factors, do not help our understanding of how disruptions occur. For that, we will turn to the interviews with adoptive parents and young people. First, we report on the survey returns from which the interview sample was drawn.

Summary

- Between 1 April 2000 and 31 March 2011, information was available on 37,335 adopted children, 5,291 SGOs and 5,771 ROs. It was known that 525 adoptions, 121 SGOs and 415 ROs had disrupted.
- The adoption disruption rate was 3.2 per cent, the SGO disruption rate was 5.7 per cent and the RO disruption rate was 25 per cent.
- Children's gender and ethnicity were not associated with greater risk of disruption.

- There was LA variation in the proportion of the placements that had disrupted.
- Age at entry to care and the number of placement moves were significant predictors of disruption for children for all three types of order.
- The biggest contributory factor to adoption disruptions was the child's age. Teenagers were 10 times more likely to have a disrupted adoption compared to younger children. Nearly two-thirds of adoption disruptions occurred during the teenage years.
- Age at placement and delay between the placement and the adoption order were also significant predictors of adoption disruption.
- Foster carer adoptions were not more stable than adoptions by stranger adoptive parents. Children adopted by foster carers had lengthier adoption processes than children adopted by strangers.
- Children who were no longer living with their adoptive families were significantly more likely to have lengthier adoption processes compared with the children whose adoptions were intact. This was the case for those who entered care under the age of four years and those who entered over four years of age.
- Children who experienced a SGO or a RO disruption were older at entry to care, older at placement and at the time of the order than children whose SGOs or ROs were intact.
- The time between entry to care and placement with the guardian was not associated with a SGO or RO disruption. The majority of children were placed with the person who became their legal guardian within a year of becoming looked after and the legal orders were made soon after.
- Disruptions were less likely if the children were initially placed with a family or friends carer and when the SGOs or the ROs were made to kinship carers. The children placed with kin experienced fewer placement moves than children placed with unrelated carers.
- Children who experienced a RO disruption were more likely to have had two or more attempts at reunification compared with those whose RO placements were intact.
- Children who experienced a RO disruption were more likely to

have had the order made quickly and within 12 months of being placed with their carer.

- Unlike adoption disruptions, most SGO and RO disruptions occurred when the child was under the age of 11 and disrupted quickly within two years of the date of the legal order. In comparison, the majority of the adoption disruptions occurred in the teenage years and more than five years after the adoption order. However, it should be remembered that data were only available for five years of SGOs and six years of ROs.

- Adoption orders were the most stable of the three orders even when age at placement was taken into account.

5   Surveys of adoptive families

Our analysis of national data produced an estimated rate of adoption disruption, as well as information on some of the factors that were associated with an increased risk of disruption. However, we had concerns that perhaps there had been under-reporting of disruptions by adoption agencies, for the reasons outlined in Chapter 2. Therefore, to examine disruptions using a different approach, our work plan included a survey of adoptive families.

A short survey was sent to adopters (n = 630) who had legally adopted a child placed by our sample of 13 LAs between 1 April 2002 and 31 March 2004 and who could be traced. The intention was to focus on the adolescent years, as our statistical analysis of national data had shown that adolescence was a particularly difficult time for adoptive families. Although many of the families were no longer in contact with the adoption agency, the survey was completed and returned by 210 adoptive parents: a 34 per cent response rate. We had no means of knowing whether those who replied were representative of the complete sample. The same survey (but open to anyone who had legally adopted a child from care) was posted online on the Adoption UK (AUK) website on a disruption thread. It was therefore completed by parents who had adopted children over a wider time period. The AUK survey was completed by 180 adopters who had adopted 310 children.

Surveys could be returned anonymously or information inserted that gave consent for the research team to make contact with the adoptive parent to discuss further involvement in the study. Some AUK adopters did not complete all the survey questions, particularly questions that asked for dates. It seems possible that adopters were concerned that they or their children could be identified and perhaps some doubted the security of an online survey. Therefore, the numbers of responses differ in the analyses below.

In total, we collected survey information on 390 adoptive families caring for 689 adopted children and young people. The children had been placed by 77 different local authorities.

The adoptive families

Most of the adopters had no previous relationship with the child at the time of the adoptive placement. There were slightly more foster carers who had adopted in the LA survey than in the AUK survey (Table 5.1).

Table 5.1
Percentage of adoptive parents who were stranger adopters or previous foster carers

Adoptive parents	LA survey (n = 210) %	AUK members survey (n = 180) %
Stranger adopters	87	93
Child's foster carers	13	7
Total	**100**	**100**

The majority of adoptive parents had adopted more than one child, with most parents adopting two children (range one–six children: Table 5.2).

Table 5.2
Percentage of families who had adopted one or more children

Number of adopted children	LA survey (n = 210) %	AUK members survey (n = 180) %
One	39	25
Two	47	51
Three or more	14	24
Total	**100**	**100**

Most of the parents who had adopted more than one child had adopted a sibling group who had all been placed at the same time.

About 15 per cent of adoptive parents had adopted two or more children who were biologically unrelated.

The adopters were asked to identify the type of agency that had assessed and approved them as adoptive parents. In both surveys, the majority had been approved by the same local authority that had looked after their child/ren pre-adoption, but more of the AUK members had been approved by a voluntary adoption agency (VAA) (Figure 5.1).

Figure 5.1
Agency that approved the adoptive parents

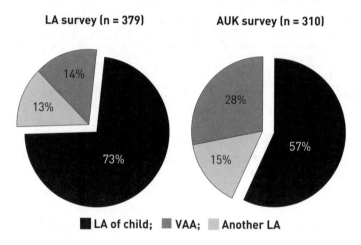

LA survey (n = 379)   AUK survey (n = 310)

■ LA of child;   ■ VAA;   ▨ Another LA

The adopted children (n = 689)

Dates of birth were supplied for 78 per cent of children from the AUK survey and 99 per cent of children from the LA survey. The children's average age differed in the two samples, as did the average length of time in the adoptive home (Table 5.3). This variation was partly due to the differering inclusion criteria for the two surveys: the LA survey could be completed only by those who had legally adopted a child 9–11 years ago, whereas the AUK survey was open to anyone who had legally adopted a looked after child. Although the LA sample predominantly comprised adopted teenagers, parents had adopted other children who were younger and older (age range 1–30 years old), as had the AUK members (age range 0–27 years old). Information was collected on every adopted child in the family.

Table 5.3
Characteristics of the adopted children (n = 689)

	LA survey (n = 379)	AUK members survey (n = 310)
Child's mean age in 2013	14 years old (SD[29] 3.88) Range 1–30 years old	11 years old (SD 5.08) Range 0–27 years old
Gender	50% boys and 50% girls	47% boys and 53% girls
Mean age at the time of adoption order	Four years old (SD 3.34)	Four years old (SD 2.78)
Timeframe in which the majority of adoption orders were made	2002–2004 Range 1986–2010	2005–2008 Range 1985–2013
Time spent with the adoptive family since the making of the order	> eight years 87% 4–7 years 11% 0–3 years 2%	> eight years 31% 4–7 years 46% 0–3 years 23%

How the adoptions were faring

The survey asked adoptive parents to describe how each adoption arrangement was faring, by selecting one of the following four categories: a) going well; b) highs and lows, but mainly highs; c) it is

---

29 SD = standard deviation.

difficult; and d) child no longer lives at home. A couple of parents complained about the categories, wanting to place themselves between "highs and lows" and "it is difficult". Nevertheless, all adopters completed this question.

The majority of adopters (66% in the LA survey and 65% in the AUK survey) described the adoptions as either "going well" or with "highs and lows, but mainly highs". Such a high percentage reporting that family life was pretty good is particularly pleasing when many were parenting teenagers.

About one in five of the LA adopters and one in four of the AUK members described family life as very difficult. In the LA survey, nine per cent of the young people had left home under the age of 18 years, as had eight per cent of young people in the AUK survey. Although the survey had been completed by two different samples, the results were very similar (Figure 5.2).

Figure 5.2
How the adoptions were faring

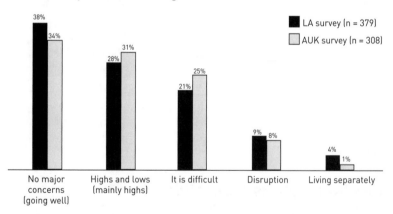

There was space on the survey form for adopters to provide more information if they wished. Some adopters were annoyed that we had seemed to assume that there would be difficulties and were only too pleased to tell us how happy they were. But many adopters took the opportunity to give more detail on the difficulties their children were struggling with, such as attention deficit hyperactivity disorder (ADHD), post-traumatic stress disorder (PTSD), obsessive compulsive disorder (OCD), autistic spectrum disorders (ASD), foetal alcohol spectrum disorders (FASD), developmental trauma, learning difficulties, aggression, difficulties in managing anger, and a lack of empathy. Inadequate support and lack of information were common themes that ran through adopters' comments. We consider those themes in the following sections, which are grouped according to the category adoptive parents selected to describe adoptive family life.

Going well
LA survey n = 143 (38%); AUK members n = 104 (34%)

In this group, many adopters described family life very positively. For example, they wrote: *100% fantastic!* and *Absolutely brilliant.* Most of the comments indicated that the families in this group were experiencing few or no difficulties and thought that their family life was very similar to that of many other families in the community. Parents often stressed that their child was embedded in the family and that secure attachments had developed. For example, adopters commented:

Extremely positive, the best thing I have ever done. My son is the light of my life. (LA survey)

It's brilliant! We are a normal, happy family. There is no difference between ourselves and other families with children of the same age, i.e. my son's friends' families. (AUK survey)

Our daughter is a teenager with the usual teenage problems. She is no more or less difficult than my own birth children. (LA survey)

Wouldn't contemplate anything different. They are "my kids". (AUK survey)

Nevertheless, a few adopters reported that, although things were going well, their child had significant difficulties. For example, one adopter commented:

Daughter has Down's and many health issues but is a delight.
(AUK survey)

In this group, parents typically reported the high quality of social work support they had received, saying, for example:

We have been well supported by our adoption agency . . . brilliant family placement officer. (AUK survey)

However, some adoptive parents stated that they did not want social work support and were pleased to be free from social workers, as in the following extracts:

As soon as we shook off social services and the courts, all our lives improved. (LA survey)

We believe our placement has worked because they knew they were adopted and the subject is EXTREMELY open and referred to often. We do not take them to "adoption events" or involve them in any post-placement schemes . . . Our kids know they are ours, we are not loaning them, borrowing them, or bringing them up for somebody else. The family is forever, surely the whole point of adoption. (LA survey)

Highs and lows, but mostly highs
LA survey n = 107 (28%); AUK members n = 97 (31%)

Although many of the adopters who selected this category described the adoption as generally faring well, they placed more emphasis in their comments on difficulties and the challenges that they were facing. Some parents commented that the lows were just part of bringing up teenagers or were associated with children's disabilities or health problems and not necessarily with the adoption itself. For example, one adopter wrote:

Child has foetal alcohol syndrome . . . lows because of problems, not lows with adoption. (LA survey)

Other parents emphasised how their child's behaviour or mental health could, after months of normality, suddenly deteriorate before returning to an even keel. These adopters emphasised how the "lows" had been very difficult to manage. For example, one adoptive mother wrote:

Child has a pattern of going along well for long periods and then sinking fast and hard occasionally. (LA survey)

In this group, adopters gave examples of the excellent professional support they were receiving:

We had a course of Theraplay, which made an enormous differ-ence ... we have just had the 10th anniversary of the adoption order and things are going well. The adoption allowance we received has made a big difference to our family. (AUK survey)

However, there were also more complaints about inadequate service provision and the word "fighting" appeared frequently in relation to receiving support. Adopters wrote about their perseverance and dog-gedness in getting help for their children, as in the following extracts:

Hard work but very rewarding and we're in it for the long haul. Fight for everything but wouldn't change it. (AUK survey)

We cannot access post-adoption support because we adopted out of our local area. We have to wait until she has lived with us for three years before she becomes the responsibility of our local authority. What nonsense this is. Meanwhile, she thrives in our loving household but the financial, emotional, physical toll taken to bring her up cannot be quantified!!! (AUK survey)

It took five years to get the right support in school. Attachment disorder, dyslexia, co-ordination development disorder and liver treatment for Hep C are just some of the issues our son has had to cope with ... I could write a book with descriptions of the myriad of challenges we have faced in parenting our son. We love him dearly and marvel at his determination to keep up with his peers, his sensitivity to the needs of his friends and his desire to do his best. (LA survey)

Major difficulties
LA survey n = 81 (21%); AUK members n = 78 (25%)

In this group, all the adoptive parents reported that their child had multiple and overlapping difficulties and had often not received appropriate interventions or support. More of the parents (36%) who had been approved by a VAA reported major difficulties compared to parents approved by a LA (22%). This is likely to be because children placed with VAA-approved adopters tend to have more special needs, but it may also have been because of difficulties in accessing additional support.

Adopters frequently used words such as "nightmare" and "struggle" in relation to accessing appropriate support services. They also referred more often to the impact on themselves, especially the exhaustion of parenting children with multiple difficulties. For example, an adoptive parent wrote:

Zero support for us as a family. We hang on in there somehow for her sake because she deserves it, we love her, and we can't contemplate the alternative. But it is at huge cost to our emotional, physical and financial health. (AUK survey)

Many parents commented on having to "do battle" with professionals to get support which, even if provided, was often time-limited and unco-ordinated. Adopters also commented on feeling personally "let down" by the failure of social workers to keep their promise of being there when needed, or of the agency reneging on support packages. For example, parents wrote:

Despite numerous professionals and social workers saying they are supporting us, we have received NO practical help until the last few months when our lives and health were falling apart. Despite extreme behaviour at home and school, CAMHS did not help us . . . it has been a nightmare . . . we finally got to Great Ormond Street Hospital . . . he needs a residential school. The last four years have been constant exclusions from a school he should never have attended. As a family, we feel totally let down . . . this could have been prevented. (LA survey)

We adopted out of county and have not received any meaningful adoption support. Every day is a challenge and we feel badly let down. My wife cannot work and we are both exhausted. (AUK survey)

[Child] has since been diagnosed with ASD and ADHD, as well as sensory issues, asthma and migraine headaches. He is a very poor sleeper and also has poor fine motor skills. Challenging behaviour and very poor relationship with his younger sister. His behaviour at home is very difficult and has a major impact on the other children and how we function as a family. He has had support from education but CAMHS are only interested in diagnosing and prescribing. There is no support to deal with behaviour and they do not want to consider attachment or the effects from his pre-birth and pre-adoption experiences. It is very frustrating as a parent. (AUK survey)

Some of the comments from adoptive parents in this group suggested that the adoption was very close to breaking down. For example, adopters used terms such as "surviving", or "only just living with us" and described how relationships were very fraught. They emphasised the impact of the child's difficulties on marital and family relationships. For example, one adoptive father wrote:

Wife has left so single parenting . . . son's behaviour a contributory factor in wife leaving. (LA survey)

However, not all the adoptive parents who selected this category were on the verge of disruption. Some adoptive parents acknowledged the difficulties, but the tone of the comments suggested that the child would remain within the family, as in these examples:

Very little post-adoption support . . . he has anger management problem and not many friends . . . detention and exclusions are commonplace. We have some good days and some not so good days. It is not all negative, we love him loads. (AUK survey)

[Child] is very difficult to live with at times but we love her and [her sister] very much and that will never change. We feel that if we had more respite care (never had any, although begged for it a few times) things would have had a chance to settle. Have felt at times like running under a bus but nobody cares or helps at such times. (LA survey)

For a few adoptive parents, the support they had been offered was excellent, as in the following extracts:

We received amazing support there every step of the way. Older child [has had] CAMHS therapy for a while, private music therapy and mentoring. That's what helped us continue. Husband died four years ago. Love is not enough. (AUK survey)

The adoptive placement went through a tricky patch...we had involvement from the social services department and faced the possibility of a disruption. At a family liaison meeting, we were supported hugely to keep going, and through the generosity of good friends and his godfather, who offered permanent lodgings for three–six months, we weathered the storm. (LA survey)

A few of the young people in this group had spent a short period in foster care and then returned to their adoptive families, and two had had short spells in adolescent psychiatric units following self-harm. A few had returned to their birth families, but then returned to their adoptive family, as in the following example:

He left at 17 years due to his stealing to feed his cannabis/ smoking habit . . . came back aged 23 years following the death of his birth mother. (LA survey)

This latter group of young people reminds us that a survey asks about the progress of adoptions at a specific point in time, and circumstances can and do change.

Children or young people who had left home prematurely
LA survey n = 34 (9%); AUK members n = 26 (8%)

Thirty-four young people in the LA survey and 26 young people in the AUK survey were no longer living with their adoptive parents. Most of the young people had left their family at 14 or 15 years of age (range 6–17 years old). Table 5.4 shows the whereabouts of the adopted young people at the time of the survey.

Table 5.4
Living arrangements for young people who had left home prematurely

	LA survey (n = 34)	AUK members survey (n = 26)
Foster care	11	14
Independent living	6	5
Pathways to independence	4	4
Residential care	3	2
Supported lodgings/supported housing provided by adult disability services	2	
Whereabouts unknown	2	1
Extended family or a friend's family	2	
Sectioned under Mental Health Act	1	
A new adoptive placement	1	
Hostel	1	
Prison	1	
Total	**34**	**26**

The reasons for leaving home were generally a combination of young people's behaviour becoming too challenging to manage, combined with inadequate support. The quality of support was a key issue for adopters in this category. It was not simply a lack of support, but adopters also reported that parental concerns were not taken seriously and/or felt that they were being blamed by professionals for their child's difficulties. For example, one parent wrote:

> *My daughter was only put back into care as the local authority would not give her a full psychiatric assessment after . . . taking and hiding knives around our family home where I had two birth children . . . The local authority never accepted the aggression my daughter displayed and failed to take on how destructive this behaviour can be to herself and especially to the family . . . The local authority seemed far more interested in blaming the family than ever looking at the possible issues.* (LA survey)

Although the majority of parents' and young people's relationships were very fraught, this was not the case for all. Some parents had a "shared care" arrangement with the young person living in foster care and at home, as in the following example:

> *Although the eldest is in foster care, we see her about once a fortnight when she comes to stay with us . . . She is presently accommodated in "foster care" but we, her adoptive parents, continue to have parental responsibility as far as we are concerned, but her reliance on us varies from situation to situation. She comes to stay with us when she has a crisis or is anxious about her circumstances. She lives between her LA accommodation and our home. Last year she moved between her birth parents (she had sought them out), her foster carer's home, her boyfriend's house, and us.* (AUK survey)

Young adults living independently from their adoptive parents

LA survey n = 14 (4%); AUK members n = 3 (1%)

Adopters provided some information on this group of young adults who had left home between the ages of 18–31 years. Three of the adopted young people were living in adult residential care homes or supported housing projects because of learning difficulties or other disabilities and were not expected to be able to live fully independent lives. Some were settled with their own families and had good relationships with their adoptive parents.

> *He obtained six GCSEs at Grade C or above and has worked as an electrician since age 18. Has had a steady girlfriend for three years.* (AUK survey)

For other adopted young people, the impact of their early experiences continued to have a detrimental impact on their adult lives. For example, one adoptive mother wrote:

> *She had been sexually abused and been to 11 schools before being placed with me and she now has mental health problems and is unable to keep a job. We were unable to access any help relevant for her. She is not an alcoholic, nor is she a drug addict, nor has she been in prison – so she is doing very well. She is still my daughter, although I parent at a distance now.* (LA survey)

Overall, the survey provided evidence that the majority of adoptive placements were going well and families were settled. The survey was first conducted with a sample of LA adoptive parents who were parenting mainly teenagers and then replicated with AUK members who were parenting mainly younger children. In both samples, most disruptions had occurred when young people were teenagers. The survey provided examples of family circumstances that, on paper, would have been categorised as a "disruption" but where the adoptive parent still had a commitment to the welfare of the young person. There were also examples of intact families where relationships had broken down and parents were waiting for the young person to reach an age when they could be asked to leave without fear of parental prosecution. The issue of how living arrangements are defined was raised in Chapter 1 and could be clearly seen in adoptive parents' comments. Although disruption was rare, some families were really struggling and were concerned about the lack of support. One parent made a plea about the research request for information: 'Please let this contribute to support for adoptive families, more than a jolly get-together at Xmas!' In addition, another parent wrote:

> Before the Government makes any changes to reduce the time it takes to adopt a child, an urgent review is required of post-adoption services and support. Social workers urgently need training in how to provide, listen and act on adoptive parents' concerns. Too much finger-pointing goes on, claiming parents need to do parenting courses.

In the next chapters, we explore these issues in detail from the information shared during our interviews with adoptive parents.

Summary

- A short survey was completed by 210 adoptive parents from the 13 LAs taking part in the research and by 180 AUK members, caring in total for 689 adopted children. The survey asked for details about their adopted children and how the adoptions were faring.
- The children in the LA survey were older (average age 14 years) compared to most of the children (average age 11 years) adopted by AUK members. The majority of children (83%) in the LA sample had been with their families for eight years or more, whereas most (69%) of the AUK members' children had been with their families for less than eight years.
- The children had been placed by 77 different local authorities. Most had been placed with adopters approved by a LA, whilst 20 per cent were placed with a VAA-approved adopter.
- The results of the two surveys were very similar. Just over one-third of adoptive parents were experiencing no or few difficulties and family life was described as going well. Where support had been requested, it had usually been provided and adopters were complimentary about service provision. For another 30 per cent of

families, whilst family life was still good, they also reported facing challenges. Often these challenges stemmed from their child's special needs and getting the right support in place.

- About one-quarter of parents described major parenting challenges with children who had multiple and overlapping difficulties. Many parents were struggling to get the right support in place. Parents reported that they were physically and mentally exhausted and that lack of support had had a negative impact on marital and family relationships. Some of the comments from parents who described parenting as very challenging suggested that families were on the verge of disruption. Comments from other parents indicated that, after a tricky patch, sometimes involving the child's brief return to foster care or an intensive intervention, relationships had improved.

- About nine per cent of the young people had left their adoptive home under the age of 18 years (average age at disruption 14–15 years old). Parents typically reported that the move out of home had been triggered by a combination of challenging behaviour, inadequate support and feeling blamed for the child's difficulties. Most parents were still active in their parenting role, although some were not in contact with their children.

Introduction to the interviews

In the next section, we focus on the findings from interviews with adoptive parents, young people who had experienced a disruption, and adoption managers. Our statistical analysis of the national data had found that an adoption disruption was a rare event. However, we wanted to understand why disruptions occurred and what could be done to help families who were in crisis. The survey findings also revealed that, although disruption was uncommon, there was a significant minority of families struggling with very challenging children. We wanted to know whether these families were "disruptions waiting to happen" or whether they were likely to stay intact.

Seventy parents were interviewed for this purpose: 35 parents who were experiencing great difficulty in caring for an adopted child who still lived at home, and 35 where the difficulties had led to a young person leaving home prematurely (under the age of 18 years). Parents were selected for interview because adoptive family life was, or had been, extremely difficult. The families are *not typical* of adoptive families generally, but may be typical of families experiencing great difficulty. We did not interview adoptive parents who described family life as "going well" or those with "highs and lows outweighed by highs". Notably, these latter two groups accounted for about two-thirds of all the survey responses (see Chapter 5).

The interviews were designed to understand more about the context in which difficulties arose, and the nature of the challenges faced by families. The interviews followed a well-established investigator-based approach (e.g. Brown, 1983; Quinton and Rutter, 1988). This method combines a "qualitative" approach to questioning but allows a "quantitative" treatment of data. It provides systematic and detailed coverage of topics and numerically analysable data whilst providing extensive case material. Interviews were usually held in adoptive parents' homes and lasted on average three hours. The method allowed us to see if there were any systematic patterns that differentiated those families whose child had left home.

The interview schedule with parents tracked the experiences of their adoption journey chronologically and the findings are presented in the same way. The chapters report on the pre-adoption experiences of parents; the early days of adoptive family life; onset and escalation of difficulties; communication and cohesion within the adoptive family; service responses to families in difficulty; and, for 35 parents, experiences of adoption disruption. The interview work with parents concludes with reflections on their adoption experience and their hopes for the future. In Chapter 14, we report on the findings from the interviews with 12 young people who had experienced an adoption disruption. This is followed by adoption managers describing the services they offered, and the challenges they were facing in delivering good post-adoption support services.

6 Interviews with adoptive parents: starting out

Characteristics of the adoptive parents

In this chapter, we begin by describing the characteristics of the 70 adopters who were interviewed and their families. The sample was drawn from those adopters who had completed the survey and had given consent to be interviewed. We consider the preparation and assessment of the adoptive parents, their experiences of linking and matching, and the introductions to the children they later adopted.

The 35 interviewees who were experiencing great difficulty in caring for a child living at home are described as the "At home" group, whilst the 35 interviewees, whose child had left home prematurely are described as the "Left home" group. Attention will be drawn to where there was a statistically significant difference between the two groups; otherwise, the analyses include all 70 families.

In 57 families, one adoptive parent (51 mothers and six fathers) was interviewed alone and in 13 families both parents were interviewed together. Most parents (83%) had been approved as adopters by a local authority (LA), whilst 11 parents (17%) had been approved by a voluntary adoption agency (VAA). Three parents (4%) had previously been the child's foster carer. Seven per cent of parents were from a minority ethnic background. At the time of their approval as prospective adoptive parents, the majority (91%) were married or living with a partner. Just six (9%) of the 70 parents had been approved as single adopters. The proportion of LA-approved and VAA-approved adopters and couple/single adopters were similar to the national picture of the characteristics of adoptive parents. There were fewer foster carer adopters in our sample compared with the national statistics (DfE, 2013a). Information on the ethnicity of adoptive parents is not collected nationally.

Family composition

Since approval, there had been some changes in the marital status of our 70 families: nine per cent of parents had divorced, four per cent had separated, four per cent had been widowed, and four per cent had a new partner living in the home. At the time of the interview in 2013, nine mothers and three fathers (21%) were parenting alone.

The majority of adoptive parents had other children living in the family home besides the young person who was the focus of the interview. Just over three-quarters (76%) of the households included other adopted children (range 0–4 children) and 23 per cent had birth children (range 0–4 children). Eleven families (16%) had both adopted and birth children living at home and one family had continued to foster. In three families, an adopted young person's own baby was also living in the family home and another family was caring for an elderly relative with dementia in the home. There were 10 (14%) adopters with no children living in the household at the time of the interview; all had experienced a disruption.

Employment

Eighty per cent of adoptive mothers in the "Left home" group were working full or part-time, as were 68 per cent of mothers in the "At home" group. Mothers commonly had careers in the health, social care or education fields, with several holding senior professional posts. We interviewed mothers who were university lecturers, head teachers, doctors, senior nurses, social workers, and those running their own businesses. Of those not working, the majority said that they were not looking for work or were unable to work because of their parenting commitments. Most fathers (92%) were working, three had retired, and two were looking for work.

Adoptive parents' motivation to adopt and early preferences

Adoptive parents were asked what had influenced their desire to adopt, how family and friends had responded to their plans, and whether they had any early preferences with regard to the children they were hoping to adopt.

The adoption choice

Just over three-quarters (n = 54) of parents had chosen to adopt because of infertility, pregnancy-related health concerns or following miscarriages. For example, adoptive mothers said:

I couldn't have children of my own, so it was a response to my childlessness. (Left home)

I married at 35 ... when it came down to it, I'd waited too late. (Left home)

Twelve (17%) adopters wanted to adopt for altruistic reasons, some of whom said that adoption had been part of their life plan for a long time:

We decided before we got married that we would have a child of our own and then we would adopt after that ... We wanted two children, one of our own and one adopted, that was the grand plan ... we're both altruistic people and we just wanted to do something to help really. (Left home)

Three adopters had been the child's foster carer and the child had become part of their family. Nearly half of the parents had parenting experience, often in a previous relationship. Fewer fathers in the "Left home" group had any experience of parenting.

Encouragement to adopt from family and friends

Some parents already had a close connection with the experience of adoption: three mothers were adopted themselves and a further 27 (39%) parents had a close friend or relative who was an adoptive parent or an adopted person. For some parents, their decision to adopt had been influenced by knowing a person who spoke positively about the experience. As one mother explained:

Our best friend, she's adopted and she talked to us about how good it had been for her ... she didn't encourage us to do it ... but her experience helped me have the confidence to do it. (At home)

While most adoptive parents said that their family and friends had been supportive of their plan to adopt, one-fifth (n = 14) said that there were key people who had been against the idea. In these instances, it was nearly always one or both of the adopters' parents who had struggled to understand or accept their desires and motivations. For example, one adopter explained how her mother-in-law could not accept their infertility:

> *I remember being told that we didn't have to [adopt], we just had to keep on trying to get pregnant, and it will happen.* (At home)

Others described how they were told that they needed their "heads testing", or were advised to get a dog instead. Adopters explained how they had hoped that the arrival of their child would change people's views.

Early preferences

Adoptive parents were asked about any preferences they had had at the outset, such as the number, age, or gender of the child/ren they were hoping to adopt. Most (60%) of the parents started out wanting more than one child; about one-quarter wanted to adopt just one child, while the remaining parents had no particular preference or had not given it much thought. Of those who expressed an initial preference on the number of children they would like, 20 per cent changed their minds following training and preparation, or because professionals presented them with the details of specific children. In most of these instances, the change was from initially wanting a single child to being matched with a sibling group, although three families took a single child when they had originally wanted more. One parent who changed his mind explained:

> *Having started with the idea of one [child] we actually read some research that suggested that when you've got birth kids, a single adopted child can feel like the odd one out and it could be better to have a sibling group. Also, I thought that I don't really want to go through this process again.* (Left home)

Only one in five of the adoptive parents had initially hoped for a baby. Most knew that being matched with a baby was very unlikely. Even so, the majority of parents expressed a preference for a child as young as possible and of pre-school age.

Just under one-fifth of parents (19%) did want an older child. These parents generally thought that there would be less developmental uncertainty, as any difficulties the child had would be apparent. A few believed that an older child would fit in better with their own work patterns and the existing family composition, whilst a couple of adopters with health issues thought that lifting and carrying would not be needed with an older child. About 10 per cent expressed no preference on age or did not mind. Just over one-quarter of parents (27%) changed their minds about the age of the child they were willing to consider. Some did so when they realised that their initial preference for an infant was unrealistic, but most changed their minds after hearing about the child with whom they were eventually linked.

Adopters were also asked if there were other characteristics or features in children's backgrounds that they had felt unable to manage. Most often, parents stated that they had not wanted to be matched with a child who had significant physical or learning disabilities, such as Down's syndrome, or with children showing serious emotional and behavioural difficulties. Adopters were also particularly cautious about children with a history of sexual abuse or those born out of incest or rape.

Overall, 39 per cent were matched with a child who did not meet at least one of their original preferences. Some parents accepted a match that contradicted several preferences. Most changes were in relation to the child's age (accepting older children) and number of children (accepting siblings). In most cases, adoptive parents did not seem to mind changing their preferences and saw it as part of the process. However, more parents in the "Left home" group (n = 16) adopted a child who did not match their original preferences compared with parents in the "At home" group (n = 11).

Preparation and assessment

Adoptive parents were asked about the quality of the social work preparation. In hindsight, 65 per cent of parents whose child had "Left home" thought that the preparation had been inadequate, as did 20 per cent of parents whose child still lived at home. Parents stated that they had felt unprepared, although a few recognised that the state of knowledge at the time their child was placed was very different to that known today. For example, adopters mentioned the recent growth in knowledge about the importance of attachment and security, the long-term impact of maltreatment, and the recognition of developmental trauma. One mother explained:

> With hindsight, nobody ever talked about attachment . . . Nobody ever covered the issue of raising a child born addicted [to heroin] and the issues that very obviously brings. To be fair, they probably didn't know very much about it. I think the research was still in its infancy. (At home)

The majority of parents saw the home assessment as a means to an end and it was tolerated. However, more than one-third of parents (37%) enjoyed the experience, with some describing it as an opportunity for personal growth and discovery. A few adoptive parents disliked the home visits, often describing poor rapport with their assessing social worker. One criticism made by several adopters was that the home study had not been sufficiently challenging or informative. One parent explained:

> What I would say is that it was probably too comfortable. I did feel sometimes that I was just able to say it, you know, give my side, but not be probed further. I'm wondering if I went back to that assessment, whether or not there were things that I should have really explored in more detail that would have been helpful. (Left home)

The majority of parents said that they had been truthful during the assessment process, but about one in five revealed that they had downplayed difficulties, or had not been totally honest because they did not want to jeopardise their chances of being approved. There were, for example, adopters who did not disclose that their marriage was under strain, that they were struggling to come to terms with a recent miscarriage, or that they were having fertility treatment at the same time as being assessed as prospective adopters. Seven of the adoptive parents knew that the panel had reservations about their application. Although we did not ask whether parents had ever been turned down as prospective adopters by another agency, three parents volunteered this information.

The preparation of other children in the household
Eight of the parents in the "Left home" group and 11 in the "At home" group had other children living in the household *before* the child was placed for adoption. Only one adopter in the "Left home" group and three in the "At home" group thought that there had been good preparation of these children by professionals. Most parents recalled little or no interaction between their existing children and the social worker. As one adopter recalled:

> I think they briefly spoke to [children] once, but it was more ... for their form filling ... just, 'Are you OK with this?' (Left home)

The adopted young people (n = 70)

The majority of adopters were parenting more than one child. Some families had experienced more than one disruption and in these instances, parents were asked during the interview to focus on the child who had moved out of home first. Other parents, who had more than one child considered challenging and living at home, were asked to focus on the child who was the most difficult to care for.

Sibling groups
Fifteen children (21%) had been placed as a single child in the family, whilst the majority (79%) had been placed with siblings. Forty-five

children had been placed with one sibling, six with two siblings, three with three siblings, and one child had been placed with five other siblings.

Age at entry to care, placement and at disruption

Compared with the children who still lived at home, the children in the "Left home" group were, on average, older when they were first placed with their adoptive families and were less likely to have been removed from their birth families as infants. Only three per cent of children in the "Left home" group became looked after at or soon after birth, whilst the same was true for 29 per cent of children in the "At home" group.

The young people who had left home were also significantly older when they entered care, at placement with their adoptive family, and at the time of the adoption order compared with the children who were still living at home (Table 6.1).[30]

We know from the statistical analyses of the national data (Chapters 3–5) that the average age at entry to care for all adopted children is 14 months, and that being older at entry to care and at placement increases the risk of disruption. The majority of children in this sample were much older than most adopted children when they entered care and on placement with their adoptive family. It is also interesting to note that most of the young people left their adoptive family as teenagers, the age range where disruptions are most likely to occur.

There was no statistical difference in the likelihood of the young person having left home by the child's gender, whether they had been placed as part of a sibling group, or whether their adoptive parent was a single parent.

---

30 Mann Whitney $U = 382.00$, $Z = -2.73$ $p<.006$

Table 6.1
Gender and age of the young people in the study

	Left home	At home
Gender	20 boys (57%)	18 boys (51%)
	15 girls (43%)	17 girls (49%)
Age at entry to care	Av. 3.8 years	Av. 2.0 years
	(SD 2.01)	(SD 1.90)
	Range 0–10 years	Range 0–6 years
Age at placement with the adoptive family	Av. 5.4 years	Av. 3.5 years
	(SD 2.15)	(SD 2.61)
	Range 0–11 years	Range 0–7 years
Age at the time of the adoption order	Av. 6.0 years	Av. 4.2 years
	(SD 2.61)	(SD 2.39)
	Range 1–12 years	Range 0–8 years
Age when left home	Av. 14 years	
	(SD 2.21)	
	Range 10–17 years	
Age at the time of the study	Av. 18 years	Av. 15 years
	(SD 2.20)	(SD 2.22)
	Range 12–22 years	Range 12–20 years

Children's family background and early history

It was surprising how little adoptive parents knew about the child's birth and early history.[31] For example, many parents did not know whether the child had been born prematurely or of low birth weight. Of the 11 children (16%) known to be of low birth weight (under 5.5lbs), three had needed interventions for drug withdrawal at birth.

Birth mothers

The birth mothers of the children had experienced the kinds of difficulties that have been reported in many previous studies (e.g.

---

31 Birth family history was assembled from the adoptive parents' accounts. There may have been circumstances of which they and/or the placing social worker were unaware.

Rushton, 2003; Selwyn *et al*, 2006a; 2010). Forty-seven per cent of the mothers had been looked after themselves and many had experienced difficult childhoods, characterised by domestic violence and/or abuse. Many birth mothers had their first child as a teenager, followed by a series of pregnancies with children removed sequentially because of neglect or abuse. Four birth mothers had previously had a child die as a result of abuse, or in circumstances where there had been existing concerns about maltreatment. Just over one-third (35%) of mothers were known to have had mental health problems. There was a high level of drug and alcohol misuse, with 61 per cent of the mothers known to have drug and/or alcohol problems. At the time of the interviews with adoptive parents, three birth mothers were known to have died: two had taken their own lives and one had died after an illness.

Birth fathers

The identity of one in five birth fathers was unknown or uncertain, but even where their identity was known, adoptive parents knew a lot less about children's fathers than their mothers. Adoptive parents had some information on 46 of the 70 fathers. Prevalent were drug and/or alcohol misuse and histories of violence leading to prison sentences for murder, assaults and gun-related offences (22 birth fathers). Five fathers had extensive histories of sexual offences and two fathers had died.

The children's history of abuse and neglect

The vast majority of all the children had been abused and/or neglected prior to placement with their adoptive families. Of the few children without a history of maltreatment, three had been removed at birth by children's services with signs of heroin dependency, and a further five children had been rejected or abandoned by their parents at birth.

More of the young people who had left home had been maltreated (Table 6.2) and from the accounts given by their adoptive parents, had often suffered more severe levels of abuse than those children who were still at home. Five children from the "Left home" group had been sexually exploited by their birth parents and other adults.

Table 6.2
Children's history of abuse and neglect

	Left home	At home
Neglect	33 (94%)	27 (77%)
Exposed to domestic violence	32 (91%)	20 (57%)
Emotional abuse	22 (63%)	21 (60%)
Physical abuse	20 (57%)	16 (46%)
Sexual abuse	12 (34%)	5 (14%)
Rejection	9 (26%)	12 (34%)
Sexual exploitation	5 (14%)	0 (0%)

The very high levels of domestic violence in the birth family home were noticeable. The children's exposure to violence was not only from fathers, but also from birth mothers' new partners and occasionally from the mothers themselves. There was a significant association between having been exposed to domestic violence and the child not living at home. Children who had been exposed to domestic violence in their early life were more likely to have had an adoption disruption than those who had not been exposed.[32] It is important to remember that the "Left home" group did not enter care until they were, on average, four years old. Therefore, they had been exposed to domestic violence and abuse during their formative years and probably including the period (about 6–12 months) when preferential attachments are formed.

Linking and matching

Adoptive parents were asked about the process of linking and matching. Surprisingly, many parents (59%) knew that they had been linked with at least one other child before being matched with the child/ren they went on to adopt. Some adoptive parents gave accounts of social workers visiting with the details of children and trying to persuade

---

32 χ^2 (1) = 10.77, $p<.01$

them to change their preferences. An adoptive parent who wanted more than one child said:

> The social worker came round with pictures of one baby boy ... and I said, 'No thank you'. I stood my ground. They [social workers] just thought they'd show me a picture of baby and she'll melt, she will go for the one [child]. I said, 'No, I really want two children'. (At home)

Sometimes adopters chose not to pursue a link when more detailed information about the child/ren and parents' backgrounds became known, or after they had been able to reflect on the situation. Sexual abuse was of particular concern, as in the following account:

> I can remember very clearly the very first child who was brought to our attention. It was a little girl, she was two years old ... she had been abused ... The social worker [explained] that if the child was sat on a settee and you went close, even at that age she would say, 'No touch Sasha', and that stayed with me. We felt in the end that we weren't knowledgeable enough perhaps to enter into that situation. (At home)

Occasionally adopters were just not drawn to the children they were linked with and, although they could not identify anything tangible, knew that a match would not be right:

> They had sent us paperwork on a boy and a girl ... there was nothing wrong with them. We read it, but it just didn't sing to us ... there was nothing there that we wanted and they said, 'Are you keen to follow this up?' We couldn't say why, but no, we weren't. (At home)

Most commonly, however, a link did not progress because the social worker decided not to take things further. Several adopters thought that they had been in competitive matches with other prospective parents and for some, repeated knock-backs were difficult to accept, as a parent said:

We were shown other profiles and we always said, 'Yes, we're interested', but then they always chose another couple over us. I think we had about three or four like that. That was hard and my husband was very close to chucking the towel in. (At home)

Adopters sometimes described how they had already started to invest emotionally in the children who they were linked to and to describe feelings of disappointment and loss when the link did not develop into a match. As one mother explained:

There was one child who we'd gone all the way down the line with . . . we'd met all the social workers . . . it was approved by panel, but the decision-maker wasn't there. Then the decision-maker went against the decision of the panel. That really threw us, because you just kind of feel you're already attached at that point . . . We had seen pictures of her, everything had been approved and agreed, and then it was 'No'. We then actually withdrew from the adoption process for about six months because we just thought, actually, we can't do this any more. This is just too emotional. (Left home)

It is important to remember that many of the adoptive parents had tried for many years to conceive, had been through episodes of unsuccessful fertility treatment, miscarriages or stillbirths and consequently had multiple experiences of loss. Links with children that did not proceed may have reawakened some of those feelings of bereavement and loss. A few adoptive parents said that, from time to time, they still wondered about how things had turned out for the children with whom they had been linked, but not matched.

The match to their child

The adopters' initial response to the proposed match was generally positive, but at this early stage and before having met their child, 40 per cent of parents said that they had had some concerns. The concerns centred on the child not meeting their expressed preferences or the growing realisation that the backgrounds, histories, and behaviours would not make the task of parenting easy. Nevertheless, most adopters thought that they were up to the challenge and, on reflection, some were struck by how overly confident and arrogant they had been at the time. A few adopters were worried about the ramifications of adoption plans that were being contested by birth parents.

Most of the adopters had seen a photograph of the child; some had also seen video footage, which was valued. As one mother said:

We did ask to see a video of her in order for me to see how she looked and how she acted, and so the foster carer did that and that just clinched it really. That was a fundamental part – for me to engage with her before we actually met her. That was very significant. I would advise anybody to do that. (At home)

Four adopters had been allowed to see the child in person before the match was approved by the panel.

Time to matching
About one in five adopters (21%) waited a month or less to be matched with their child, 43 per cent waited one–six months, 13 per cent waited 7–12 months, and 23 per cent waited a year or more. The majority of links and matches were led by the social worker, although about one-fifth (21%) of adoptive parents found the child themselves by searching in publications such as *Be My Parent*.[33]

Introductions

The time spent introducing the child and the adoptive family ranged from 1–56 days. A usual pattern was introductions lasting about 14 days, although nearly two in five children (37%) moved into their adoptive home within a week. Thirty-nine per cent of adopters thought that, overall, the introductions to the children had been handled well, 31 per cent rated them as reasonable, whilst a similar

---

33 *Be My Parent* provides profiles of children waiting to be adopted in England and is published by BAAF.

proportion (30%) thought that the introductions had been badly handled. Poorly managed introductions were mentioned far more frequently by adopters whose children had left home. Children were statistically more likely not to be living at home if their adopters considered the introductions to have been handled badly.[34] There were three main reasons why introductions were thought not to have gone well: poor timing, poor planning, and rushing.

Poor timing

Some parents described how little thought had been given to the timing of the introductions. Some children had moved into their adoptive homes on or around key events such as a birthday or Christmas or at times when support from adoption workers was absent or extremely limited (for example, bank holidays). One child moved into his adoptive home within days of his birth mother having a baby that the child knew she was planning to keep. Parents explained how the lack of attention to timing only added to what was an already stressful situation. One adoptive father recalled:

On the Friday we were [suddenly] asked to bring the girls home for one night and then take them back the next day . . . we're talking about 350 miles . . . and we had to make a success of a four-hour journey. Normally, a social worker comes down and takes them back, but because it was a bank holiday, 'Oh, you can do that; we haven't got anybody. You will have to bring them back.' (Left home)

Poor planning

Adopters spoke of arrangements that had not been properly thought through, such as one adoptive mother who had been given B&B accommodation in the street adjacent to the birth mother's house. Another mother described how she had been left to organise her own accommodation during the introductions:

---

34 c^2 (1) = 7.00, p<.05

I don't think anything [children's services] did was planned well. There was no helping me out, nothing towards the costs, no thought about how would I get there . . . So I went down and stayed with my brother. I slept on his sofa for the introductions. (Left home)

The introductions were particularly exhausting for parents adopting a sibling group, especially when the children lived in different foster placements. One father thought that the plan of introductions had failed to consider the strain on both him and his wife. He explained:

The social workers said it was the most gruelling set of introductions they had put anyone through . . . Three children, three different foster placements and they moved in individually over four weeks. I was trying to work from home full time, but I was starting work at four in the morning, and then spending a few hours driving around [the county], meeting the kids, and coming back. It was planned with military precision, but I don't think it was considered very well . . . the stress on us was not taken into account . . . at the end of that we were absolutely exhausted, which put us on the wrong foot. (Left home)

Rushed introductions

There was a feeling amongst several adopters that the introductions had been rushed. Such hastiness was often linked to the children's fostering situation. A few foster carers had issued an ultimatum to the local authority, giving a date by which the fostering arrangement must end, because they wanted the child moved on, or they had booked a holiday without foster children. Parents described how rushed introductions had impeded the transition between the foster and adoptive families. For example, one mother explained how she had been persuaded to accept a plan of introductions, even though her husband was not available that week. The social worker insisted that his involvement was unnecessary. The school-aged child moved into her adoptive home within a week, having met her prospective father only twice. The adopter subsequently discovered that the foster placement had been on the verge of disrupting. In the event, the prospective adoptive father chose not to legally adopt the child, leaving his wife to proceed as a single parent.

Support from social workers during the introductions

The quality of the support given by the assessing social worker during the introductions had a bearing on how well the adoptive parents thought the introductions had been handled. Forty per cent of the adopters whose children had left home and 63 per cent of those whose children were at home rated their social worker as supportive and available when needed. For example, parents said:

She was there if we needed her, we could phone her. She was very supportive. (At home)

Outstanding. She was at the end of a phone all the time. (At home)

About one-third of all adopters considered the social worker neither supportive nor unsupportive during this time – some did not think that their involvement was needed. However, about 20 per cent thought that the social work support had been inadequate. A few adopters had a strained relationship with their social workers, as in the following examples:

I don't think we got much support really. We had a rather lame social worker . . . who was hopeless actually. So I wasn't particularly looking for any support from him because I didn't value him. (At home)

Our social worker was hideously stressful. She was bloody awful. I couldn't wait for her to leave. (Left home)

Some felt that, during the introductions, social workers were so preoccupied with other agendas that as prospective parents, their support needs were overlooked:

There was very little response to actually how we were feeling at the time. We were told the foster carer had booked a holiday, which did not include these two children and that if we didn't go ahead they would be put into temporary foster care. After the first overnight stay, my ex-husband and I both had a bit of a wobble and there was no time to discuss it – we spoke to our social worker on the phone and we got the, 'Oh, this is perfectly normal! Everything's fine, everybody has this kind of experience.' (At home)

The [social work] focus was very much on the foster carer and how she was feeling, which I felt was strange at the time. 'Marjorie [foster carer] is not dealing with this very well; it's very upsetting for her.' So the pressure was then on to make sure she was all right and so we were very mindful of trying to not upset her. (Left home)

A few adopters had received no support at all because their social worker was on leave, had resigned, or had retired around the time of the introductions. It was suggested that the absence of professional support had led to missed opportunities for reflection:

The social worker who had been involved with Stacey up to that point left and a new social worker had arrived . . . so between the foster carer and me, we managed the transition. When the [new] social worker first came to visit, it was after Stacey had already moved in. So we did it completely with no professional input, but the reality was that I had no check and balance. I had no-one saying, 'Where are you up to today? What do you feel about that? What does that raise for you?' (Left home)

The foster carer's role in the introductions

The foster carer had a key role in making the introductions successful. Most foster carers (61%) were judged by parents to have been support-ive and considerate, a few (9%) were described as neither supportive nor unsupportive, whilst just under one-third (30%) were thought to have behaved in ways which had hindered the introductions and transition.

Supportive foster carers

The majority of adoptive parents described the foster carer as welcoming, friendly and helpful during the introductions. Typically, these carers shared information about the child's routines with the adoptive parents and provided more detail about the child's history. Adopters explained:

> She told us what he likes to eat, what his routine is, how he is with animals and how he is with other children, what he didn't like – he doesn't like to be rushed. In fact, I remember writing it all down at the time. She was very helpful. (At home)

> She told us a bit about the life story . . . and how that fitted in, and who was who, and all that sort of thing, reassured us really. (At home)

The more experienced foster carers supported the prospective parents by helping them to understand the process and explaining what to expect during the introductions. One adoptive mother said:

> We had a really experienced foster carer who knew inside out what she was doing. She had done loads of children and she was very good . . . wonderful woman. She was able to tell us what would happen next, I guess that's helped. She was able to explain why some things were done some ways, like, for instance, the first meeting she let us go outside with Daisy but she kept observation from the window and that sort of thing. (At home)

Experienced foster carers were also able to help the child to prepare psychologically for their forthcoming move, as in this example:

> She [foster carer] was totally on the ball, really helpful, really prepared the girls, and really understood the whole process.

She was telling us what was going to happen. She understood not just the procedure, but the emotions involved and she understood what the girls needed. She had just this huge understanding. (Left home)

Adopters valued the actions of foster carers who made a point of talking with the child about their prospective adoptive parents between visits and who helped the child to understand that the foster placement was temporary but they were now moving to a new perm- anent family. Foster carers hosted "goodbye" or "celebration" parties for the children, some put together memory books, life story books or photo albums for the children to keep. Occasionally, adopters even stayed overnight at the foster carer's house during the introductions so that childcare responsibilities could be handed over gradually, in a familiar and safe environment.

Unsupportive foster carers

About 30 per cent of adoptive parents described how the behaviour of foster carers had hindered the introductions and transitional arrange- ments. This was more likely to be reported by the parents whose child was no longer at home.[35] Typically, in these situations foster carers were described as having difficulty letting go of the child, sometimes because they had wanted to adopt the child themselves or because they were inexperienced and thought to be struggling with their own feelings of grief and loss. Adoptive parents described the following situations:

On the day that he actually came to stay, [foster carer] just handed him over at the door. She was crying and Jacob was crying. I just don't think that was good . . . it was like a parcel being passed over really. She should have come in or we should have gone to the park or something and done it that way. She was just breaking her heart. She was very close to Jacob. (At home)

---

35 $\chi^2 (1) = 3.916, p<.05$

They were first-time foster carers, quite inexperienced, but they had had the children for 20 months . . . and they had become quite attached to them. They found it very difficult to stick within the arrangements of the appointments . . . it created a lot of anguish really. Sometimes we'd turn up and they wouldn't open the door, or they'd taken one of the children out. Yes, it was very tricky. (Left home)

Some parents recognised the negative impact this had on the children, who had not been given psychological permission to move on. The day of the move itself could then be very traumatic for everyone, as in this example:

I do remember [adopters' social worker] commenting that the foster carer was not properly prepared by her social worker . . . The foster carer needed a lot of support in order to say goodbye and let go . . . Robbie sobbed and sobbed and he was only little. He was just four and he was clinging to the roof of the car, and we had to just keep taking him off, because he didn't want to get in. (Left home)

A few foster carers were thought by adoptive parents to have been critical of their parenting abilities. Rather than provide guidance and support, several parents felt they had been "set up" with childcare tasks in which they would be seen to struggle and fail:

I thought that the foster mum would be showing me how she does things. I think because I was young, I was about 27, and she was quite old . . . It's like she wanted to see me fail. So she went, 'Now give her a bath', and stood back and watched me. And I was expecting her to show me her routine so I could copy her routine. And it was like she wanted to see me do it wrong. (At home)

Strangely, two foster carers would not allow the prospective parents upstairs in their house, so the opportunity to bathe the children and be involved in their bedtime routine was missed. Certainly, for one couple, this related to the foster carer's disapproval of them as gay adopters.

Some foster carers had wanted the child out of their home as quickly as possible and did not want to jeopardise the imminent move. Typically, this group of carers did not share important information, downplaying or denying difficulties shown by the children. For example, parents reported that information about seizures, development, and aggressive or sexualised behaviour had not always been disclosed. Parents said:

> The foster carers were very supportive to us on the surface, they were nice to us . . . but I don't think they were very honest. A lack of honesty comes up a lot . . . I don't think they informed us of her issues and I don't actually think they helped her issues either. (Left home)

> She was a very nice lady but throughout the whole of the thing, what permeated for me is she wanted her gone . . . she didn't reassure me really about what was starting to present because the child I met was not the child that had been described . . . this child that presented to me wasn't slightly developmentally delayed, she was very delayed. (Left home)

Some parents were upset by derogatory or negative remarks made by foster carers about the child, for example, harsh comments about the child's physical appearance or their lack of potential. One foster carer went as far as to say that the child was unloveable. It is possible that the adoptive parents' accounts of these seemingly cruel and unkind remarks may have been made by carers who were reflecting the way that the children felt about themselves. Children may have felt that they were unlovable and unwanted. Children with deep-seated insecurities can, in their interactions with adults, provoke adult behaviours that confirm their negative view of themselves.

The insensitive way in which the children's personal belongings were dealt with by the foster carers upset a small group of adopters.

Sadly, bin bags were occasionally used to pack up the children's belongings. A handful of children arrived in the adoptive home with insufficient or ill-fitting clothes and footwear and very few personal possessions; the foster carers may have kept everything for their next foster child without regard for the importance of these items for the child's sense of identity. The importance of comfort objects (such as a blanket or soft toy) in making a transition to a new family was also sometimes overlooked, as in the following example:

> *When they came to live with us, they came with nothing. Oscar didn't even have a cuddly toy. Not even any clothes, so that was all a bit [upsetting]. The first day we brought them home, we took them to Asda to get them some clothes.* (Left home)

Poor quality foster care

Nine adopters were certain that their child had suffered abuse and/or neglect whilst in foster care and a further nine suspected maltreatment. The abusers or suspected abusers included the foster carers, their partners, and older children living in the foster family. In three instances, the abuse or suspected abuse occurred during episodes of unsupervised contact with birth family members. Sometimes information about maltreatment only surfaced after the child had moved into their adoptive home.

Eleven other adoptive parents thought that, whilst looked after by the LA, the child had received inadequate care. Most often, parents thought that their child had lacked sufficient stimulation whilst in foster care and, as a result, had not made satisfactory developmental progress. Foster carers caring for several children, all of whom had very specific needs, and those struggling with their own personal issues, such as bereavement, were identified as factors that had compromised children's development. One father, for example, described the situation in which his daughter's needs were overlooked:

> *It was not the right environment for Josie in a sense because [foster carers] just didn't have the time. They had taken on too much . . . I couldn't have looked after [foster carer's] disabled*

daughter on my own, let alone two other children, she was absolutely amazing . . . But with the best will in the world, the interaction for Josie was mainly coming from her lying next to a severely mentally and physically disabled child. Josie was largely left on the floor all day and then she was sleeping 14 hours. A four- or five-month-old baby, having to be woken up – so she'd obviously just completely shut down. (At home)

Other parents described a lack of warmth in the child and carer relationship, describing the foster carers as "cold", "professional" or "clinical". As two mothers explained:

One thing that she used to do, and she told us that we could do this with him, is to leave his bottle of milk in his crib at night so he could just grab it and have it in the night. That said something to me, you don't really do that . . . It's not very safe because he could choke. How would you know? (Left home)

She was meticulous actually and met all his physical needs. She said to us, 'I'm not here to show him affection or love, it's your job'. So, she just did the basics. She said, 'I've had him as a favour to [local authority]. I don't have babies but he was a favour.' (At home)

Other aspects of poor care that worried adopters included shouting and smacking by the foster carer and failing to provide the child with a proper diet. When we combined the number of children known or suspected to have been abused and those who were considered by the adoptive parents to have received poor quality care, we found that over two-fifths of all adopters (41%) had serious misgivings about their children's well-being whilst in foster care.

Meeting important people in the child's life

In addition to speaking to the child's foster carer, 37 per cent of adopters met and spoke to one or both birth parents, whilst 19 per cent met members of the child's extended family. The majority of these meetings had been constructive and the adoptive parents were pleased that they had occurred. It enabled them to see the mother in a different light, and many spoke of feeling sorry for her. Adoptive parents were more critical of birth fathers. Nearly one-third (31%) of adopters also had the opportunity to speak to the agency medical adviser or another health professional, and a similar proportion had met with the child's teacher or nursery worker. Two adopters had attended a life appreciation day, and a handful had met with other professionals, such as the independent reviewing officer who knew the child.

Goodbye meetings – the final contact visit

Twenty parents were aware of final face-to-face meetings having taken place between the child and the birth parent(s). Most adoptive parents knew little about these or what sense the children had made of them. The few parents who were given information about the meetings usually described events that lacked adequate professional support. One mother explained:

She was totally traumatised by the goodbye meeting. Luckily we knew about those feelings from the social worker . . . we had a full account from the social worker about how it went and what happened. It was a party tea at a regular place they used to meet. [Social worker] documented the whole thing with photographs . . . cards and presents were swapped and kisses, quite a big event. Then birth mother got in a taxi and went, and Amy was left. Then there was the aftermath of how she struggled back at the foster placement . . . unfortunately nobody really joined up to handle it properly and support her. When she'd said goodbye to her birth mum and aunts and uncles and so on, she was dropped off at the foster carer's house and they were out. The only person who was in was their teenage daughter. (Left home)

Another child who had witnessed his father's severe physical and sexual violence towards his mother and siblings was left believing that his father would "come and get him".

95

They had their goodbye visit with their birth parents the day before they met us. [Child's] dad had said to him, 'Yeah, I'm all right with you being adopted, I'll come back for you when you're 14 or 15, I'll come and get you and I'll write every week.' . . . They wandered round with [the social worker] a bit behind . . . They all went off on a little train on their own and [the social worker] waited for it to come back. So there was at least 15 minutes on their own, so I don't know what else was said. Who knows? (Left home)

Some parents knew that the final contact visit had occurred just a few days before the child was introduced to them. Parents also knew that fairly frequent contact with birth parents had suddenly ceased when the introductions commenced and they wondered what explanations their child had been given. For one family, the "goodbye meeting" with grandparents and the birth mother occurred six months after placement. The adoptive mother described the meeting:

Suzanne [child] was taken off into another room and then shortly after the social worker came in and said, 'Suzanne's very distressed, it's OK with the birth mum if you come in'. We went into a room, and there was, I'm going to use this word, a posse of social workers. There were four social workers sitting there . . . Mum had hold of Suzanne and she was very distressed because she hadn't seen her for a year. Why put a child in that situation? (Left home)

Missing information
Forty-eight adopters (69%) thought that they had not received all the information they should have had about their child prior to placement. Parents said that details about the birth family or child's history and important medical information had not been shared with them. The existence of such information only became known to parents after their child had moved in and often after the adoption order had been made. A few parents thought that information had not been shared with them due to an oversight by the placing authority. However, the

majority were certain that important information known by social workers had purposefully been withheld. One mother described her experience in detail:

> *I realised there was just loads of information that we didn't have. So, under the Freedom of Information Act, I asked for access to the children's files . . . two of the documents that came through were judges' reports and it turned out that the birth father was examined for the court to see if he was able to understand pro-ceedings and to give instructions to his solicitor. The psychiatrist found him to have either schizophrenia or a schizoid-type con-dition . . . These judges' reports, obviously they had all been made before we met the children, so this information was known by social services, despite us saying explicitly that we didn't want any serious mental health issues to deal with. They lied to us because I actually asked outright if anyone in the family had a serious mental illness and they said, 'No, [birth father] is a unique man but he does not have mental health issues'.* (Left home)

Even when parents were given information, they were not usually helped to understand its significance, for example, parents com-plained that the developmental challenges the children would face in the light of their early trauma were not explained. Two parents were told by their assessing social worker to "read between the lines" of a report provided by the placing authority. One father said:

> *They [social workers] should be helping us to read between the lines, they shouldn't be telling us to . . . Actually, there should be nothing written between the lines, it should be explicit.* (Left home)

Overall readiness to adopt

After completing the introductions and listening to the foster carer, social workers, and other professionals, the majority (74%) of adopters had few concerns and thought that their partner felt the same way too. As one mother said:

I guess we didn't know what we didn't know. We were aware that our energy levels needed to be superhuman, but after the introductions, I don't think at that stage there was anything that was alarming us. (Left home)

Just over a quarter (26%) of adopters did have concerns, with some beginning to worry that there were more difficulties than they had first thought, or that they were not feeling an immediate connection with the child. Most of these adoptive parents talked things through with professionals and were sufficiently reassured to proceed. Seven of the parents did not voice their concerns, as they felt they were embroiled in a process over which they had little control. One mother explained:

At the time I don't know if I felt I could [raise concerns] . . . I didn't feel strong enough or empowered enough to say, 'Can we stop this a minute, I'd like to talk about this a bit more'. I didn't know that I could . . . I always thought of myself as quite a strong individual . . . but you're so vulnerable . . . I don't think people recognise how vulnerable you are in the process because of your own need and desire. (Left home)

Even at this very early stage, some parents felt that they had already made a commitment to the child on which they could not and would not renege. Thirty-eight per cent of parents had been matched with a child or children who did not fit with their original preferences and 30 per cent of parents had experienced poorly managed introductions. Rather than being bolstered and ready for placement, about one-third of adoptive parents were already feeling stressed and tired, with their emotional resources depleted by failed matches and difficult relationships with foster carers and/or social workers. Into these families were matched children who were older than most children who are placed with adoptive families and who had suffered significant harm. In the next chapter, we describe how children and adoptive parents settled into life as an adoptive family.

Summary

- Seventy adoptive parents were interviewed: 35 whose child had left home under 18 years of age, and 35 whose child lived at home, but where parenting was very challenging.
- The majority (75%) had chosen to adopt following infertility or pregnancy-related health concerns. Nearly half of the parents had previous parenting experience. At the time of the research interview, 12 were lone parents. Just over three-quarters of the adoptive households included other adopted children and 23 per cent of adopters had birth children living at home. In three families, an adopted young person's own baby was also living with the family.
- The adopted young people were on average 16 years old (range 12–22 years old) at the time of the interview. Those in the "Left home" group had left on average at 14 years old (range 10–17 years old). The young people who had left home were significantly older on entry to care, at the time of their adoptive placement, and when the adoption order had been made compared to the children who were still living at home.
- A comparison of the "Left home" and "At home" groups found no statistical difference in the likelihood of having left home, based on the child's gender, on being placed as part of a sibling group, or on placement with a single adoptive parent. However, children who had been exposed to domestic violence were significantly more likely to have left home than those who had not been exposed.
- More (65%) of the parents whose children had left home described the preparation for adoption as inadequate compared with those parents whose child still lived at home (20%).
- Many (59%) of the parents had been linked with one or more other children before their child was placed. Adopters described how they had begun to invest emotionally in these children.
- Thirty-nine per cent of parents were matched with children who did not meet their original preferences. More of the parents whose child had left home had seen their preferences changed.
- Most (70%) introductions seemed to have gone well. Poorly

managed introductions were associated with children having left home.

- Most parents received good support from social workers during the introductions and transition. About 20 per cent described support as inadequate, with transitions planned when social work support was unavailable, or arranged to meet the foster carer's needs rather than the needs of the child.
- The role of the foster carer during the introductions and transition was crucial. The majority of foster carers (61%) were welcoming. About 30 per cent of foster carers were less helpful and obstructed the move. Lack of support from the foster carer during the move was associated with later disruption.
- Two-fifths (41%) of adoptive parents had concerns about the quality of care that their child had experienced whilst in foster care.
- Sixty-nine per cent of adopters thought that they had not received all the information that was available. However, most had been able to talk to important people in the child's life and 37 per cent had met with one or both birth parents. These latter meetings were generally appreciated and they enabled some adopters to see birth mothers, in particular, in a more positive light.
- Immediately before the child moved to their adoptive home, the majority (74%) of adoptive parents had few concerns. Some who were worried talked things through with professionals, but others felt that there had been no real opportunity to raise issues. Even at this early stage, parents were committed to proceeding with the adoption and felt that there was no going back.

7 Settling into adoptive family life

In this chapter, we describe how the parent and child relationship began to develop in the first few months of the adoptive placement, and the early impressions that parents had about their child. We consider briefly parents' satisfaction with social worker support before the adoption order was made and discuss two key events in early adoptive family life: the children's transfer to nursery or school and their transition to becoming legally adopted.

Parent and child relationships

Adoptive parents were asked how family life had felt in the early days of the placement, and how easy or difficult it had been to start feeling close to their child. The majority of adopters spoke positively about their early experiences as a family. For example, one mother said:

> *It was wonderful, it was lovely, it was really beautiful. The only thing we noticed is that she didn't smile a lot, and we thought that was just Daisy. Suddenly after six months, she started laughing and we were stunned.* (At home)

Despite feeling that things were generally going well, many adopters said how tiring it had been to parent their child in the early days and emphasised that parenting had not been without its challenges. The parents whose children had left home were more likely to say that the child's presence had not felt right from the start.[36] Whilst four-fifths (80%) of adopters whose children were at home reported that the early days had felt right, the same was true for just less than half (49%) of parents whose children had left home prematurely. As adopters in the "Left home" group explained:

---

36 Fisher's exact=.02

In the early days, when they first moved in, there was nothing, we were like four individuals and this is what I'd always feared. Four people who've got no shared history, no shared memories. How the hell are we going to make a family out of this? (Left home)

It felt very strange indeed . . . [The children] were both rather remote, because they didn't know us. They weren't interested in adults and they had the usual superficial charm of children from the looked after system. They were very used to manipulating adults to get what they needed and we came under the full glare of manipulation. I found Poppy very hard work. I couldn't get a sense of the person and I found that very distressing. (Left home)

Forty-three per cent of adopters reported no difficulty in bonding with their child in the early days. Just over one-third (34%) said that both parents had difficulty bonding with the child, 20 per cent said that the difficulty lay in the mother–child relationship, whilst just three per cent said that difficulties were only between the father and child. Interestingly, adopters who described both parents as having difficulty in bonding were more likely to have their child still living with them, whereas those children who focused their resistance and avoidance on their adoptive mother's attempts to parent them were more likely to have left home.[37] One mother described the difficulties she faced managing overt aggressive behaviour from her son:

It's always been very, very challenging. My husband didn't feel that, it was strictly between me and Kieran – he had something about the mother from day one. He kept me at arm's length for three years, he wouldn't let me anywhere near . . . and I'll tell you something, which I absolutely am adamant about, is that I felt threatened from day one with Kieran . . . Kieran has made me feel very ill at ease – always. (Left home)

---

37 Fisher's exact = .04

Early observations

Adopters were asked if anything in particular had struck them about the child or their behaviour during the first few months of living together. Many parents talked at length about the early days and often, but not always, this included their observations about troubled and troublesome behaviours shown by their child from the outset. In this chapter, we identify briefly the range of early impressions reported by parents. We will see that some families were under serious strain soon after their child moved into the adoptive home.

Parents often mentioned that they quickly became aware of their child's difficulties in connecting with others, describing children who from the outset were "flat", "frozen" or "unavailable" emotionally. Children's resistance to accepting intimacy and comfort worried adopters in these early days, and many (50%) described avoidant and resistant attachment styles. As one mother recalled:

> He showed all the signs of trying to be super-independent and that he could look after himself. If he fell over, he would jump up and not make a sound and just carry on, even if his knee was bleeding, he wasn't going to show anything – nothing could hurt him. He would put up a massive shield, as I realise now, to try to protect himself. (Left home)

Other adopters were struck by their child's indiscriminate affection in the early days of the placement and a few parents thought that their child was too compliant. Some children were parentified,[38] and adopters described how these children struggled to allow someone else to care for a younger brother or sister. Parents also observed intense jealousy between some siblings. There were also children who arrived in their adoptive home, not knowing how to play. As parents recalled:

---

38 A parentified child is where a parent transfers the role of emotional and/or physical responsibility of parenting to a child. The child may become responsible for their parent and/or siblings. Maltreated children have often had to care for parents and siblings.

He couldn't play. He could do things like ride a bike round and round, but I sat down with a pile of Duplo and built a police station and the robbers escaped while the police were asleep and things. My birth children would have joined in and taken over. He just watched, and when I suggested he did it, he simply re-enacted exactly the same scenario. (Left home)

She didn't know how to play . . . she was quite mystified about throwing a ball, and I remember like it was yesterday buying her wellies and saying, 'Right, we're going to find all the puddles', and I was saying, 'Come on, jump!' (Left home)

Parents also reported sleep problems and nightmares, as illustrated in the following account:

He would start shrieking in the middle of the night, night terrors, he'd just scream, and you'd go in there and he'd be wide awake. Well, he would be eyes open, but he was asleep. (Left home)

Parents often described the children's early behaviours as controlling and manipulative. With so many of the children having lived in unpredictable and stressful environments, with no adult to help them make sense of the situation, it is perhaps not surprising that these key signs of trauma surfaced. Children were also angry, defiant and pushed boundaries. Some adopters were taken aback by the extended tantrums and rages shown by the children or their displays of antisocial behaviour. One mother explained:

His birth mum had taught him to spit in people's faces during her visits, so that was something that did occur initially . . . which we got used to, but you would pick him up and it was a bit of a shock. (At home)

Several parents described how children repeatedly told lies or showed obsessive-compulsive traits. A few were terrified of certain sounds, or disliked the feel of specific textiles or sand. Other children wet or soiled themselves or self-harmed. One mother, in describing some of these behaviours, said:

> It felt brilliant for a couple of days [after he moved in] and then John put his hand in the door and banged it, so self-harmed. He said, 'I've dropped my drink, but you don't need to hurt me, because I've already done it . . . He smeared; he's always smeared, from day one. There was never a day when there wasn't poo put on the bathroom wall, ever, until he left. (Left home)

In this family and in others, there was a growing belief amongst parents that they had not been told everything they needed to know about their child and that the child was far more traumatised or developmentally delayed than they had first thought.

Odour

This was sufficiently important for a couple of adopters to mention their early difficulties in coming to terms with the unfamiliar smell of their child. These mothers said:

> He smelt strange to me and I think his odour became something that I had to try and overcome . . . He would want to be cuddled close and I would be cuddling close thinking, 'Why don't you smell right?' I never told a soul at the time because it sounded like such a strange thing to say, and I guess quite primal really. (Left home)

> And the thing I remember was their smell – the smell was a very alien smell – a very strong smell in the bedrooms. You don't think about that when you have children, and I bought air fresheners, and then that was OK, because it overrode. It's something very basic but they do smell different. (Left home)

We do not know if the adopters were just recognising that the children smelled different or whether the children's smell was indicative of the extreme stress the children were feeling. Stress produces a different kind of body odour to the smell of sweat caused by heat or exercise. Another explanation is that it was not the children who smelled strange, but the adoptive parent's perception of smell had changed. Research (Krusemark *et al*, 2013) has found that anxiety can turn innocuous odours into aversive and unpleasant smells. If you are feeling very anxious, the environment can smell bad. We also do not know if children also experienced the odour of their new home and parents as noxious. It is important for professionals to recognise that smell has an important role to play in the physical closeness new adoptive parents and children feel towards each other and enable families to talk about this without fear of ridicule. Intervention may also be needed to ensure that negative feedback loops are not established that keep children and parents physically apart.

Some adoptive parents also described their initial difficulties in recognising the way in which familiar smells seemed to comfort or agitate their child. Research (e.g. Keller, 2009) suggests that odour memories are processed differently in the brain to other memories and that odour-evoked memories are more vivid and emotional than memories stimulated by other means. Certainly, some parents described how their child reacted quickly to smells that they associated with early memories:

We went to this camping place, they had only been here a few weeks really, and they spent the entire weekend hanging around the toilets, the sluice area. They loved it there, but I could not understand why they were playing around the toilets, obsessed with it. But it's the smell: it was very familiar to them. (Left home)

If you went anywhere, he could smell smoke a mile off, which was not normal . . . he had this thing about smelling smoke. Then he used to tell us about when he was in a fire and they had to crawl on the floor to get out. We found out that his grandma burnt the house down while the children were inside. (Left home)

While the majority of the parents' early impressions centred on aspects of children's behaviour that concerned them, not all the observations they had in the early days were negative. A few said that they very quickly recognised how bright or funny their child was. Several adopters were struck by how easily their child had seemed to settle, and how smoothly things seemed to be going. As one mother said:

> I was really shocked that she settled just like that. I really thought that she wouldn't settle as quickly, but she just seemed to settle straight away. It surprised me because I thought she would be crying a lot because she would be unfamiliar with where she is, and unfamiliar with the smells and the sounds. (At home)

Although at the time some adopters thought that the early days were going well, a few said that they now wondered whether the ease with which their child settled was in fact an early indication of their lack of attachment to their previous carers.

Settling into nursery and school

Just under half the children (49%) were of pre-school age when they moved in with their adoptive family. The majority of parents used childcare provision for these children before they started school. Most went to nursery, but some were cared for by child-minders, grand-parents or au pairs. About two-thirds of adopters thought that the children had settled well into their childcare routine, whilst a third reported that there had been some difficulties.

Thirty-six children (51%) were already of school age when they moved in with their adoptive family. Adopters described how they had been strongly advised to start their child at their new school almost immediately. More than one-quarter of these parents thought that their child had started school far too quickly. Several adopters felt passionately that their child had needed longer to settle at home, to help develop relationships within their new family. The following accounts illustrate the strength of feeling held by some parents:

In hindsight, I would have liked a month at least, to be honest, just for her to be here and not be rushed into school . . . to give her some good quality time as a one-to-one. Even if we'd have gone to the park, gone shopping, gone swimming – done things to try and bond when my other children weren't around, so she could find her niche and wasn't competing with the others. She was hoisted out of another family, thrown into a family that does everything differently with two other children that are older and then, 'Oh, let's go to school and learn your times tables and come home and do your homework'. Hold on a minute, what's more important? (Left home)

Social workers insisted that Nathan went straight to school. I wanted him to stay at home and they insisted he start school . . . He really shouldn't have been started, he needed to be here with us, and I regret that more than anything. I knew it was the wrong thing, but we just kept getting overruled . . . I knew he needed to be here. I wanted him to stay home. He wasn't statutory school age. Would it have killed them for him to have an extra six weeks at home and then review it for the summer term? (At home)

Contact with social workers

Before the adoption order was made, the child's and the adopters' own social worker usually visited the adoptive home. A few parents had no recollections of social work visits. Most parents (87%) reported that the relationship with their own social worker was good and that the visits had been helpful. Parents said:

It was great . . . like an auntie coming to visit . . . she was very nice, very experienced and had been doing the job a long time. (At home)

If you had to judge it [social worker's ability], I'd say 110 per cent, because she was there at every turn . . . at any time of the day, out of hours, it didn't matter. (Left home)

However, 40 per cent of parents whose child had left home and 29 per cent of parents whose child still lived at home said that they had not been at all satisfied with the child's social worker. Parents complained that they felt sidelined during visits, that social workers frequently changed or had little knowledge or understanding of their children and that promises made by social workers were not kept. Two parents described their experiences:

What made me very uncomfortable was, she did lots of visits to the children shortly after they had moved in, which I found quite stressful and I felt I was treated like I wasn't important – like it wasn't my house. She would just walk through the front door, go up to the children's bedroom, do stuff with the kids, be there for an hour and a half and I'm thinking they need feeding and I don't know what to do. I felt excluded and not in control of the process at all. (Left home)

She was leaving, rarely saw her, she told me she would pass on [child's] file to the next social worker and that her life story books would be prepared . . . but it never was. (Left home)

According to parents, a small group of children became very unsettled by the regular visits from social workers. Sometimes parents thought it was just the presence of social workers that had made the child fearful that they were about to be moved again. A few parents described how children used to hide when social workers visited. As one mother described:

We were sat in the garden having something to eat when [social worker] came, and as soon as he realised she had come, he legged it to the bottom of the garden. She shouted down to him, 'Zak, you must come and see me and if you don't I'm going to chase you'. I thought, this is a child, he's just moved in with us, I don't know what's gone on in his past, he might have been chased, and she's saying that! Well, anyway he was petrified and when she had gone he sobbed and said, 'Don't let that lady ever come back here'. So I rang up and said, 'Could we have a different social worker?' and they said, No, we couldn't. (Left home)

Other parents explained how information shared insensitively by social workers had upset their child. For example, a mother described the distress felt by her child when the social worker announced that the birth mother had recently had another baby. The adopter said:

Well, Sonia was all over the place . . . back to square one and I was really angry and I said, 'Why did you have to tell her?' and she said, 'Because she's not legally yours yet'. (At home)

The making of the adoption order

Adoptive parents were asked how close they had felt to their child at the time the adoption order was made. Just over half of parents reported feeling very close at this time, whilst nearly one-third described feeling slightly close. However, 12 (17%) adopters (eight whose child had left home and four whose child still lived at home) did not feel close at all. Eight of these parents thought that neither they nor their partner were close to the child at this time.

Whilst most parents did not delay applying for the adoption order, 12 parents did not legalise the adoption swiftly. Predominantly, delays were adopter-led and were linked to the challenges they were experiencing in caring for their child and fears of losing support once the order had been made. One order was delayed when birth parents contested and in another instance, a social worker's absence held up the court process.

Irrespective of their concerns, most adopters (83%) described feeling very satisfied and pleased that they were now their child's legal parent. Parties and celebrations took place to mark the day. Just six parents admitted feeling wary and hesitant about the future, including one mother who had quickly sought the adoption order, fearing that the longer she waited, the less likely she would be to go ahead with it. Some parents hoped that once the adoption order was in place, their child would finally settle and accept that they were a part of a permanent adoptive family.

However, for some families, the parent–child relationship did not improve but deteriorated, whilst in other families new and/or more complex patterns of behaviour emerged during adolescence. In the next chapter, we focus on the particular behaviours and the events that ultimately led to the young person having to leave their adoptive home.

Summary

- Many parents described the early days of adoptive family life positively. However, there were also difficulties in parent and child relationships. Fifty-seven per cent of parents described difficulties in bonding with their child. Some children resisted intimacy and attempts to comfort them. There were also children who were over-compliant, indiscriminately friendly or very aggressive.
- Families where the early difficulties were centred on the mother and child relationship were more likely to have disrupted compared to those families where both parents had early difficulties in feeling close to the child.
- Parents reported that odours evoked early memories in their child and some children sought out familiar smells, even when these were unpleasant. Occasionally adopters were troubled by the strange and unpleasant smell of their child, which affected parent enjoyment of physical closeness, and served as a reminder that the child was not biologically theirs.
- Some of the children's behaviours, such as self-harm, night terrors, soiling, manipulation and control, alarmed parents and they began to worry that information had been withheld and/or that the children were more traumatised than they had understood to be the case.
- One-quarter of adoptive parents whose adopted child was of school age thought that their child had started school too quickly after moving in. Parents wanted the opportunity to begin to build relationships with older adopted children, rather than face another stressful transition into a new school.
- Most (87%) adopters felt that they had a good relationship with

their own social worker, but they were less positive about the child's social worker. Complaints were that social workers changed frequently, broke promises and, in a few cases, children were frightened and unsettled by their visits.

- At the time of the adoption order, most parents were pleased to be making this commitment. Just six parents were hesitant and wondered whether they were making a mistake.

8   The behaviours that threatened the stability of adoptions

In this chapter, we identify the point at which serious difficulties began to surface in adoptive family life. It should be noted that the families in this study were sampled either because the child had left the family, or because parenting a child living at home was very challenging. The severity of the behaviours described is not typical of all adopted children. We describe the nature of the problems experienced in the adoptive families and draw particular attention to the difficulties that were the most challenging, and those that ultimately led to the young people leaving their adoptive home. We also provide some context to the situation, by considering what was happening in families at the time the difficulties emerged or escalated.

Parents typically described one of two patterns to the onset of difficulties.

- The first pattern was characterised by an early onset of difficulties, often from when the child was first placed, with increasing intensity during adolescence. This pattern was the most common and reported by 80 per cent of parents.
- The second pattern was characterised by difficulties that began at the time of puberty, often quite suddenly and with rapidly escalating intensity. This latter pattern was reported by 20 per cent of parents.

We begin by describing the behaviours that parents found difficult to manage in the years preceding puberty and examine how the behaviours increased in intensity as the children grew older. Parents were asked to identify when serious difficulties in caring for their child first began. Typically, parents said that they had started to find parenting seriously challenging two–three years after placement, usually when the children were seven–eight years old, and that difficulties had escalated when children were 11–12 years old.

Early onset of difficulties within the adoptive family

In describing the serious difficulties they had faced in parenting young children, adopters identified a range of behaviours that had compromised both the children's development and their own relationship with the child. Parents often used concepts from attachment theory to describe these behaviours and relationship difficulties. There were also parental concerns about children's mood and self-esteem, their cognitive capacity and about biologically based impairments such as insensitivity to pain. These complex and overlapping difficulties are recognised as features of developmental trauma (Schmid *et al*, 2013). Descriptions of the behaviours that parents found most challenging during the primary school years follow.

Difficulty forming close attachments

Many parents reported that their child did not respond well to offers of intimacy and comfort. These difficulties had not usually been recognised whilst children lived in foster care, but they quickly became apparent in the adoptive home, where the expectations of family life were different. Some parents described how they worked hard to help their child develop more secure attachments, often reading widely on the subject and attending courses. It was through researching the difficulties they were experiencing that some parents first learnt about attachment theory and about the vulnerability of abused and neglected children to attachment difficulties. Despite their increased understanding of the situation and their efforts to forge closer, more secure and loving relationships, many parents felt that they were just not connecting with their child in the way in which they had hoped. As one mother explained:

> She [child] was always very much at arm's length . . . we didn't feel close to her. She wouldn't let us; it wasn't for want of trying. We did lots of attachment parenting things and she wasn't engaging in them at all. (At home)

As well as coping with avoidant and resistant children, adopters described their difficulties in parenting children who were too clingy, as well as those who were indiscriminately affectionate. Parents gave concrete examples of the way in which these relationship difficulties caused problems in family life, as in the following account:

> We were going to mother and toddler groups and she would disappear off, go to other mums, ask to be taken to the toilet by anybody. [She was] overly affectionate with men – any man, tried to kiss the postman. At the doctor's surgery, she would walk round the waiting room and just climb up onto people's laps, things like that. (At home)

Manipulation and control

In the context of these serious relationship difficulties, many parents described the impact on adoptive family life of living with children who were manipulative and controlling. Parents described children who showed little ability to compromise and who needed to control their environment and those around them, which in turn led to significant tensions within the adoptive family. As one mother recalled:

> It was all about control, she had to be in control, she would have to be in control of my husband, and she would quite often try and divide us in opinion. It was like warfare, to be honest with you: psychological warfare. (Left home)

The difficulties in dealing with children who tried to dominate siblings caused considerable concern for parents. Such difficulties were very apparent when the children were at play. As one adopter explained:

> Reuben doesn't show any particular attachment to his siblings. He controls them and uses them to his own ends . . . they very much lost the ability to play because if they were in the same room as him and playing, he would always want to get involved, get their attention, take over, control them, which essentially meant stop them playing. (Left home)

It was not just play between siblings that provided opportunities for the child to exercise control over situations. One father described his experience of trying to play with his child:

I found him very difficult to play with when he was a child . . . Tom was always totally controlling from a very early age. So if I was trying to play Lego with him, I'd start building something and a little hand would come over, smash up everything I'd done, and make me do it his way. So in the end . . . I would sit there holding bricks for him, or put them where he told me to . . . and actually that is a pattern with him that he makes you do it his way or no way. (At home)

Parents described children who repeatedly lied and stole from within and outside the home. Children sometimes arrived home from school having "acquired" other children's belonging and often items of low monetary value. As one mother recalled:

She took somebody's glasses out of lost property and wore them for a while and the teachers didn't notice. She would wear somebody else's shoes. You could open her drawer at school and there would be lots of other children's pencils and pens. (Left home)

Anger and aggression

Parents described their difficulties in coping with incredibly angry and volatile young children who were unable to regulate their emotions. Rages and tantrums could escalate quickly and last for several hours. Young boys, in particular, showed serious levels of physical aggression, which was often directed towards their adoptive mothers:

I think it was very apparent from the beginning that it was not going to be easy. Some of the outbursts were difficult, and by that point [adoption order] Joe had broken my nose, he was headbutting and things like that . . . He'd behave in such an unpredictable way. (Left home)

He was insecure and angry all the time, and he attacked me a lot, broke things around the house, and damaged things. He did odd things, like he tried to set fire to the house a few times. (Left home)

Some parents described the strategies they had used to manage their child's angry outbursts, which usually involved preventing them physically from lashing out. One mother explained how she was able to contain her five-year-old son's rages by 'tucking him under my arms'. Some parents had been advised by professionals to hold their child during aggressive outbursts to reduce the likelihood of them hurting themselves or others. However, this was not always easy, as one mother explained:

> I was sent on a positive handling course, so I'd have to hold her . . . that was before she went to secondary school . . . I remember once she grabbed my glasses and headbutted me, that was when I realised that I wouldn't perhaps be able to do that any more. (Left home)

From the outset of the adoptive placement, some parents were also dealing with sibling violence. There were children who could not be left alone together for fear of one child hurting another. There were also other aspects of sibling dynamics that affected the cohesion within adoptive families. These are discussed further in Chapter 9.

The children's aggression sometimes spilled over into their school lives. Parents described how they were regularly contacted by the school with complaints about their child's aggressive behaviour. As two mothers explained:

> I was getting daily phone calls and emails, multiple times a day from the junior school complaining about her, 'She's done this, she's done that, what you are going to do about it?' . . . Pushing people down steps and chucking chairs at staff. (At home)

Whilst some parents described their child as the instigator of conflict at school, others explained how their child's aggressive behaviour was sometimes in response to the goading and bulling they endured as an adopted child.

Low mood, poor self-worth, sabotage and self-harm

Adopters described the difficulties they faced in parenting young children with a low mood and poor self-esteem. Some young children expressed self-loathing or even a wish to die. As two mothers recalled:

> *He would sit there banging himself in the head and banging his head against the wall, 'I hate myself, I am rubbish. I want to die.' And I thought, I've never heard a four-year-old talking about wanting to die. I'm sure at four I had no concept that could happen – you think that you're going to live forever when you're four or five.* (Left home)

> *Saul always used to say, 'I'm bad, I'm a bad boy, me' . . . and if I ever told him that he was not a bad boy, he was a good boy, he'd get angry about that. He believed he was a bad boy, and he still believes that.* (Left home)

A small group of parents were dealing with very young children who self-harmed. Children were headbanging, pinching and scratching themselves, and some seemed to draw comfort from self-inflicted pain. As one adopter explained:

> *He would have these horrendous grooves, absolutely horrendous grooves in his nails . . . I was trying to think, why is he doing this . . . and the pain [is terrible] when I've done it to myself . . . he was damaging the nail bed to cause these grooves, but obviously that's his pain, he was wanting to inflict pain on himself.* (Left home)

Nearly three-quarters (73%) of the children struggled to accept praise or respond positively to attempts to show them that they were cared about. Children sabotaged experiences to ensure a negative adult reaction, as illustrated in the following account:

> *He couldn't cope with you being happy with him, or praising him, so when he was made head boy at junior school he kicked a football boot through a stained glass window, so that he'd be in trouble for the rest of the year.* (Left home)

Children often did not care for their possessions and some purposefully ruined items. As two mothers explained:

When she was little, any dolls would have their arms broken off or their hair pulled out; nothing was ever treasured or cared for. (Left home)

The first Christmas, we bought them a teddy bear each and he broke the head off. He rejected it totally and to have broken the head off, he must have used extreme force. (At home)

Sexually inappropriate behaviour

Several children showed inappropriate sexualised behaviours at a young age, usually to siblings but occasionally to other children at school or nursery and nearly always in the context of having been sexually abused themselves. Two parents described their child's behaviour:

Sometimes I would hear James [sibling] giggling and Alex would be on top of him and he would be trying to hump James. He would be lying on top of him, kissing him inappropriately. (Left home)

My underwear started to go missing, a lot, until it all disappeared. And I asked his sister what's happened to my underwear . . . and she said, 'It's Billy, he's taken your underwear, even out of the wash basket and he's had it in his mouth, in his backside, and he made me do the same.' (Left home)

Cognitive deficits

Parents described a range of difficulties that the children showed in their thinking and learning. Some children had learning difficulties or other conditions linked to cognitive impairment (a table of children's diagnoses is set out in Chapter 14). Adopters described great difficulty in parenting children who seemed to have impairments in learning from experience and linking actions to consequences. Parents described how children did not seem to learn from mistakes, could not accept responsibility for their actions, and did not respond to offers of rewards for good behaviour.

In the years before adolescence, parents described having the most difficulty in managing aggression, self-harm and sexualised behaviour. However, puberty and adolescence brought many more challenges, as the intensity of these behaviours escalated and became more dangerous and the safety of everyone in the adoptive family was compromised.

Onset or escalation of difficulties during adolescence

Many parents described a rapid escalation of challenging behaviour in their child as they approached puberty. Adopters reported that children were on average 11 years old (range 5–17 years, SD 2.9) when behaviours escalated. While 80 per cent of families had always had some difficulties, one in five families saw the onset and escalation of difficulties at puberty. In the late onset group, parents often described a very sudden change in their child's behaviour. One mother said her child had gone to bed her usual self, but came down the next morning a different person. Other parents likened the change to a switch being flicked. One mother, who had enjoyed a warm, loving relationship with her son until he reached puberty, explained:

> He ran away when he was 12, we had the police out, the helicopters, and when they brought him back they said, 'We're going to see more of this boy, his attitude is unbelievable'. He just turned from this lovely little kid into this very angry person . . . it was like a switch. (Left home)

Parents were asked to identify the challenging behaviours shown by their child at the point at which difficulties in family life had escalated (Table 8.1).

Anger, aggression and control during adolescence
Parents reported that 35 (92%) of the 38 boys and 25 (78%) of the 32 girls had been physically aggressive towards others. Much of the aggression shown by the young people occurred within the adoptive home.

Violence within the adoptive home
Whilst some parents had suffered injuries such as broken bones, black eyes and extensive bruising as a result of the physical aggression

Table 8.1

Adoptive parents' reports of behaviours that were very challenging

	Left home		At home	
	n	%	n	%
Defiance and flouting boundaries	33	97	30	86
Verbal aggression	31	89	29	83
Physical aggression	30	86	29	83
Destroys things	25	71	27	77
Difficult behaviour in school	29	83	25	71
Difficulties forming or maintaining friendships	29	83	27	77
Sabotages intended positive experiences	26	74	25	71
Runs away	23	66	17	49
Actual or threatened self-harm	18	51	19	54
Sexualised behaviour (age-inappropriate)	14	43	8	23
Depression/low mood	14	40	18	51
Makes allegations against others	14	40	12	34
Anxiety/OCD	13	37	20	57
Serious crime	10	29	1	3
Alcohol misuse	8	23	5	14
Drug misuse	8	23	2	6

shown by the young person, equally as frightening was the intimidation and coercive control that the young people exerted within the family. Many parents described the psychologcal abuse they endured. A few also mentioned sexual and financial abuse.

Parents did not describe the common adolescent boundary-testing behaviour shown by many adolescents, nor the occasional squaring up of sons to fathers, but behaviours intended to dominate and control parents, who had to change their own behaviours to accommodate the threat of violence. This type of abuse, known as child to parent violence, was statistically associated with children not living at home.[39] It was shown by 27 boys and 14 girls. Boys were significantly more likely to use this type of violence;[40] several were described by parents as superficially charming, but lacking empathy and with little concern about the impact of their behaviour on others.

In criminal justice and social work research, interest is growing in child to parent violence, with published articles mainly appearing in the last 10 years.[41] There is no single definition of child to parent violence, as it describes a wide variety of physical and psychological behaviours designed to control, coerce and dominate the parent and family members. Paterson and colleagues (2002, p 92) described child to parent violence as:

Behaviour considered to be violent if others in the family feel threatened, intimidated or controlled by it and if they believe that they must adjust their own behaviour to accommodate threats or anticipation of violence.

In this definition, there are two elements. First, the emphasis on behaviours designed to control; and second, the change seen in the behaviour of those affected. In this study, we applied this definition to the data from the interviews. One of the major difficulties that parents faced was children and young people being aggressive inside and outside the home. Aggressive child behaviours were described by 60 of the 70 parents and, using the above definition, 41 of the 70 families were or had been living with child to parent violence.

Children who had been violent towards their parents from early on in the placement typically continued to be so as they got older. Aggressive outbursts that had been manageable when children were younger became much more of a problem as young people grew taller and stronger. Parents explained how children's behaviours became

---

39 χ^2 (1) 11.667, p<.001
40 χ^2 (1) 5.337, p<.021
41 See http://holesinthewall.co.uk/, a useful blog by Helen Bonnick (social worker) collating key articles and news on child to parent violence.

more intimidating and difficult to manage as they moved into adolescence, not least because the physical balance of power shifted when young people became stronger and taller than their parents. There was another group of children whose violence only began around the time of puberty.

Many parents described feeling vulnerable and frightened by their child's behaviour. Some parents could not bear to be alone at home with their child for fear of being physically attacked, bullied or dominated. Although mothers were the main target of the child to parent violence in the adoptive home, some young people lashed out at siblings and fathers too and in one case at elderly grandparents. Family pets were also harmed. Parents described the difficulty they faced in coping with their partner being assaulted by the child. A mother described one such instance on the day her daughter left home:

> She beat her dad up, she just started punching, and punching, kicking, and punching him, absolutely going berserk, I mean unhinged berserk. He's a very gentle giant, never ever laid a finger on her . . . She always used to bully him quite a lot and something inside me just snapped. He used to be like a saint with her really, because she has been very hard work and she just punched and punched and kicked him. I just got in the middle and I slapped her round the face, which I regret, but I did slap her. (Left home)

Adopters described also how the child to parent violence had a profound effect on siblings in the adoptive home. As two mothers explained:

> Martin [sibling] said, 'Mum, if James [study child] is still here when I come home from college today, I'm moving out. I don't know where I'm going, but I'm moving out and I'm going to the police . . . I cannot watch you and Dad being beaten up any more.' (Left home)

> Billy [study child] was becoming more and more aggressive towards me. I remember Freddy [sibling], who was six at the

time, came up, and gave me a toy gun so I would have something to defend myself with. (Left home)

In sharing accounts of the serious sibling aggression that occurred in the adoptive home, parents nearly always described it in the context of the study child as the instigator of the violence. On occasions, brothers or sisters were themselves moved out of home temporarily or sent to a boarding school to keep them safe. Other parents had put locks on doors to enable siblings to retreat from escalating conflict. Sibling violence often brought the situation to a head when parents realised that they could no longer keep their children safe from one another. One mother, for example, described the incident that ultimately led to her son leaving home:

He hit her on the temple . . . he cornered her in the shower upstairs where he knew she couldn't get away, and I heard her cry out . . . I ran to the bottom of the stairs and I shouted up the stairs, 'Come away from her'. He came to the top of the stairs, and he looked right down and made eye contact with me at the bottom of the stairs, went back and thumped her again in exactly the same place. I knew when he hit her that we really couldn't keep either child safe . . . I had already burnt out and my husband had burnt out before me. (Left home)

The following extracts, all from different interviews, illustrate the type and severity of child to parent violence shown within the adoptive families.

Adopters' accounts of child to parent violence

She's physically attacked me – she's been in the cell a few times [after assaulting me]. I thought that might help, but she doesn't care . . . When she was smaller I could pick her up and put her in a room. I've not been able to do that since she was nine or 10 . . . she's always been huge and the problems are just escalating because there's not a thing I can do . . . She's verbally aggressive, destroys things . . . made allegations against my brother. What she's done is sabotaged all my support networks as well . . . she just wants to control me . . . she really bullies me, stops me going into her room, puts her foot in the door, finger in my face, telling me to fuck off and laughs because I can't do anything about it because she's so much physically bigger. It's domestic violence, that's exactly what it is. (At home)

She started to put knives around the house . . . knives went missing and we found them in her bedroom. Why did she have them? She wouldn't say. This is where silence is so powerful, no explanation. What really freaked me out was when I took the washing out of the washing basket and as I put it down on the floor, a carving knife fell out. [Birth daughter] saw it and said to me, 'Who was that meant for, Mum, is it you?' And I thought, oh my goodness. (Left home)

I am physically frightened of him. I feel it's like living with a husband who beats you, where you become a doormat because you're tiptoeing around, rather than upset the apple cart. I don't think I'm parenting very well now because I'm frightened of him. (At home)

He would do things like hold us hostage in a room and scream and shout for two hours and we weren't allowed out. (Left home)

From the minute he got up to the minute he went to bed he just terrorised us . . . threatening us with knives . . . throwing stones at us, throwing buckets of water at us, squirting us with bleach . . . the TV was locked in his bedroom...You would be walking along and he would suddenly just punch you in the back for no reason . . . You couldn't even leave the dogs with him. If they were laying in here and Freddie walked in they would leave and I've known one of them to wet herself [in fear]. [Husband] was beaten round the head with a broom. I can remember one night . . . we went to bed and lay there and I can remember crying and then he came in and he punched me in the back and he said, 'Yes, you cry you bitch'. (Left home)

She's always been violent with me; she is a bit with her dad but in particular with me. I'd got this black eye and I'd been to CAMHS and we sat talking about it. Do you know what annoys me more than anything . . . I turn up at CAMHS with a black eye and all they say to Claire is, 'Oh, that's not very good, is it?' If she'd have turned up with a black eye, whether I'd done it or not, all the authorities would be down on us like a ton of bricks, but because it's a child [perpetrating the violence] it's accepted, but it's domestic abuse whether it's from a husband, a mother, a child, your brother, whatever. I said to them if it was my husband who'd blacked my eye, you'd all be encouraging me to leave him but because it's a child it's accepted, and it isn't acceptable. She's been violent right from the beginning, but it's escalated with her age, because she's stronger and I'm getting weaker. This is why I'm at the end of my tether. (At home)

Use of knives

We were surprised to find that 19 (27%) parents, without prompting, reported worrying behaviour shown by their child around the use of knives. Parents described children who had used knives to threaten, intimidate or control others. Girls as well as boys had used knives. Whilst some parents explained how children grabbed knives and wielded them during angry or distressed outbursts, others reported much more calculated behaviour. One mother, for example, described how her son would pick up a knife, make eye contact with her, then slowly and deliberately put it back down. Another described how her daughter ran her finger up and down a knife blade during an altercation with her father. Two parents had found knives hidden in their child's bedrooms and around the home and three others reported that their child had taken knives out of the house; in one instance, into school. One young person had committed a knifepoint robbery. Young people had also used other weapons with which to threaten or intimidate others, such as scissors, but it was the use of knives most often mentioned by parents. Two adopters described their experiences:

She would be walking around with knives at night. She'd threaten her brother with knives, she would be stabbing furniture . . . we used to barricade our door because we used to think she was going to stab us at night . . . I sat down with the psychologist and the first thing he said is, 'Jessica has much more severe complex mental health difficulties than post-traumatic stress disorder'. (Left home)

Robbie [sibling] was in his room and I was in the kitchen. Suddenly Daniel [study child] came in, got the bread knife, got it at my throat, and said, 'I don't want to hurt you but I've got to'. I don't know how I managed, but I got him to get away and I just quickly rang the police . . . and that's when things started really going to pot . . . Daniel wrote 'DD 9.00' on the chalkboard and he went, 'You know what that is, don't you?' I went, 'No'. So he went, 'Nine o'clock D-day, that's the time you lot are going to die tonight'. He took a knife in to Robbie and said, 'This is the knife you're going to die with tonight'. (Left home)

Oppositional behaviour and running away

Many of the children who had been controlling in their younger years refused to accept parental authority in their teens. The young people wanted more freedom and were angered by the boundaries that parents tried to set. One mother explained how her attempts to protect her daughter were rebutted:

She didn't want to be looked after, she didn't want any of that, she didn't need it. It was fine if she was sending sex texts to all these boys about [a sexual act] . . . It was fine if she wanted 600 friends on Facebook – No, she didn't know who they were, but they were friends of friends, saw no danger in that. (Left home)

As family life became more difficult, many (n = 40) young people began running away from home or going missing for lengthy periods.

Some young people in the "Left home" group ran away and never returned to the adoptive home, whilst others returned on many occasions. More of the young people (63%) who had left home had been reported to the police as a missing person than those (22%) who still lived at home. Young people who had run away sometimes went to stay with other adults whose motivation for befriending the young person was questioned by parents. Several parents were sure that their child had been exploited, sexually or otherwise, for example, young people were meeting single adult males. One young person moved into a business premises where he slept and was supplied with alcohol. Young people who were running away often stayed with a "family" whose characteristics seemed to resemble those of their birth families. They moved into chaotic households, where drugs and alcohol were often provided and in some instances where there were many young people passing through. Most of these "families" were well known to children's services and to the police. It was unclear whether young people were seeking to answer troubling questions about their identity and gravitated towards families with whom they felt some affinity, or whether their vulnerability had led to them being targeted and preyed upon by adults and gangs who wanted to use them for other purposes.

Adoptive parents found themselves powerless to intervene in these situations. Police and social workers often visited the place where the young person was staying for a welfare check, but if young people were over the age of 16 and stated that they wanted to remain there, neither the police nor social workers were prepared to act and did not seem to ask too many questions. One mother, for example, described how her daughter, aged 16, went to stay with the family of a school friend. A social worker visited her at the friend's home to assess the situation. Members of this household had histories of violent crime, sexual abuse and serious mental illness. The social work involvement resulted in the *school friend* (aged 15) being put on the "at risk" register, but it was considered acceptable for the adopters' daughter to remain living in the household. The adoptive mother said:

What really got me was the social worker maintained that Josie was in a safe place ... What she said was, 'She's being fed, she's warm, it's OK'. She closed the case. Josie was still there. We wanted her to go into care temporarily for her to get away from this family. (Left home)

Police did intervene with some young people, for example, in one instance when Special Branch found guns at the address where the child was living. Parents thought that their children were extremely vulnerable in these situations, particularly as they believed that their child's emotional age was much younger than their chronological age. Parents reported that a few young people had tried to persuade or encourage their younger siblings to run away with them.

Lack of self-care

A few parents described how their child (usually girls) showed a lack of self-care. Several mothers described particular difficulties in encouraging daughters to deal appropriately with personal hygiene during menstruation. As one mother described:

She did used to leave horrible things in her bedroom – used sanitary towels, and then she went through a stage of weeing in her knickers and leaving them for me to pick up. (Left home)

Another mother described the difficulties she faced with her son's behaviour:

He'd walk around wiping his bottom and come in and have a conversation [about it], which is fine if you're in the house on your own, but if you've got friends for dinner, when you're 13, this is a bit odd. (Left home)

Eight parents were also concerned about their child's growing dependency on alcohol and/or drugs. Misuse of alcohol was often linked with violent behaviour and stealing. By their mid-teens, three young men were described by their parents as dependent on alcohol.

Serious criminal offences

Many of the young people who had left home had been involved with the criminal justice system: 19 had been charged with assault and 12 young people had appeared in court and been convicted of serious crimes such as rape and aggravated burglary. Some parents thought that their children had been dealt with leniently by the courts, because of their "previous good character" and the background of the adoptive families. Six young people who were living at home had also been charged with offences. Several other children had been arrested following an assault on a parent, but the parents had chosen not to press charges. An adoptive mother described her son's escalating involvement with the criminal justice system:

> He was arrested for burglary when he was about 13; he was arrested for robbery when he was about 14, then thefts and assault. He has been arrested loads of times for possession of cannabis. He has been arrested for possession of crack cocaine . . . been in and out of court, there have been loads of referral orders . . . he's been arrested for knifepoint robbery. (Left home)

Sexualised behaviours

About one-third of parents had concerns about the inappropriate sexualised behaviours shown by their adolescent child. Many of these young people had shown inappropriate sexualised behaviour as young children, but in adolescence, the behaviours became more risky and often involved underage sex with strangers. Parents reported children as young as 12 exchanging grossly inappropriate text messages of a sexual nature, or using social networking websites where they exposed themselves to sexual predators. One mother, describing her daughter's behaviour, said:

> She gets on the internet and she is contacting older people, adults, in their 20s, for sex. It first happened a couple of years ago. She'd have been 14 . . . first it was Facebook and it was inappropriate people and from all over the country. (At home)

There was a small group of young people who had engaged in serious sexually deviant activity, for example, the sexual abuse (including rape) of younger children, the making and distributing of indecent images and videos on the internet, stalking, and the obsessive viewing of pornography. There were also concerns about other types of inappropriate behaviour, as illustrated in the following extract:

> He had taken his clothes off and laid down in the road in front of a car, so the school phoned us and said, 'We've had a phone call from a member of the public' . . . He had pulled his trousers down and laid down in the road with his trousers round his ankles, exposing himself. (Left home)

Attention-seeking behaviour

Parents described their difficulties in coping with young people who fabricated stories or made threats, which triggered an intense reaction from others – behaviour that some parents thought was designed to gain attention and sympathy. As one mother explained:

> She told people she was raped at the age of two . . . the sorts of things to get a big reaction from people – sympathy. She's ramped that up another stage and started talking about suicide . . . 'I'm going to take tablets' . . . but she's gunning for some sort of attention, any sort of attention, from anybody. Quite a lot of her friends have got upset with her when they find out it's not true . . . she uses the flow of information to control friendships – that means they get fed up with being manipulated. (At home)

Two adopters explained how their children began to act out aspects of a fantasy life that they had created. One mother described how her son had told his tutors that his adoptive parents were dead. He pretended to have undergone surgery and used crutches to get around college, he persuaded his mother to help him with college projects that did not exist, and he told elaborate and false stories to friends and their parents about murders within his birth family. The young person was thought to have believed aspects of these stories to be true.

There were other children who had made allegations against parents, family members or teachers, which had resulted in the adopters being subject to a child protection investigation. Section 47 investigations are considered fully at the end of this chapter; suffice to say that most parents refuted these allegations. Some parents thought the allegations had been made by their child as a mechanism for drawing attention to themselves, or to control their parents, or because the child thought that it was a way to become looked after again and so escape the tensions in the adoptive family.

Stressful life events and children's difficulty in coping with change

Parents were asked if there had been other events in the family's life at the time the child's behaviour became very challenging. Many parents stated that their child had difficulty coping with any form of change and that the upset caused by change lasted much longer than would be expected. Just under half (46%) of parents identified particular events that had upset their child around the time that serious problems emerged or escalated. In a few cases, a single event had set off a chain of events, which led ultimately to the child moving out of the home.

Developmental changes
Puberty was a key turning point in the escalation of difficulties for many children. Three adopters specifically mentioned the difficulties associated with early puberty (under the age of 10 years) and 20 per cent of parents stated that difficulties only began at puberty.

Educational transitions
The move from primary to secondary school was thought to have caused additional stress for many children. Parents described how children had not coped well with the larger, more impersonal nature of secondary education and the increased responsibility expected of them.

Peer relations

Bullying at school was a possible trigger for some children's problem behaviours, as were friendship difficulties. About one-third of the children were known by their parents to have been bullied at school because of their adoptive status.

The school curriculum

Two parents identified the teaching of attachment theory on psychology courses at school or college as the specific trigger of distress: both young people were left with the belief that their own early neglect and abuse had permanently marked them and that there was no hope for them to become well-adjusted adults. They were fearful that they would repeat the mistakes of their birth parents and were led to understand that they had no capacity to make a good parent. One of the mothers said:

> He came home and he said we did (attachment theory) and there were all these names that said, 'If you don't have good relationships you're doomed. You're doomed for life.' And basically Graham came home with that message . . . my future is doomed. (At home)

Home life became very difficult in another family following the child's involvement in a debate at school about children's rights. It brought to the fore painful memories about the abuse she had suffered in her early life, when she felt that her rights had been overlooked, and that no-one had listened.

Changes in the adoptive family

As in many families, there was additional stress brought on by other events such as parental separation/divorce, house moves, and changes in the household composition – birth children were born, new adopted children arrived and older young people left home. One mother described how her son's challenging behaviour escalated around the time she gave birth:

Things got very much worse when [birth child] was born and in the run up to that. Oscar would have been approaching eight, he had huge school issues . . . He was absolutely terrified of me having a birth child and sending him back [to care]. He was going to burn the house down and kill the baby and at that point, his relationship with me became difficult because he went, 'Well, you're going to reject me anyway, so let me do it for you'. There was physical and verbal aggression mostly towards me, but towards other children at school, that's why he got excluded. Not the best [year] . . . it was one of those crazy bittersweet awful wonderful years. (At home)

Parental illness and death

A few adoptive parents developed serious medical problems, such as heart disease and cancer. The fear of losing a parent once again was difficult for some children to cope with. One mother explained:

In May 2011, I was diagnosed with breast cancer . . . the word cancer; Fiona has experienced that word cancer, because it was featured in her birth families on either side. She thought I was going to die. She just saw the worst side of it and felt again she would be rejected. I had to reassure her that wasn't the case at all. (At home)

Two adoptive fathers had died suddenly and in one of these families, the child's grief had manifested in anger and resentment towards his mother. He started to behave in ways that seriously worried her:

We had a garden shed with guinea pigs and Daniel actually went into the hutch to sleep. He sat on the shed roof. It was bizarre behaviour. He would be prancing around in the field with cows, would sneak his guinea pigs into school. (Left home)

The death of extended adoptive family members also unsettled children – the death of grandparents in particular. In one family, three of the four grandparents died within a year of each other. A pet dying was also noted as a traumatic event for adopted children and their families.

Changes in the birth family

Events occurring within birth families also detrimentally affected children, for example, children discovered that a sibling had returned to live with a birth parent or that their birth mother had gone on to have another child, and in two instances that a birth parent had died. Changes in contact arrangements also triggered difficulties for children, such as new letterbox arrangements being set up with siblings whom the child had not known existed, ongoing court disputes about contact, and unplanned contact made through social networking websites.

Disclosures of abuse

Difficult behaviours escalated for girls following their disclosure or decision to reveal more about earlier sexual abuse. Two children revealed that they had been sexually abused whilst living with the birth family, whilst a further three had been abused whilst living in their adoptive home, by an adult outside the family. The insensitive professional responses to some of these disclosures added to the child's distress.

Poor quality support

Some families reported that the support they had been given by agencies had helped to hold the family together (see Chapter 10). However, it is important to note here that some interventions were thought by parents to have triggered the escalation of difficulties, especially those that were badly timed, poorly thought through, or cut short. As two parents explained:

We wanted support for Martin . . . because of his age [14] . . . we wanted him to be able to understand things that had gone on in a more mature way . . . understand more about his past. Social services had three sessions with him, they had a roll of wallpaper and did a timeline, but it was horrific, made matters a whole lot worse, three one-hour sessions and that was it. They told him all the bad things that had happened to him, then said, 'Sorry, that's all we can afford,' and that was that . . . He had all this information, but what was he to do with it? He was better off not knowing really, than being told then dropped. (Left home)

We always said to him, '[Birth mother] couldn't look after you'. We never said one negative thing about her . . . But it obviously clearly wasn't enough. The social worker said, 'It's time we need to start telling him a bit more, because he says he doesn't want to live with you any more, he wants to go with his birth family'. So she told him about the birth father first of all and had to explain what he had done . . . The next day his behaviour escalated and he started running away a lot more. (Left home)

From the accounts provided by parents, it was clear that many children had really struggled to cope with changes that occurred in family life. Moreover, some of these events, such as bereavement, divorce, and illness, were likely to have reduced the parents' own capacity to cope.

Allegations

Twenty-six (37%) of the children had made an allegation of abuse against an adult, which they claimed had occurred whilst living in their adoptive home. The allegations were mainly against adoptive parents, but children had also accused wider family members (such as grandparents, uncles, and cousins) of abuse. Some children had made multiple allegations against a range of individuals.

Most accusations resulted in a brief investigation by social workers or police officers, who quickly found that the allegations were, in all probability, spurious and had been made by the young people to draw attention to themselves or to punish or control their parents. Nevertheless, parents explained how the accusations had fractured relationships and caused great tension within the adoptive family. One mother, for example, described how her husband, the child's adoptive father, had "shut down" after the child alleged that he had assaulted her. He withdrew to his bedroom each evening at 8.30pm in order to avoid his daughter. Another mother described the tension in the household that remained after her child made what was described as an unfounded accusation of assault against her stepfather:

> I'm always going to be living in fear now of her making another allegation . . . I don't dare leave her on her own with [partner]. Not because he's going to do anything to her, but because of what she's likely to say . . . I'm still terrified that we're actually going to go through all this again, she's going to come out with something else. It's like living with the Sword of Damocles over your head, it's horrible, and at some point, if she does make another allegation then I'm going to have to say she cannot stay here. (At home)

Some parents described how they had been accused by their child of assault after dealing with an altercation or aggressive outburst from the child. One mother, in describing one such incident, explained the predicament she then faced in the months preceding her son's move out of home:

> I was in the kitchen and Oliver [study child] had come in, leapt on my back, and brought me down by my neck. My [husband] came in, I was on my back, and Oliver was on top of me. My husband got him off . . . next day the police arrived because my husband had left two marks on him. He had told school, 'Daddy has done this to me'. So we had the police round, I had got this massive bruise on my back, and they said when they had interviewed Oliver they could tell he was just making things up, and they could tell it was a restraining thing, but they said, 'If you restrain him in future you're not allowed to mark him'. So it doesn't matter that he marks you, and he's hitting [husband], he's sometimes hitting his brother, we daren't restrain him. (Left home)

Child protection investigations

Perhaps one of the most unexpected findings to emerge from the interviews came from the 19 adopters (13 families where the child had left home and six where the child was still at home; 27 per cent of all those interviewed) who revealed that they had been threatened with or subjected to a child protection (Section 47) investigation. This was a sensitive matter for parents to talk about and there may have been other instances that were not revealed during the interviews.

In nine families, an investigation was triggered by an allegation made by a child against a parent. In all other cases, social workers had initiated or threatened parents with an investigation. Adopters thought that social workers were concerned that they were neglecting, scapegoating or emotionally abusing their child. One adopter was never able to establish why a child protection investigation was started.

Adopters had often rung children's services for help and had been directed to the children and families team rather than post-adoption services. It was difficult to know whether the adopters' tone of voice, their desperation or the way they spoke about the child had triggered social workers' concerns. It would not be surprising if parents, in their distressed state, had sounded angry or cold. Many were worn down, worn out and frightened. It is also possible that children's social workers viewed the cause of children's challenging behaviour as neglectful or inadequate parenting. Although all parents refuted these accusations, a few did state that on occasions they had responded aggressively, been critical or had lacked warmth. Parents described how they had struggled to convince social workers that their parenting capacity had been compromised by the difficulties they had been experiencing, often for many years, and not that their child's difficulties had emerged as a consequence of their poor parenting.

Most parents were outraged by the accusations; some were devastated, as their integrity had been brought into question. Perhaps unsurprisingly, adopters described how a child protection investigation or the threat of proceedings against them had soured their relationship with children's services. Parents explained how they had lost their trust in social workers, as one mother explained:

I got a letter [from children's services] – it totally annihilated my integrity . . . and at that time that's all I had, I had nothing else. If you can imagine, your family is breaking down, you've got one daughter that's petrified [of her sister], you've got another going into care, you don't know what the hell is going to be happening the following day, and you get a letter to say, 'We consider your behaviour abusive', because I've asked for psychological assessments . . . We go into a system and we're put in with other abusive parents. I am not an abuser. Don't you dare treat me like one . . . I have to remind people actually that a lot of these issues were about long before Christina met me . . . I cannot be responsible for Christina's low self-esteem, and yet we are blamed . . . All I've ever done is to ask for help and it hasn't been there. (Left home)

The impact of child protection investigations or threats of investigations were felt throughout the family. They affected marital relationships and employment. There were several parents working in a professional capacity with children, such as social workers, teachers and nurses, who were fearful of losing their professional credibility, their opportunity for promotion or even their job. As one mother explained:

It was awful, because it [investigation] went through to my employers, it's made me so ill, I was off work for two months. I went on antidepressants . . . I feel they have destroyed me. My professional integrity is gone. (At home)

Professionals working with the family were themselves sometimes divided in opinion over the decision to instigate a Section 47 investigation. Splits were described between adoption social workers and children's social workers, in conflict over the best way to manage the difficulties. In most cases, the adoption worker was overruled. One adopter explained how a child protection investigation came about and described the reaction of other professionals:

They sent the intensive support team round who suggested some sticker charts. I asked this lady, 'Why are you suggesting it? What do you think it's going to achieve? How long do you think it's going to take to achieve it?' And her response was, it could be a long-term solution. So I specifically said to her, 'I'm not refusing to do this, it's just that I don't see the point of it, and you don't seem to be able to explain to me how it will help' . . . They then decided that it was a child protection issue because we were blaming and scapegoating Andrew for the problems within our family and therefore emotionally abusing him. So they started a child protection investigation . . . we had our post-adoption social worker there [at the meeting], and our lady from CAMHS and both of them said they were absolutely shocked and appalled. They had never had any concerns about our parenting whatsoever. (Left home)

Some parents were aware of many other adopters who had been through similar experiences. As one mother said:

We've been through a child protection investigation, which obviously came out as nothing to investigate. Every adopter, I think, has to go through one at some point in order to be a real adopter! (At home)

While this adoptive parent was able to recall the event with a certain amount of sarcasm, most parents said that they had been scarred by the experience and were left feeling betrayed by the professionals whom they had trusted.

Summary

• Serious difficulties in parenting children most frequently emerged when the children were young (pre-pubescent). Early onset difficulties were characterised by complex and overlapping child behaviours often consistent with features of developmental trauma. Many parents described a rapid escalation of difficulties in adoptive family life as children approached puberty. For one in five families, difficulties did not emerge until the child entered puberty.

- Anger and aggression during adolescence was a major challenge for adoptive families. Child to parent violence was shown by 41 young people (57%) and was statistically associated with children having left home. Knives were used by 19 children to threaten, intimidate or control others. Boys were statistically more likely than girls to show child to parent violence.

- Parents also described difficulties in coping with teenage children who were oppositional and showed inappropriate sexualised and attention-seeking behaviour. Eleven children (16%) had engaged in serious criminal activity – all but one had left home.

- Forty children (57%) had run away or gone missing from home. The police had often been involved in locating the children. Some went to stay with adults whose motivation for befriending the child was questionable and parents feared that children were at risk of exploitation.

- Just under half of parents (46%) identified life events or other stressors that they thought may have contributed to the escalation of the child's difficulties. These included developmental changes in the child associated with puberty, school transitions and the school curriculum, bullying, changes in the household composition, illness, death, events in the birth family, changes to contact arrangements, disclosures of abuse, and poor quality support.

- Twenty-six children (37%) had made an allegation of abuse against an adult whilst living in the adoptive home. Adoptive parents were most commonly accused, but so too were other family members. The majority of allegations were concluded after a brief investigation by social workers or the police and with no further action.

- More than one-quarter (27%) of parents revealed that they had been threatened with or subjected to a child protection investigation. This sometimes followed an allegation made by the child but, more often, it was generated from social workers suggesting that parents may have been emotionally harming or neglecting the child. In the main, parents were outraged or devastated by the accusations and vehemently refuted the allegations. Parents felt betrayed by social workers.

9 Family relationships, birth family contact and communicative openness

In this chapter, we focus on the factors that had an impact on the communication and cohesion within the adoptive families. We consider the quality of sibling relationships, birth family contact (including the physical and psychological presence of birth parents), and the openness of communication between the child and parents about adoption and the child's history. In this chapter, the term "study child" is used to differentiate the child who was the subject of the interview from their siblings. The chapter concludes with a particular focus on the 35 families who were still intact at the time of the interview.

Sibling relationships

The vast majority (93%) of the children in our study had been or were living in adoptive families with other children. Parents were asked to describe how well their children got on together. Most parents described typical sibling relationships, involving the usual bickering and jealousy, but also loyalties and closeness. Siblings defended each other and sometimes reminded parents that the study child was "just being a teenager".

Sibling relationships were often described as difficult for parents to manage when each child in the sibling group had special needs. Children in the "Left home" group were significantly more likely to have had very difficult sibling relationships (Table 9.1).[42] Difficulties were mainly between adopted siblings, and 17 per cent of the children had strained relationships with the birth children of their adoptive parent.

Fractious relationships between siblings had usually been evident

---

42 χ^2 (1) 7.00, $p<.016$

Table 9.1
Parent reported sibling relationships

Sibling relationships	Left home (n = 31) %	At home (n = 34) %
Conflict most of the time	48	18
Get on very well most of the time	29	41
Ups and downs	23	41
Total	**100**	**100**

from the very early days and adopters described how the strained dynamics between their children had been central to the parenting challenges that they had faced over the years. We asked parents to describe the kinds of sibling behaviours that worried them. In the "Left home" group, parents were most concerned about the serious physical aggression and sexually inappropriate behaviours shown by the study children to their siblings. They also worried about the ways in which the study child had bullied, manipulated and controlled brothers or sisters. In comparison, in the "At home" group, it was more often verbal rather than physical aggression that most worried parents, as well as jealousy and behaviours intended to exclude. Interestingly, the majority (75%) of adopters in the "Left home" group said that sibling conflict had usually been initiated by the study child, whereas only 40 per cent in the "At home" group believed this to be true. The majority of the "At home" group of parents were more likely to say that the child and their sibling were *equally* responsible for causing the conflict.

In describing the serious conflict between their children, many parents focused on the physical aggression shown by the study child to a sibling. As well as the violent outbursts (which one parent referred to as a 'rage that has to be noticed'), it was also the intimidation and the unpredictability, the not knowing when the next incident would occur, that distressed siblings. Parents also reported sexually inappropriate behaviour between the siblings and embarrassment and shame felt by siblings when the study child's behaviour affected their own friendships or life in school. A mother described how her daughter taunted, goaded and humiliated her brother:

There's lots of antagonism towards her brother, 'You're fat, you're stupid, you're a nerd, nobody likes you, I don't know why Mum adopted you'. It's the verbal attacks . . . but she can be physically aggressive as well, so she will hit him and kick him. What worries me most is when she's around he withdraws, so he just goes, 'Do you know what, I don't even want to engage in this. I want to stay out of her way'. She does invade his space; she'll go into his room and go through his stuff. Every time she walks past his bedroom door she will push it open and make some stupid comment, or she'll be talking about her boobs in front of him and he's uncomfortable with that, he doesn't like that. Actually, she has gone into his room when he had a friend there, pulled down her trousers and knickers in front of him and the friend . . . I told social services, to me that's really worrying behaviour. (At home)

A common strategy for managing the conflict was for siblings to avoid each other. Brothers and sisters spent long periods of time out of the house or alone in their rooms. They also avoided having their friends come round to the house, ashamed of what they might witness. Siblings' disengagement could lead to extreme situations, as illustrated in the following extract from the interview with one adoptive mother:

When Cora [study child] was about 13, James [sibling] stopped speaking to her and he withdrew from her completely and he didn't speak to her again until she left home [aged 15] and we had to live and manage that within the family. I tried to talk to him about it and I told him off about it . . . He said, 'She can't deal with me, I can't deal with her, I'll just take myself out of the equation'. We try and encourage him to be compassionate about Cora's difficulties, but we also have to keep an eye on him, how he's coping and managing. It was absolutely unmanageable. (Left home)

A strategy used by adoptive parents was to split the caring responsibilities so that each parent cared for one child, in a conscious effort to keep their children apart. In some families, parents never allowed their children to be alone together or share rooms, even on holiday. Another parental strategy was to ensure that bedroom doors could be locked to ensure that other children could retreat safely to their rooms. As one mother explained:

> To keep [child's sibling] safe we say, 'Go on your computer or go to your room' . . . There have been times when we've had to go into this safety mode, which is why he's got a lock on his door. (At home)

The risk of both serious physical and psychological harm posed to siblings within the adoptive family was so great that occasionally the siblings themselves were moved out of home to keep them safe. One mother, who had sent her birth son to boarding school, explained tearfully:

> I suppose that's been the hardest thing for me in some ways – Tommy's relationship with John [adopters' birth child] and it's why John is now boarding – because Tommy bullied John . . . John is just softer and he's not angry and he almost let himself be the victim at times. He doesn't walk away from it, he can't understand all the anger, and so that's been really hard. (At home)

For some parents, sibling conflict had devastated family life and several parents described how the aggression between their children had ultimately led to their child's move out of home – the situation often coming to a head when parents realised that they could no longer keep their other children safe. The demands of parenting more than one child meant that many parents (68%) said that they had felt guilty that the study child's siblings had received less attention than they would have wished. Parents described how they had been so preoccupied with parenting the study child that they had taken their "eye off the ball" with their other children, and in some instances, this had led to a sibling's own behavioural and emotional problems not being recognised. Parents knew that their other children felt keenly the disproportionate amount of time that the study child had taken up. One mother described feeling very upset by her daughter's recent comment that life was always all about her brother and that she sometimes felt quite lonely in her family.

A few parents with both adopted and birth children mentioned the ongoing difficulties their adopted child faced in accepting that their birth history was different to that of a sibling. Some parents described an undercurrent of inferiority felt by their adopted child that could not be shaken off. The adopted child sometimes sensed the easier relationship their parents had with a birth child, which only added to the adopted child's difficulties. On the other hand, some of the older birth siblings were able to show great tolerance and restraint in their behaviour towards the study child and were able to provide relief, through humour, in situations of conflict.

Marital/partner relationships

The children's challenging behaviour had put the adult relationships under intense pressure. Tensions built up between the parents as the children played one off against the other, or created instability by splitting the parents (seeing one parent as all bad and the other as completely virtuous). In the previous chapters, we have seen how mothers in particular bore the brunt of children's anger and distress, which could leave them feeling isolated. Some mothers described their own behaviour as obsessional and of becoming "hard to live with", as they became totally focused on trying to find ways to help their child. There were also families where fathers were always the "bad guy", although this was far less frequent. As parents struggled to manage the challenging behaviour shown by their child, a few parents described their relationship strengthening. For example, a mother said:

We talked about it an awful lot. A lot of it [aggression] was aimed at me. He [husband] would come home early from work . . . he supported me. [At home]

Difficulties in some marital relationships emerged specifically in the management of child to parent violence. Fathers frequently struggled with their response to children's aggression and parents spoke about the complex feelings that violence in the home aroused. Some fathers feared allegations of child maltreatment if they tried to restrain children who were attacking their wife or other children. Several fathers had been attacked themselves, including one who had suffered a broken arm. Fathers described feeling impotent, disempowered and unable to protect loved ones. As one father explained:

> One of the things that people don't recognise is that it's very stressful being a husband when you are having to witness your wife suffering violence . . . and you can't protect her, you can't step in and stop it. It leaves you in a very confused position . . . The fact that you are out at work and you can't control what's going on at home. You're not sure when you get home whether one of them will be dead. (Left home)

Fathers' responses to violence were often polarised. Some men withdrew and avoided dealing with conflict, while others imposed very strict disciplinary boundaries. Two fathers admitted to having "lost it" and had retaliated to protect their wife or other children. One mother, in describing the impact on her husband, explained how he responded to conflict:

> I think my husband had an undiagnosed nervous breakdown as a result of it . . . he hasn't always disciplined him as well as he might, because he's frightened that he's going to hit him. So he tends to just walk away. (At home)

Eleven relationships had ended. Nine husbands had moved out of the adoptive home, as had two wives. In all but one instance, the child's challenging behaviour was said to be a major factor in the parents' separation. As one mother said:

> If we hadn't gone ahead [with adoption], I would probably still be married to my ex-husband. We'd gone 24 years to that point;

there wouldn't have been much to get in the way. But, that's life.
(At home)

A couple of parents were angry with their ex-partners, particularly if they refused to have contact with the adopted child, but more often, the lone parent was accepting of the stress that had led to the relationship ending. As one mother explained:

At the beginning, we were trying to work together on it. We were both in shock . . . to start off, we went to "managing teenagers"-type courses . . . His dad moved out because he just couldn't cope any more . . . People keep telling me, 'You've got to do this'. And you do this but the behaviour still carries on. The contracts didn't work, the sticker charts didn't work . . . we did all of it. (Left home)

Parents had often been forced to make choices about which relationship to prioritise. Some parents had chosen to continue parenting their adopted child at the cost of losing their partner or of other children having to leave the family home. Other parents had chosen to ask that their adopted child be returned to care to ensure that the rest of the family stayed together. A few parents had struggled to make an either/or decision. One mother, talking about her husband, said:

I think if he could have just left the children he would have done, but he wouldn't leave me and therefore he stuck with them because I couldn't make that either/or choice. But if he could walk away from them, he would do. (At home)

Birth family contact

Parents were asked about birth family contact – specifically, the contact between the child and their birth family prior to moving in, plans for contact post-adoption and the contact that had actually occurred. Two types of contact were considered: a) face-to-face contact involving the child; and b) letterbox contact (Table 9.2).

Table 9.2
Number of children in contact with their birth family over time

		Contact occurring pre-placement (n)	Contact plan post-placement (n)	Contact at the time of the interview (n)
Birth mother	Face-to-face	38	7	12
	Letterbox	3	49	19
Birth father	Face-to-face	15	1	2
	Letterbox	2	21	7
Siblings	Face-to-face	22	18	17
	Letterbox	2	10	8
Extended family	Face-to-face	16	7	7
	Letterbox	1	12	4
Foster carer	Face-to-face		14	8[43]

Pre-adoption contact

Before moving in with their adoptive parents, the majority of children (60%)[44] were having contact with their birth mother and 21 per cent had contact with their birth father. One-third (34%) of children also had contact with siblings living elsewhere and 24 per cent with extended family members. Contact was nearly always face-to-face. One in three children had no contact with any family members around the time of the introductions.

Plans for contact post-placement

Most often, the social work plan for post-placement contact was to cease face-to-face contact and replace it with letterbox contact. Letterbox arrangements were set up between the adoptive family and 67 per cent of the birth mothers and 30 per cent of the birth fathers. Face-to-face contact was planned for seven children (10%) with their birth

---

43 Plus a further eight families where only the adults had contact – foster carers had become friends of the adoptive parents.
44 Two birth mothers had died, as had three birth fathers.

mother and one child with his birth father. Four children had no plans for any contact with parents or adult relatives. Most adoptive parents agreed with the contact plan, although over one-quarter had mixed feelings or did not agree with it. Those who were less satisfied with the plan usually thought that too much contact had been agreed. For example, in one instance, arrangements had been made for the child to visit a birth family member every six weeks. After complaints from the adoptive parents that this was unworkable, contact was reduced to five times a year, but even so, this was in a contact centre with a different social worker collecting the child each time. After a while, the adopters insisted that they supervise contact. The husband did this, as the adoptive parents thought that he would be less threatening to the birth mother. Unusually, two adoptive mothers wanted face-to-face contact with the birth family when social workers had planned letterbox, and one adoptive mother wanted more frequent face-to-face contact than planned. These parents (without the social workers' knowledge or involvement) organised face-to-face contact with birth family members, but in all three cases, serious complications with the arrangements ensued. In one family, for example, an adoptive mother established informal contact with birth grandparents, but this enabled the birth mother to make unsolicited contact with the child when the child's birth grandparents disclosed his whereabouts. In another instance, the frequent physical presence of two mothers unsettled and confused a young child, who started to show more challenging behaviour at home.

Post-order letterbox contact

Adopters listed a catalogue of challenges and difficulties that they had experienced with letterbox contact over the years. Difficulties have been reported in many other studies (e.g. Neil, 2004; Selwyn *et al*, 2006c). Letterbox contact was not usually reciprocal, with adopters describing how they had regularly sent letters, but received nothing back. As a result, some had stopped writing. This lack of reciprocation also affected children. As one mother explained:

Paul said, 'Mummy, why do you still let [birth parents] hurt me?'

And I said, 'Could you explain?' He said, 'Well, you write and they never write back and they still hurt us and I don't want you to tell them about our lives now, because I don't want them in it'. I said to my other child, 'What do you think?' And she agreed. I thought, well, I cannot be part of something that's hurting my children. (Left home)

When communication from birth parents stopped abruptly, as it sometimes did, adopters described how children became anxious or distressed, convinced that birth parents had died. It was often difficult for adopters to establish why the letters had stopped. The content of letters could also be inappropriate or insensitive, leaving parents unsure whether or not to share the correspondence with their child, for example, photos of birth parents playing with other children or of family events, such as weddings, were enclosed. Two mothers described the difficult situation they faced when the birth mother sent cards to one child, but not the other, and others described the difficulties of trying to manage different types of contact for siblings who did not have the same birth parents. Letters from birth mothers were sometimes too "claiming" of the children and both adopters and their children found the content of these particularly distressing:

When she was about eight or nine, I gave her the card she'd got from her birth mum . . . It said, 'Happy birthday to my precious daughter', and it had lots of things about her personality – 'You are fun-loving', you're like this and very specific things. It was quite inappropriate because she doesn't know her to be able to say that. Emily absolutely hit the roof, she just went into a red rage, tore it up . . . She said, 'I don't want her to say it's from Mum because she's not my mum'. (At home)

As they got older, several young people insisted that the arrangement cease, telling their parents that they did not want their personal information shared with their birth parents. Correspondence also stopped because adoptive parents found it particularly hard to write to birth parents about family life when their child was struggling and

151

relationships within the adoptive family were difficult. As one mother explained:

> What do you do, do you put a spin on everything? Just think if you were receiving the letter and read that your child is having all sorts of problems and there's not a damn thing you can do about it. It's just passing the burden down the line to someone who can do nothing, so is that a good thing? I don't know. (At home)

Post-order face-to-face contact with birth parents

Adoptive parents described a number of difficulties with the few face-to-face contact arrangements that had been planned with birth parents, not least the reluctance or refusal by some children to attend these meetings. There were also the challenges of managing very difficult child behaviours around the time of birth parent contact. Most face-to-face contact was overseen by the adoptive parents, but in two instances, it was supervised by children's services. In these cases, the contact was considered unsatisfactory by the adopters, as the child was still treated as though they were a looked after child and the adoptive parents' status went unrecognised. For example, one mother described her dissatisfaction with a proposal by the contact co-ordinator for a birth mother to take the child swimming whilst the family support worker "supervised" from the side.

However, adopters also described aspects of face-to-face contact that they thought had been beneficial, for example, birth mothers could answer questions that the child had about their past. In two cases, a close friendship had developed between the adoptive and birth mothers that both had found beneficial.

Contact at the time of the research interview

At the time the young person moved out of their adoptive home, or at the time of the interview (for the "At home" group), over half of the letterbox arrangements had ceased or had never got off the ground. Letterbox contact with birth fathers had ended more frequently than arrangements with birth mothers.

Thirteen (19%) children were having face-to-face contact with a birth parent. Four of the eight *planned* face-to-face contacts with birth parents had ended, but eight other children (11%) were having face-to-face contact with birth mothers that had *not been planned* at the start of the adoption, as were two young people with their birth fathers. This included one child who was in touch with both birth parents. In three instances, adoptive parents had asked children's services to re-establish contact with the birth family at their child's request. Two of these mothers believed that their teenage child had become so preoccupied with meeting the birth mother that their own relationship with their child was at risk had they not facilitated the contact. On reflection, all three adoptive parents thought that making contact with the birth mother had been the right thing to do.

Three other children had been in direct contact with birth parents via Facebook. One adopter thought that although the initial method of communication had been inappropriate, it had been a positive experience for her child to meet his birth mother. The benefits were less clear for the two other young people. For another child, face-to-face contact with her birth mother began after the birth mother arrived unannounced at the adoptive home. This created a huge amount of turbulence within the adoptive family.

Sibling contact remained stable over the years (see Table 9.2). Several parents arranged for their child to have contact with their previous foster carer, even though some had been advised by social workers that it would be best for the child to have a clean break.[45] These arrangements were usually considered by parents to have worked out well. Foster carers had provided support to adoptive parents, and there was little suggestion that such contact had been unhelpful or difficult for the child. One mother, who did describe some early difficulties, realised that the nature of the contact had not been fully explained to her son, who initially thought that he might be returning to foster care.

---

45 This approach was common 10 years ago, as it was believed that maintaining contact with the foster carer would prevent children making a secure attachment to their adoptive parent.

Satisfaction with contact

In the main, adoptive parents had been satisfied with the way in which birth family contact had worked out. For some parents, the cessation of planned contact had suited them. Adoptive parents had been least satisfied with birth mother contact, although there was no trend to their dissatisfaction – nine adopters had wanted more contact with birth mothers, whilst eight had wanted less. There were similar feelings about contact with birth fathers and siblings.

Social media

We asked parents whether there had ever been any difficulties with birth family contact through texts, email or Facebook. Whilst 20 per cent of parents said that this had been the case, many more feared that they would be addressing such difficulties in the future. The contact made via social networking websites had caused upset in some adoptive families. One mother, whose child had responded to a social networking request from his birth mother during a particularly turbulent time in his adoptive home, remarked:

> *Facebook was the thing that really messed it up for us. Facebook actually put the nail in the coffin for us.* (Left home)

Some adopters whose children had used social networking websites commented that it was not contact per se that had caused problems, rather the unsupervised and unregulated way in which it had occurred. However, even when parents had tried to exercise some control over the situation, difficulties ensued. For example, one mother, on discovering that her son was communicating with his birth mother via Facebook, contacted the local authority for advice. Social workers facilitated a reunion between the child and his birth mother, but failed to consider the impact on the adoptive mother. She described it as an experience that badly affected her. She explained:

> *They did a reunion when he was 14, but I was in the room . . . the emotion was so intense, they were just holding each other and holding each other and wouldn't let go. I was just sitting there*

and then I went out and said, 'That was really hard to sit there', and [co-ordinator] said, 'Yes, it's the first time that's ever happened with the adoptive mum in the room at the same time'. I don't think I should have been in the room, it was the most emotional thing I've ever been through and I felt that emotion, I was just a quivering wreck . . . I think it was because we were quite early ones with the Facebook thing, but I think it's happening an awful lot now. (Left home)

Some young people had made Facebook contact with cousins or siblings, but were then subjected to unsolicited communication from others in the birth family with whom they did not want contact. One mother described the upshot of the contact her daughter had with a birth family member, who passed her details on to the birth father:

Last Christmas Eve, Sarah unexpectedly got a text from her birth father, no warning – a text message with a photo of his face saying, 'Hello, I'm your dad, it would be really nice to meet you sometime'. (At home)

Three adopters described how their children's birth families had waged campaigns through social networking websites in an attempt to locate and retrieve children. These and other adoptive parents described seeing photos of their children online – occasionally the very pictures that they had sent to a birth parent as part of their letterbox contact.

As we have seen, after having been placed for adoption, a significant minority of children (n = 17, 19%) did have face-to-face contact (planned or otherwise) with birth parents. Adopters held mixed views about the impact of such contact. Whilst some reported that the physical presence of a birth parent had compromised the stability and cohesion within the adoptive family, others, particularly those whose *teenage* child had sought out contact with birth parents, described how adoptive family life had become more settled once their child had met a birth parent. Evidence from these families would suggest that there is a need for post-adoption support services to be developed that would enable adolescent children to re-establish safe contact with a birth parent or where the social worker would act as a go-between. Some young people did not want contact but wanted answers to questions that only their birth parent could supply.

It should be remembered that the majority of children had not had any face-to-face contact with birth family members as they were growing up in their adoptive families. Their birth parents were rejecting and abusive, or their lives were so chaotic that it would have been unsafe for children to see them. Yet, birth parents continued to play an important part in children's emotional lives.

The psychological presence of birth parents

For some children, their early memories of abuse and neglect had haunted them, causing nightmares, flashbacks and fears that they would be "found" by the abusive birth parent. Adopters said:

For years, he had nightmares about his birth dad coming to get him in a white van. He couldn't go into his bedroom without the blackout blind having to be shut... Even up to the day he left here, he couldn't go into that bedroom without shutting the blinds. (Left home)

She still gets quite a lot of nightmares. It's stopped taking over her daytime so much, so concentration in school has got a lot better. But she likes to sleep with the light on. She won't have the door closed. She has a lot of nightmares about being abused... really quite intense nightmares where she is crying and screaming. (At home)

Sixty-three per cent of the children had been adopted over the age of four years old and had memories of their early lives and maltreatment. One mother, whose son was placed for adoption as an older child, reflected on his insecurities about belonging within the adoptive family. She remarked:

For these big children going into adoption... they have long-

standing loyalties to their birth families, which you cannot set aside. They are real and they are legitimate; even if their families are appalling, they're legitimate, they're part of them. So you can't pretend they don't exist. (Left home)

Other parents talked about young people who were preoccupied with finding their birth parent(s) or who had deep-seated fears that they would become like their birth parent. This seemed to be more of a concern for boys whose birth fathers were shadowy figures with little known about them except for histories of violence.

Previous research (e.g. Neil, 2004) has highlighted how birth parents often failed to take account of the child's growing maturity in the letters that they wrote. In this study, adoptive parents reported that children too held in their minds an image of their birth parents taken from the pictures in their life story books or from their early memories. Children did not think about their birth parents getting older. For example, one adoptive mother explained what had happened when she asked her son why he was looking at pornographic sites:

[Mother said] 'What were you doing?' He said, 'It wasn't me, it was the lad next to me, he was on this porn site and there was this girl on there and she looked just like my birth mother', and I said to him, 'Was she a young girl? How old was she? Was she about 19 or 20?' And he was like, 'Yes'. And I said, 'But Peter, your birth mother is 30-odd now'. (At home)

Although about one-quarter of children had had face-to-face contact with a birth parent, it should not be assumed that contact had made family openness and discussions about adoption any easier. It is possible to have contact and for communication within the family to be closed. Conversely, an adoption can be "closed" but the communication within the family can be open (Brodzinsky, 2006). We were interested to know whether the level of openness about adoption was related to risks of disruption.

Talking about adoption within the family – communicative openness

In simple terms, communicative openness refers to a process within the adoptive family characterised by open and honest communication, which supports adoption-related emotions and which embraces the meaning of adoption (Brodzinsky, 2005, 2006). The level of communicative openness can vary between a child and each parent, as well as between different adopted children in the same family (Wrobel *et al*, 1998; Hawkins *et al*, 2008). Brodzinsky found that communicative openness was a stronger predictor of children's adjustment than having contact with the birth family (Brodzinsky, 2006).

The theory builds on the work of Kirk (1964), who wrote about the inherent balancing act that adoptive parents must perform between acknowledging, but not overemphasising, the impact of adoption on family members. Kirk described the negative impact on adoptive families who collude in secrecy and denial about adoption (families who deny the difference), but also on those families who insist that the sole lens for viewing the family and its interactions is through adoption (families who insist on the difference).

Communicative openness seems to be particularly important in adolescence, as adolescents who perceive greater communicative openness in their families report more trust in their parents, fewer feelings of alienation, and better overall family functioning (Kohler *et al*, 2002; Brodzinsky, 2011). However, previous research has also found that parents can underestimate the difficulty children have in raising the subject and talking about adoption. Children can feel disloyal or fear that they might upset their adoptive parents if they mention their birth family.

Parents talking to children about adoption

Parents were asked how easy they had found it to talk about adoption with their child. Just over three-quarters (77%) said that they had found it easy, with many parents emphasising the effort they had made to keep the subject of adoption open for discussion. Parents described a "drip feed" strategy, whereby they gradually shared more information with their child as they matured. However, while parents said that they found it easy to talk about adoption, their children often wanted to avoid the subject; therefore, parents often felt that they were talking "at" rather than "with" children. Whilst most of the parents thought that they acknowledged their difference as an adoptive family, other parents thought that they were following social workers' instructions by emphasising the difference. For example, one parent said:

> *You wonder why you have to beat yourself up and keep reminding her that you're not her dad because the adoptive system is, 'You must let your children know that they're not yours' ... which you do to the point of driving yourself stupid about it ... When I speak to people I say, 'Nina is adopted' ... and I'm thinking, why have I done that? What have I said that for?* (At home)

When asked a more specific question about the ease with which adoptive parents had been able to talk to children about their birth parents, fewer (62%) reported that this had been easy. Parents described treading a fine line between wanting their child to understand the severity of the circumstances that had led to their removal from birth parents, yet feeling a need to spare the child from the appalling detail of their early history. As a result, adoptive parents were sometimes quite vague when talking about birth parents, which did not always satisfy children's curiosity and might have fed their fantasy of returning to live with their birth family.

For some adopters, a one-off meeting with the birth parent/s (prior to adoption) had helped them to communicate more openly and honestly with their child about the adoption. Parents described how these meetings had given them a better understanding of the difficulties and adversities birth parents (particularly birth mothers) had faced, which in turn had led to feeling greater compassion. Having met birth parents, some adopters felt more assured in speaking to their child, especially about a birth parent's feelings. However, as difficulties escalated within adoptive families, some parents' views about the birth parents hardened, as they realised the long-term impact of their child's maltreatment. One parent said:

It's like I live with these people. I've never met half of them, but I live with their ghosts ... Even now if he's anxious the main thing to do is feed him, because he's still food-orientated. He used to have terrible nightmares of turning into a skeleton and dying, because he was so hungry. (Left home)

Children talking to parents about adoption

We also asked parents how easy or difficult they thought it had been for their child to talk to them about adoption, their birth parents and their early life. Parents thought that most children had struggled to talk about each of these areas; this was the case more frequently for children in the "Left home" group (Table 9.3).

Table 9.3
Children's difficulties in talking about adoption – parents' reports

Child had difficulty	Left home %	At home %
Talking about birth mother	75	51
Talking about birth father	80	63
Talking about adoption	77	57
Talking about the past	71	57

About three-quarters of the children who had left home had had great difficulty in talking about adoption-related issues. Some children had simply refused to talk about anything to do with adoption, despite parents working hard to create the opportunities for honest and open communication. Some parents said that the young person had never asked any questions about their adoption. One mother, for example, could not talk to her son without him becoming angry. He had forbidden her to mention anything even vaguely related to his adoption. She explained:

I think he's very mixed up about his beginnings, very mixed up, but I'm not allowed to talk about it. I do agree with people when they've said, 'You need to talk about adoption'. It's not that I don't agree with them, but he wasn't wanting to do it, so I couldn't . . . I think he's got huge issues about it. (Left home)

Another parent said that at any mention of adoption, his daughter would put her fingers in her ears and say: 'La la la'. Parents were sometimes unsure of how much their child remembered or how accurate their recall was when the memories were controlled by an elder sibling who stated definitively what had and had not happened. Children were also unsure about their early lives, as they could not always differentiate between memories, flashbacks and dreams. One parent said:

Sometimes you get a little flick of the eyes and you think maybe she does remember something, but you would never know . . . she would never tell you. (Left home)

Just 19 of the 70 children talked openly about their pasts, for example, they could remember and talked about having to pawn their toys at the fish and chip shop to get food, being thrown downstairs, house fires, being strangled, shouting, seeing their father hit their mother and being given heroin.

In most families in the general population, adolescents confide and communicate less with their parents than do younger children; adolescents are notorious for giving parents the "silent treatment". Following this pattern, adoptive parents too described a reduction in communication about adoption during the teenage years. There is a paradox here, in that at the time when adopted young people want and need to know more about their histories, they are least able to ask. Parents were aware though that the feelings and questions about adoption were just under the surface. One mother recalled a conversation with her 13-year-old daughter who came home one day and unexpectedly asked:

'Are they still alive?' And I said, 'Who are we talking about?' She said, 'My birth family', and I said, 'I don't really know'. So she said, 'Well, I'd like to know', and I said, 'OK'. (At home)

Most parents recognised that young people were thinking about their adoption and birth family, even if they were unable to ask questions. For example, one adoptive parent said:

Sometimes I go into her room and I find all her books [life story]. She visits it more than I was expecting her to, so she's obviously still churning things over in her mind. (At home)

A few young people talked about their birth families outside the family, using this to gain kudos and celebrity status, saying, for example, 'I bet you haven't had XYZ [severe types of abuse] happen to you?' but would not engage in any real discussions of the issues with their parents.

Children's worries

About 54 per cent of adoptive parents thought that their child worried about being adopted and had many worries about their birth families (60 per cent of those who had "Left home" and 49 per cent of the "At home" group). Parents reported that children worried about whether birth parents were still alive, about siblings still living with or returning to live with the birth family, being traced by family members, and about who would care for them in the future. Several young people were aware that their behaviour was different from that of their peers and asked their parent, 'Why am I like I am?'

Parents were also aware that their child's adoptive status made them more vulnerable to bullying. Thirty-one per cent of the parents knew that their child had been subjected to taunts and bullying right through their school careers. For example, one mother said:

She had all this right through schooling: 'Why are you adopted? Didn't your mum and dad want you any more?' (At home)

Unfair treatment did not always end in school and for some continued into their employment. One mother described how her daughter's new job seemed to be going well until her daughter rang to say she had been sacked. Her employer had asked for a form to be completed that checked the records of criminal offences, on which she was asked to record all previous names and other personal details. When she refused to write her birth name, her birth mother's maiden name and previous addresses, she was sacked. Although her social worker supplied the details from the Home Office website that showed that those adopted under the age of 10 years old were excluded from this requirement, the young person continued to experience discrimination and a lack of awareness from employers.

Overall, there was no statistical difference between the "Left home" and "At home" parents' self-reported ease in talking about adoption-related issues. However, there was a difference between the groups in the parent-reported ease with which their children could talk about the subjects. The majority of the children who had left home had great difficulty talking about and communicating their feelings about adoption and their birth families, and many young people had refused to discuss the topics at all.

The "At home" families

In the previous chapters, we have compared the "Left home" group with the "At home" group and have been interested in understanding why some children stayed at home whilst others had left. Previous research (e.g. Sinclair *et al*, 2007) has shown that sometimes children continue to live in permanent placements, but family life is unhappy. In these instances, a move may be preferable to stability. We were keen to understand whether the "At home" families were likely to disrupt in the future, or if there were certain factors that kept them together.

Parents in the "At home" group were asked about how well they were able to communicate with their child and whether they had ever thought that their child might have to leave home. The majority (n = 28, 80%) of parents had at some point thought that their child might have to move out of home, and only seven parents had never considered this as an option. Parents said:

> Yes [thought about child leaving], on a couple of occasions when he's been extremely violent . . . I think I've got a duty of care to

protect [sibling] as well . . . but then there's always that mother thing kicks in. You think . . . I've made a commitment to this, and then an hour later when everything's subsided and I think, 'OK, you can do this, come on, pick yourself up and just get on with it'. So I guess yes, there have been those times where I just thought I can't do this any longer, but they're relatively short-lived.

Some parents only felt able to continue living with the young person because they could see an end in sight. Parents described how they were waiting for and encouraging their children to leave home to go to university or college, or to employment, such as the army, which offers living accommodation. Other young people, because of the extent of their learning difficulties or mental health problems, were not expected to be ever able to live independently as adults. Parents were hopeful that sheltered accommodation or residential care would be made available when the young people reached 18.

When parents were asked what had kept them going, some found it hard to identify why their adoption had not disrupted. Parents talked about commitment, their bond to the child, maternal feelings and responsibility. A few parents simply said, 'She's my daughter/son', or said that they could never be responsible for splitting siblings:

It's funny; I think my worry has been that [my husband] will leave because it's too awful for him. I just feel like I have made that decision that he's my son. I'm not going to give up on him, which is awful because I suppose what I'm saying is, I'm more likely to give up on my husband.

The "At home" group of parents were asked about their daily lives and about how much they did together as a family. Most parents reported reasonable levels of communication but there were a small number of families where communication and cohesion were minimal. In the following discussion, the families have been grouped by their response to questions on family communication and their views on whether the young person would still be living with them in five years' time.

Families at high risk of disruption (n = 6)

In six families, parents and young people were no longer communicating with each other in any meaningful way and were, to all intents and purposes, living separate lives. Parents and children often had minimal contact with each other and did not eat together. One mother said:

Ryan goes out in the morning and comes back at 10 at night.

At the time of the interview, three parents were close to asking that their child be taken into care. As one mother said:

Twice we've got close [to disrupting] and I'm feeling close at the moment.

Another mother was waiting for her daughter's 16th birthday so that she could move her into a hostel. Typically, these parents were exhausted and had given up. They had stopped looking for help and advice. Some expressed a hope that perhaps relationships might be re-established in the future.

Families at moderate risk of disruption (n = 14)

This group comprised parents who could usually find a way to manage challenging behaviour shown by their child, but often described "walking on eggshells". The quality of the communication in the family was variable and stressful situations at home could quickly escalate. As one parent said:

Sometimes we eat meals together; sometimes we manage to do it. He'll talk to me. And that's because of the bond that we had, we have still . . . What's his view of OK isn't a million miles away from my view of OK, and we have to compromise somewhere, don't you?

These parents were less certain about what the future might hold. They talked about their responsibilities and concerns for the child's future. Some worried that adult services might fail to provide accommodation for those young people who would not be able to live independently or that behaviour would become too challenging. For example, one mother said:

I just couldn't leave the kids, and I feel Michael is more my responsibility because I made a deliberate choice to adopt him and because of his background and things. I'll stick by him. I am very worried about it, as he gets older, how I'm going to cope with that, particularly once he's bigger than me. That really worries me, being on my own with him. But I know that there's a lovely little boy in there and I can't leave him. But, I suppose it depends on how bad his behaviour gets. But actually, I'm really hoping there's something in there – I think he'll be all right, touch wood.

Families at low risk of disruption (n = 15)

In this group, parents thought that there was a good level of communication within the family. The children talked to parents, sought out their company, and were intimate. Most ate meals together as a family. Often, parents had been able to see some improvements in their child's difficulties. In these families, young people too seemed to want to remain living in their adoptive home. Parents said:

Last night we all watched television together, and we had just been on holiday together . . . we had a very nice holiday . . . I would say it's getting better.

She's always very adamant that she's glad that she's adopted . . . this is where she wants to be . . . keeps me going when things are bad.

Some young people were in residential or boarding schools, returning for weekends and during holidays. This had helped keep three families together, although getting the funding in place had usually been tricky. Respite care had helped a couple of families to stay intact:

I was always very much thinking that this is something that we ought to be able to resolve as a family, and I think at the end of the day we probably did, but we did need that help [respite]. If we hadn't had that, I don't know quite how things would have worked out.

Attribution

Most of the parents whose children were still at home thought that the cause of their child's difficulties was outside their or their child's control. The parents did not feel guilty because of their own failings or blame the child; instead, they attributed the difficulties to the child's early life experiences, such as brain damage, effects of foetal alcohol spectrum disorder and/or maltreatment. For example, one mother said:

Even when I was very low, I thought this isn't her fault ... she's just the product of abuse. And that's what made me stick with her.

It was not possible to know whether external attribution had arisen from a parent's own personality or from reading about their child's difficulties, or whether contact with professionals had shaped that view. In the next chapter, which focuses on seeking help, support and interventions, we will see that the reverse was often the case with adoptive parents whose child had left home, as those parents reported that they felt blamed for their child's difficulties.

Summary

- Most (93%) of the children were or had been living in families with other children. Sibling relationships were considered typical for the majority of children, but just under half (48%) of the children who had left home and 18 per cent of the "At home" group were in constant conflict with siblings. Sibling conflict had often been present from the early days of the adoptive placement. Parents of the children who had left home described physical aggression, and coercive and sexualised behaviour between siblings as the most worrying behaviours. Verbal aggression most worried the parents of the children still at home.

- The majority (75%) of parents whose child had left home thought that the study child usually instigated sibling conflict, whereas the majority of parents in the "At home" group thought that both children were equally responsible.

- Warring siblings usually avoided each other and the preferred parental strategy was to keep them apart. This created splits in some families, with one parent caring for the study child and the other parenting the remaining siblings.

- The child's challenging behaviour had put marital relationships under intense stress. Some marital relationships strengthened but 11 marriages had ended.

- Fathers struggled with how to respond to their child's aggressive behaviour and felt disempowered, resulting in discipline being difficult to implement.

- At the time of placement, one in three children had no contact with adult birth relatives. Letterbox arrangements were the most frequent type of contact planned post-adoption and eight children had planned face-to-face contact with birth parents. At the time of the interviews, 13 (19%) children had face-to-face contact with a birth parent. In the main, adoptive parents were satisfied with the level of contact, although newly established contact through Facebook was difficult to manage.

- Evidence from the study would suggest that post-adoption support services should be developed to ensure that re-established contact is safely managed and that children have a place where they can get answers to the questions they have.

- About three-quarters of the children who had left home had difficulty talking about adoption-related issues and many had been poorly prepared for adoption. Parents thought they worried whether birth parents were still alive, about siblings living with the birth family, being traced by family members, and about who would care for them in the future. Some children were thought to be preoccupied with thoughts about their birth mothers.

- Most parents stated that they had tried to keep the subject of adoption open but did not find it as easy to talk about birth parents. Parents found it difficult to know how much information to share, how to talk to children about particularly harrowing histories or how to write to birth parents when children were having difficulty at home or in school.

- Most parents were aware that it was important to be open about adoption-related issues, but communicative openness was not possible when children were unable to voice their thoughts and concerns.

- Parents were aware that 31 per cent of the children had been bullied about being adopted during their school career. There were also two examples of discrimination continuing into the workplace.

- Most (80%) of the families whose children were still at home had thought about asking for the child to be removed. Some families were waiting for the child to reach 16 or 18 years old when they would be leaving the family.

- Families said that they had remained intact because of their commitment, their bond with the child, feelings of responsibility and because the child was theirs. Families that were likely to stay together had seen some improvement in behaviours and/or attributed the cause of the difficulties to factors outside their or their child's control.

10 Seeking help and support

When adoptive families began to worry about their child's difficulties, 71 per cent of the parents whose children were at home and 49 per cent of the parents whose adoptions later disrupted had lost touch with the agency that had approved them. Twenty-nine (41%) of the families had moved house since the child had been placed, but parents stated that the move had made little difference to the services they received. The first step in getting support was for professionals to acknowledge that there was a problem, and, for most adoptive parents, this was not easily achieved. Many parents spoke about the battles they had to get support. One mother said:

> *I just sat on the phone all day long, just phoning everybody – the doctor – social services – post-adoption support . . . I thought, I'm just going to sit and phone and phone, until somebody takes notice of me.* (At home)

Some parents, especially those who were employed as teachers, social workers and counsellors, found that social workers underestimated their need for support and overestimated their coping capacity. Parents spoke about the paradox of how in their professional role they were working with children and advising other families in difficulty, but were unable to help their own family. One parent commented:

> *I understand all the theory of why it's happening but it doesn't help when you're in the middle of it.* (At home)

Other parents stated that the difficulties they reported were minimised by social workers and not taken seriously. One parent said:

> *I suppose people are trying to make you think it's just normal behaviour . . . it's not, the knobs are turned up . . . it's not normal behaviour. I've seen your children; they're not behaving anything like that.* (Left home)

Parents reported great difficulty in getting professionals to understand the problems they were facing. A phrase that was frequently used by parents about their interaction with professionals was, 'They just don't get it!'

Overall satisfaction with support services

The majority of adoptive parents were dissatisfied with the overall response from their LA. In particular, 38 families complained about the difficulty in accessing services and eligibility criteria that acted as a deterrent. Parents described arguments between the placing and receiving local authority and between children's services, education and health authorities about where responsibility for support lay. Parents said that agencies had "passed the buck" and were surprised that support packages could not be ratified by the courts. One adopter described their experience:

We were using the court to try and fight for a support package, and being very surprised to find that the judge had no powers to order any. The judge was very concerned and practically begging the LA to do something. They were saying, 'No, it's health', and then you find out you're stuck between health, social work and education and because they're not working together, they're not coming up with a holistic package. (At home)

Assessments that recommended expensive support packages were often denied. For example, one mother, reflecting on what might have been if support had been received earlier, said:

They throw money at her now. If they would have put in the money they've put in in the last year, I would have had Family Futures, which is what I wanted. I asked for a referral, we had a report done just with us and nobody took any notice. In fact, do you know what, I very much doubt if anybody read it. (Left home and child in residential care)

Other families had only assessments and no services. For example, a

171

full assessment completed by the specialist team at Great Ormond Street had been sent to the local Child and Adolescent Mental Health Service (CAMHS), only for the family to find that, rather than implementing the recommendations, CAMHS were doing an assessment of the assessment.

Support packages that were in place were sometimes stopped when the child had been placed out of area and the receiving LA refused to continue after the three-year period had ended. Some parents had been on "waiting lists" for post-adoption support, as both children's services and CAMHS were short-staffed. Even when therapeutic services were provided by local authorities, they were usually time-limited (about six sessions) and/or provided many miles away from the family's home.

Adoptive parents also reported eligibility criteria that prevented children from receiving the services they needed, for example, in some LAs, autistic children did not meet the disability criteria and therefore could not receive support from the disability team. One mother, whose child had diagnoses of Asperger's, sensory processing difficulties and severe pragmatic language disorder, said:

> Because they don't count Asperger's, or autism, as a disability, they can say, 'No'. So that was a dead end. The post-adoption social worker tried really hard. The post-adoption team tried to refer us to everybody but they all came back and said that she does not meet the criteria. (At home)

Many children had complex and overlapping needs that did not fit the tight criteria demanded for intervention by agencies. Adopted children were often unable to access CAMHS or youth offending teams (because they were not currently looked after children), and in one case were unable to access LA services because the child had a post-adoption social worker and this was deemed to be the "wrong kind of social worker".

Assessments of need

Adoptive parents were asked if they had known that they could ask for an assessment of need. Most were unaware of the entitlement but 27 assessments of need were started: seven assessments were never completed, eight were completed but no services were provided, and 12 assessments resulted in the provision of services.

Support from local authority adoption teams

The majority (83%) of the parents had received some support from LA post-adoption services; this included the parents who had been approved as VAA adopters. Support had been sought from the LA by VAA-approved parents for reasons such as the VAA had closed, the family had moved too far away for the VAA to support, and the VAA was unable to provide intensive support services over many years. Ten parents had no support from LA post-adoption services: nine of the 10 had tried to get support but been told there were no services and to ring Relate, the police, or go to their GP.

Some adopters described "wonderful long-term support" from the whole LA adoption agency. More frequently, there was praise for individually named social workers who were described as "a lifeline". One-quarter of the parents who received support from post-adoption services rated social workers as the most useful support they had had. One parent said:

She's been with us every step of the way. Yesterday, for example, we had the child's review at school and she came along to that. Because she realises how difficult it can be to get people on board. She's been a godsend. I'm going to put her name forward for social worker of the year. (At home)

Parents who spoke warmly about social workers had received good support from a consistent worker and often this was combined with a package of therapy provided in-house or purchased privately by the LA. Families appreciated the detailed work that post-adoption social workers had undertaken to improve relationships within the family. Sometimes the relationship work was individual work with parents, or

173

family or filial therapy. In a few cases, mother and child counselling was provided. Most of the relationship work was intended to improve the parents' skills in managing and understanding the complex behaviours of their child. Parents valued training on therapeutic parenting and filial therapy, describing it as, "outstanding" or "immensely helpful" and offering "considerable insights". Another parent said of training on attachment and emotional regulation skills:

> It explained systematically for the first time why I saw different symptoms, and that was critical, because if you try to think from first principles about what is going to work . . . sometimes the symptoms are just so misleading . . . You have to somehow decide which bit you're going to work on because you can't do the whole lot at once. It's a thing at a time, and reward it, compound it, integrate it, remind them, give another little reward, keep moving forward positively, forward with lots of praise and enthusiasm and success . . . So I've got [daughter] to a point where she can catch a bus across town. (At home)

Adopters also appreciated financial support. This was particularly important for those who had adopted sibling groups, as it enabled parents to pay for a home help or cleaner so that they could spend time with the children. Practical support had been important for a few parents, such as the LA providing help taking to and picking up a child from school and help with birth family contact issues. One parent praised the out-of-hours foster care and adoption advice line that was run by experienced foster carers. She described the support as "brilliant".

A few parents complained that, although they were visited regularly, there had not been one consistent worker. Services were also promised but did not materialise:

> We contacted (the social worker) and he promised us the earth, and then we never heard another thing from him . . . He promised he would keep in contact, that he would get us some help, and some form of counselling – but nothing came. (At home)

Other adopters spoke of feeling patronised and "patted on the head". They became increasingly frustrated that they were being told that they were doing a "good job" but offered no additional strategies or solutions. Other parents said they had been offered ineffective services or services that they did not want. In particular, those parents whose child had left home reported that they kept being offered the same package of parenting classes when the child's behaviours were becoming more and more difficult to manage. One parent, who challenged the support offered, said:

> [Social worker] suggested that we go on a parenting course, and when I pointed out that we'd had 250 hours of parenting support from CAMHS and other seminars and things, and that I didn't really understand what a parenting course would give us, they told us that we'd refused to engage and they were closing the case. So I had to say, 'No, I'm not refusing to engage, I was just asking the question'. (Left home)

It was not that parenting courses were discounted – many parents had found them useful when difficulties began to emerge. The problem was that the same parenting courses continued to be offered, as the child's behaviour grew more extreme and out of control. Parents thought that social workers were failing to understand just how desperate they were, as one mother said about attempts to access some help for her very vulnerable daughter:

> She'd been running away a lot. She was given the phone numbers of men that she'd never met and she'd just call them and say, 'I'm at such-and-such station', and they'd say, 'I'll pick you up', and she'd go missing for days. She went missing during the riots; we had no idea where she was. Post-adoption said, when we went to see them, 'Would you like to go on a parenting course?' (Left home)

Children's behaviours were often puzzling and parents tried to educate themselves to help their child. They read everything they could find and often thought they were more knowledgeable than the professionals who visited. Some parents described situations where social workers were too ready to label difficulties as attachment disorders before ruling out other possibilities, for example, some adopters described social workers as "not having a clue" about children who had foetal alcohol syndrome.

Life story books and life story work

One of the social work interventions that parents often spoke about was the importance of a good life story book and later life story work. Occasionally a child had arrived in their adoptive placement with a good life story book created by their social worker, as in the following example:

> *[The social worker] went back into the house after the police had rescued the kids and she went and searched and got all the photographs and stuff . . . she had the foresight to do that and to build up the life story books . . . It's been a really useful tool.* (At home)

Other books were virtually non-existent, of poor quality or factually inaccurate. Occasionally, students nearing the end of a placement had been tasked to prepare books and with little obvious supervision. As one parent commented:

> *The life story book was of very poor quality. It had been given to a social work student to do . . . we had photos with the wrong captions . . . which makes you think what else is wrong? It undermines confidence.* (At home)

Some children used and were interested in their life story books right from the start of their adoptive placement. One mother described how her son would focus on the pictures of his birth in the hospital:

> *And he'd say, 'Who was looking after me?' . . . And I'd say, 'The nurses were looking after you', and he'd say, 'Well, who? . . . Who was holding me?' And I'd say, 'The nurse is holding you, look,*

she's holding you!' and he went, 'She's not even looking at me'.
(Left home)

Many children did not seem to have been well prepared for placement and adoption. Some children were said to have brought misconceptions with them into placement and had incorporated the inaccuracies into their adoption story. One mother described the challenge she faced, as her son's foster carer had told him that the fairies had found him a new mummy.

Life story work began in response to requests from adopters for help. Life story books had usually been written for young children, which became unsuitable for young people, as they got older and wanted more detail about their personal history. Events in the birth family, such as the death of a birth mother, also sometimes triggered a young person's wish to revisit their early life and fill in the details. In a few instances, the post-adoption life story work was described by parents as well executed and beneficial, for example, a mother explained how a social worker had written a new life story book with the children. She said that it had helped her realise that, as an adoptive parent, she was doing her best and had done some good things for the children. Another mother described how sensitive life story work had helped her family:

Working with the social services, talking to them about his origins . . . he was really struggling; we were having a lot of behavioural problems with him over the last couple of years about it. [Child would say] 'You're not my real mum and dad', but then we got the sessions . . . and [worker] tells him about his abandonment . . . Oh, that was horrible. But they did it so well and he totally accepted it, he's not spoken about it since. We'll chat away about things, we talk about adoption and things like that, we've looked at his book. It's weird, that was burning at him, it was really burning and you could tell but now he knows . . . having that discussion, him knowing, seems to have really helped. (At home)

More often, however, life story work was thought by parents to have been unhelpful, even detrimental to children. We reported accounts in Chapter 8 of poorly handled life story work that was considered by parents to have been directly responsible for the escalation of children's difficulties. Sometimes social workers had started life story work but failed to see it through; others had approached delicate subjects with seemingly little thought about the effect on children, as in the following examples:

> They agreed that this social worker was going to do various things . . . he started pieces of work but they were never finished. He'd do a piece of work with the boys such as a drawing to express their journey through life and it was never finished. (At home)

> So she [social worker] came in and said, 'Right, we're going to do some life story work', and they (children) just looked at her like, 'What the hell's that!' . . . So she said, 'Did you know that so-and-so and so-and-so are your half-siblings, your half-brother and sister, and they said, 'No' . . . So she said, 'Do you know what a half-brother and a half-sister are? Do you know what that means?' And they said, 'No', and she said, 'It means that your mother had sex with another man'. Well, our two just scooted. John went down behind the armchair, Lisa shot across the room under the table, and she [the social worker] looked left and right and there they are, cowering in different places, and she slammed the book shut and she said, 'I feel like Billy-no-mates . . . Oh well, I won't bother with that again!' I just looked at her, I thought 'Oh dear', and it was like this every time she visited, they were just petrified.

Individual social workers also undertook direct work with children, but from parental descriptions it appeared that some workers were inadequately supervised and did not understand the possible impact of the work on the child or the parent. One parent vividly described the aftermath of a direct work session:

> One time we were walking back from a session . . . he was

keeping his distance, probably about five metres away from me the whole time, but then he would run up to me and try and push me under a bus, and then he would run off, and I couldn't get near him. Then he would run up to me and grab my hair and pull it, and then run away again. And then he would run up to me and spit in my face, and then run away again. And so I just thought the only thing I can do is get home ... We got to the train platform and I just stood there, and I could see out of the corner of my eye he was behind me, and then he just started to cry, and he couldn't stop crying, and then he was going, 'I'm sorry, I'm sorry'. So then, we came home. (Left home)

Provision of respite care

Many families wanted respite but local authorities were extremely reluctant to provide it. Eleven adoptive families were able to have a break as the LA had developed ways of providing respite without making the child a looked after child. Some children had been linked with a "buddy" or support worker who took the child out for a few hours each week, or the LA had paid for a child-minder.

[Worker] took him out, giving positive experiences and to give us respite, so we had six hours a day on Saturdays. (Left home)

Private educational tuition (bought with the adoption allowance) also enabled the parent to have a couple of hours' break each week. For two families, the LAs had either partly or fully funded the costs of a PGL-type (activity-based) holiday for the child. Families whose child had left home reported that respite would have been more valuable before the situation deteriorated.

I think we could have done with respite care much earlier on. We were certainly making it clear what difficulties we were having. What we didn't know is what the solution was, and they weren't offering anything other than emotional support, as in sitting there and listening to us moan about how terrible it was. (Left home)

For most families, respite seemed to be provided as a last ditch attempt to keep the family together. In some LAs, respite could only be provided in two-week blocks and by making the child a looked after child. One parent, recounting her discussion with the social worker about respite care, explained:

> So they said, 'We can take him off your hands and put them in foster care for a week'. And we said, 'No, we're not talking about that, we don't want that, because it wouldn't do the boys any good. We're talking about could somebody have them for a day so we can go shopping and go to the cinema, or overnight so we could have a meal out with friends?' The response was, 'Can't be done, they would have to go back into the care system'. There's no way in the world we are exposing our boys to that, never ever. (At home)

Parents who asked for respite thought that they were treated badly by social workers and made to feel guilty.

Support from adoption support agencies

Four of the 11 adoptive parents approved by a VAA rated their VAA as providing the most helpful support of all the agencies, and reported that the social worker had supported them consistently. However, the child's needs were such that all the parents had had to seek additional help elsewhere.

Ten parents were able to get support from adoption support agencies such as Catchpoint, Chrysalis and the Post-Adoption Centre. Parents rated these services as very helpful. In addition, five adoptive parents paid for an assessment by Family Futures, but could not afford the cost of treatment and their LAs refused to pay. Adopters commented on how short-sighted this had been, as one parent explained:

> [Family Futures said] 'This is what we intend to do, it will cost over three years £75,000', and the local authority said, 'No way, that's far too expensive; we'll do it in-house'. So the residential unit now costs £250,000 a year. (Left home)

Three adoptive parents rated the support they got from specialist teams at Great Ormond Street or from the Maudsley Hospital as the best intervention they had experienced.

Many of the adopters had used the AUK message boards for advice and support and three adopters had completed the *It's a Piece of Cake?* training programme. The support from AUK was valued by adopters but one parent was critical of their decision to end the volunteer list of peer supporters, as she had found this very helpful.

Contacting the emergency duty team (EDT)

Thirty-two of the 70 parents had contacted the EDT service asking for help. More of the parents (69%) whose children had left home had rung the EDT for help than parents whose children were still at home (23%). One mother rang the EDT in tears, saying that she could no longer manage. She was advised to get a friend to come and sit with her and that an email referral would be sent to the post-adoption support team and she would receive a call on Monday. She said:

> No-one contacted me. I then phoned up and said, 'Have you had this email?' 'We haven't got a team'. That was her response and she laughed . . . to laugh when someone is in such desperate need. (Left home)

Another parent, talking about the response from EDT, said:

> Only thing that there was, was the emergency duty team, and I rang them up one night to say, 'I'm really worried my son is going to hurt me, he's threatening me with things', and they said, 'Have you had problems before?' And I said, 'Yes, it's a long history, he's going to throw something quite heavy at me now'. It was a plant pot, and he smashed it against the wall, and I said, 'He's just thrown it at me, and I'm really worried', and she said, 'Have you tried after-school clubs?' And I just thought, OK, there's no help here either. So, every time it was so inappropriate, it was the wrong support, it was non-existent. (Left home)

None of the adoptive parents reported a helpful response from the EDT and the advice often given was to phone the police.

Support from other LA teams and family support agencies

Adoptive parents and young people had also been in touch with and had received services from a range of other social work teams, such as the crisis intervention team, youth offending and pathways to independence teams. Adoptive parents were not positive about these interventions and complained that the teams were not prepared to consider the child's history. For example, one mother, describing her contact with the family resource service, said:

> They only look forwards and they weren't looking back at the trauma. I could spout all the theory at him and he said, 'I'm not really interested; I want to know what she's going to do now'. (Left home)

Parents were sometimes referred to family support services whose typical referral was a neglectful and abusive family where essentially it was the parenting that was the problem. The interventions they provided were designed to improve the quality of parenting, teaching parents how to play with their child, and form positive relationships. They were unused to working with families where the problems were thought to lay in the trauma that the child had suffered.

Support from Child and Adolescent Mental Health Services (CAMHS)

There were many complaints about mental health services for adopted young people, with parents describing similar problems to those they had experienced with children's services. Parents complained about being unable to access CAMHS because of two-year waiting lists; the child's difficulties being too complex for the service; there being no therapeutic services for children with attachment difficulties; and only being offered medication. In five cases, children refused to go for counselling. Eighty-three per cent of the parents whose children had left home and 69 per cent of those whose children were at home had tried to get help from CAMHS. Mothers explained:

> He had a tantrum at school that was so bad the teachers had to hold him down and then he wet himself, it was that bad. And he'd run away from home, it was awful. So I just kept referring to CAMHS. I said, 'We need help, we need help'. (Left home)

> [CAMHS said] we want to meet you as parents and deal with you. We went along for about a year and then I said, 'Look, things have to start moving now, you need to do something for Keith, and he needs some therapeutic input for him. Thank you very much for having us in. You pat us on the knee and tell us what wonderful parents we are, and how supportive we are of him.' (At home)

Some parents did parenting classes to try to get support for their child, but they were of limited use and were reported to be useful only when the difficulties were not severe. Parents said:

> They kept banging on about parenting classes, and I thought they're going to throw me out if I don't say yes. So we went and did some parenting classes . . . so we did that to tick a box. To be honest, the most useful thing that was said to us was, 'Play with your kids every day'. And that's the thing I always come back to. It's all about relationships. And so it was nice to be reminded of that. (At home)

Adoptive parents complained about the CAMHS they were offered and gave examples, such as the child being seen by many different workers and not developing a rapport; parents only being given videos on attachment to watch; being offered no service but told to hide the knives in the house; and CAMHS insisting on working only with the parents or only with the child.

Parents complained about how patient confidentiality was used to exclude them from the content of therapeutic sessions, leaving them unprepared for the aftermath. Mothers described the after-effects of individual child therapy, as in the following two examples:

Something was happening; we couldn't work out what. I didn't know if it was positive at the time because Kathy would come home, she'd look to try and needle me, to pick a fight and I would just ignore it. Then she would either just explode or what sometimes also used to happen, she would go to her room and howl like an animal. She'd be as rigid and stiff, it wasn't a seizure or anything like that but she'd lie on the bed and she would howl and I'd go in and I'd say, 'It's all right darling, Mummy's here.' And she just had her arm across her face and it was just like a wolf, it was like an animal in pain, and I'd try and bend her body. It wouldn't move, so I'd have to try and get her onto my lap, like trying to cuddle an ironing board really, and have her on my lap. She would just howl . . . it made me feel ill really, but I'd just hold her and say, 'It's all right, I know you can't hear or see me but Mummy's here and Mummy will always be here and you're safe'. (Left home)

I'd just hold her for as long, however many hours it went on for. I'd tell the therapists [about the impact]. I would always email them or phone them but they never actually said 'Aha, that's because we talked about xyz'. It was in total confidence and even though they were little children, we were not allowed to know anything about it. (Left home)

In four cases, CAMHS was only provided after the child was admitted to an Accident and Emergency Department following self-harming, or after the police had made a direct request for a mental health assessment. One child, who was referred urgently to the CAMHS crisis team by the General Practitioner (GP), ended up being admitted to a paediatric ward in hospital because there were no child and adolescent mental health professionals available after 10 pm. Her mother said:

They sent her to this assessment ward and then the CAMHS nurse turned up the next day and she was great . . . because she said exactly what I had said to the school the afternoon before – we need some individual psychotherapy . . . we need some family therapy. (At home)

In another case, a young person's ongoing therapy was abruptly stopped because she disclosed sexual abuse and the therapist said she was unable to cope with '*that* kind of information'. The parents reported that the girl's behaviour deteriorated from that point. Many of the complaints were about the type of intervention offered. The local CAMHS teams offered what they could provide in-house, so if, for example, the therapists were trained in CBT, that was what the child got, irrespective of whether this met the child's needs.

They couldn't really help with girls who had been sexually abused by their birth family. They didn't really have the resources, but they would do some cognitive behavioural therapy. We had them every week for about three years. [Interviewer asked] 'Did it help?' 'No'. (Left home)

Lack of expertise in working with sexual abuse, developmental trauma and attachment-related difficulties were very apparent in the descriptions that parents gave of their attempts to get appropriate help from local CAMHS. One parent was told that, 'because there is no evidence base for treating attachment disorders, [local] CAMHS would not give an attachment disorder diagnosis'. Without a diagnosis, the parent was unable to get appropriate services. Young people who appeared to be showing the early signs of psychosis were not identified and referrals were not made to more specialised child and adolescent mental health services.[46] For example, one parent said:

And the [therapist] said, I wonder if Cassie has epilepsy? So we spent the whole [year] investigating for possible epilepsy, because Cassie had been seeing her birth parents in a wall, in a

---

46 See NICE guidelines on psychosis and schizophrenia in children and young people: http://publications.nice.org.uk/psychosis-and-schizophrenia-in-children-and-young-people-cg155

brick wall. I got her to draw what she saw; she was saying things like, 'I could see those people again' ... I got her to draw and it was her birth parents. She drew them, the man had a dagger dripping blood, the woman had a cigarette and a bottle of vodka. She said, 'I can hear their voices'. I said, 'Well, can you write on here what they're saying?' She drew big bubbles out of their mouths and it said things like, 'We're going to get you; it takes a long time to die, take your last breath, and things like that'. (Left home)

In this example, the child went on to have further tests that identified abnormal frontal lobe activity. However, although there was now an explanation for some of the behaviours, none of the professionals involved knew how best to intervene.

Nine adoptive parents were complimentary about CAMHS and spoke highly of assessments, individual therapists, and emotional support provided by other specialists such as ADHD nurses. Good support from CAMHS was often provided by joint-funded Tier 4 services (within children's services) that included post-adoption social workers, counsellors and psychologists who specialised in attachment difficulties; or from the special team at Great Ormond Street. Adopters described dyadic developmental psychotherapy, breathing techniques, family and filial therapy, play therapy, art therapy, cognitive behavioural therapy and anger management as being helpful. Joint funding of residential schools was also viewed as helpful. One mother, whose child was developing a severe mental illness, said:

I phoned CAMHS and they sat with me and that was lovely because they couldn't give me anything else. That's all I needed, I didn't know what to do, they didn't know what to do either ... She was in such a mess ... in a catatonic state ... blood everywhere (from having pulled a tooth out). They said, 'It's not you, get a doctor'. A GP came and medicated her and said she needed to see a psychiatrist. (Left home)

A mother who was the only parent to be provided with CAMHS

support after the child had left home was very complimentary about the help she had received.

I had individual counselling and that was very helpful. It went on for about six months . . . it was really important to be able to talk because I don't have any family close by and only one or two close friends. So it was just somewhere to go through all my feelings and stuff. [Left home]

Support from education services

About half of the 70 adoptive parents stated that educational professionals had been helpful and offered support. Individual head teachers, teachers, teaching assistants, special educational needs co-ordinators and educational psychologists were named. Eleven parents thought that, of all the agencies, educational professionals had provided the most helpful support.

Twenty-six of the children had a statement of special educational needs (17 behavioural, emotional and social difficulties; six autistic spectrum disorders: five moderate learning difficulties; and one speech and language communication difficulties). At the time of the interviews, 40 children had attended mainstream schools but 13 of these children were only able to do so with intensive support, such as a one-to-one teaching assistant with them all day. The remaining children were educated in day special schools (n = 18), residential EBD (emotional and behavioural difficulties) schools (n = 5), private schools (n = 3), university (n = 2), a specialist school for traumatised children (n = 1), and one young person was an inpatient in a psychiatric unit. Some of the residential placements were joint-funded with health or children's services. Three parents rated staff in the residential schools as being the most helpful support they had received from any agency, and it appeared that residential provision was helping keep these children in their families.

The vast majority of children had shown challenging behaviour in school and some had spent periods of up to a year out of education; five had been permanently excluded and had attended pupil referral units, and three residential school placements had broken down. Some parents complained that the academic expectations for their children were low and that classroom disruption was avoided by appeasement, as in the following example:

> *He was just struggling, not huge trouble, because he just didn't have any concentration, so he would just walk around. I think he got parked a lot, they just gave him something to play with and left him. He has a slight obsessive tendency, so he would go and sharpen his pencil 20 times, and on his way past, he would knock somebody's shoulder, or take something off someone's desk, minor disruption, but still, when there are 30 in a class, it's disruptive.* (At home)

A few families used their own strategies to keep children in school, for example, in one family, the young person stayed at home with her mother every Wednesday, and this just about enabled the young person to make it to the end of the week. Another family took the local education authority (LEA) to court to ensure that their child was provided with specialist residential provision.

Although many parents were grateful for the support from schools, others complained that teachers had very little understanding of the needs of adopted children. Parents volunteered to go into school and talk about the implications of foetal alcohol syndrome or developmental trauma, but these offers were declined. Parents also gave examples of curriculum subjects that created stress for the children, such as drawing family trees and being asked to talk about their births. Some schools were also thought to have found ways of avoiding providing educational support, for example, one child's assessment stated that she had learning needs that were 'dyslexia and dyspraxia-like'. As this was not a definite diagnosis, no formal support was provided. Other parents thought that the additional money the school received for special needs was spread around the school and not spent specifically on the children for whom it was intended. One parent described writing to the headmaster asking for appropriate care within school.

He [headmaster] phoned me up and said, 'I want bells and whistles going on before I'll do anything'. So when I saw the consultant I said, 'Would you write to this teacher?' And she wrote to him and said, 'I have no doubt that this child needs extra help . . . and help specifically in the transition to secondary school'. (Left home)

Parents also talked about how the behaviour of their child caused embarrassment or brought shame on them and their family. In the school setting, some had felt ostracised by other parents. Adopters were unable to get support from parents with similarly aged children. As two mothers observed:

One of the hardest things was the school gates . . . people shouting at me . . . somebody sent their husband to shout at me, which was fairly hideous. (Left home)

Even on her first visit to secondary, I got the walk of shame. I went to pick her up and all the other parents were collecting their smiling children but I got the, 'Can I have a word with you, please?' She hadn't even made it into the school yet! (At home)

Parents were aware of multi-agency meetings having taken place for 57 per cent of children who had left home and for 47 per cent of children still at home. Most of the meetings had been convened by children's services but one-quarter had been convened by the LEA and three per cent by the health authority. These meetings could be overwhelming for parents:

The first one I went to there were masses of people, even a detective . . . I was in shock. They said, 'Don't worry, it's just a normal thing that happens.' (Left home)

Support from other agencies

Adopters were also in touch with and received support from a range of other agencies, such as the police, adoption support agencies and health professionals. Parents had also sought advice from MIND, the Autistic Society, MENCAP, Sir Martin Narey, Dan Hughes, the NSPCC, YMCA, Mumsnet, Parentline Plus, and Young Carers. Twenty-one adoptive parents (30%) had contacted their MP for help.

Just less than half of the adopters had paid privately for therapy or counselling. Sometimes parents had thought that this had been necessary when the LA was able to fund only the first six sessions of therapy and the parents felt that more was required. Other parents paid in the hope that their child might work with a private psychologist rather than having to attend a clinic.

Support from police

Fifty-two (74%) of the families had had involvement with the police because of the child to parent violence, running away, being at risk of sexual exploitation or criminal activity. Most of the families described the interventions by the police as "brilliant" – coming to the house to talk to the child, supporting mothers and, for those children who were self-harming, using their powers to hospitalise them and request mental health assessments. Three families stated that the police were the most helpful of all post-adoption support services. As one parent explained:

> This is what they don't tell you in prep [preparation course] – you can expect to be on first name terms with the police in your local area. The police officers who came when she ran away, they took one look at me and said, 'Oh, I remember coming to your house'... The neighbours are all sticking their heads round the curtain: 'Oooh, what's going on?' But the police have been fantastic. (Left home)

As with other agencies, there were also examples of the police trying to pass the responsibility on to another agency, as in the following example in the police response to child to parent violence:

> When an incident happens, social services say phone the police. I phone the police and they say, 'That's not our problem, phone

social services'. I can't tell you how many times I have stood at my front door talking to a police officer . . . arguing with him and social services on the phone at the same time, emergency duty team arguing with them both, each of them telling me it's the other one's responsibility. And [young person] witnessed all that so she thinks she can do exactly what she wants. (At home)

Support from community health services

Occasionally adoptive parents did meet a professional outside the adoption field who seemed to understand and grasp the gravity of the situation. For example, one mother, talking about her GP, said:

The GP's response has been brilliant. It felt like she had quite a holistic picture, because she spoke with [the child], she really listened to what he was saying, but at the same time, when he left she said, 'How's it for you, because I can see that must be really challenging to manage?' Someone who just kind of acknowledges, whereas I felt that the adoption social worker had no idea really, what it was that we were dealing with. And in fact, the adoption social worker didn't even meet [the child]. (At home)

Another mother spoke about the sensitivity shown by the dentist to her child who suffered with severe anxiety. She said:

He saw her every week in the summer holidays and he fissuresealed her back teeth. He said, 'I'm going to do one tooth a day'. And that's all he did. And it's just amazing and it's just the luck of the draw. You never know if you're going to find somebody like that versus the other people who just don't get it at all. (At home)

Sometimes diagnoses helped parents to understand why their child had difficulties in so many different areas of development. For example, a diagnosis of sensory integration disorder by the occupational therapy service enabled parents to work on what might be helpful, as the parent explained:

We worked out why she couldn't balance on her bicycle, why she was a bit slower learning to swim and swing on the swing and things like that, and we got a trampoline just to help ground her and balance and so on. We did therapeutic brushing, we then got a link to do some therapeutic listening, which we tried as well, just in terms of the headphones, and she wasn't that keen on it. I personally think it made a difference, but she didn't want to continue with it. She's got her Pilates-type ball that she tends to bounce around and lie on and push against the wall, so things like that, just in terms of helping her to ground herself. So that was quite useful. (At home)

Feelings of blame, guilt and isolation

As the difficulties increased, adoptive parents spoke of feeling increasingly alone and blamed. Adopters spoke of professionals' unwillingness to consider the child's history; the following extracts are representative of the vast majority of adopters' views:

There's this undercurrent of, it must be something they're doing. There's no acknowledgement of the fact that she is like that because of what happened to her before she came to live with us. (At home)

You're shooting the wrong person, and I get really sick of that, because we were trying to do something that was good. Give us a bit of help please! (Left home)

Adopters spoke of feeling alone in their attempts to negotiate with other agencies and find appropriate help. Many parents talked about having files and files of correspondence and of having spent hours trawling the internet trying to find anything that might help. The extracts below are typical of adopters' responses:

I kept phoning everybody. I've never hidden anything. I trawled the country to look for if there's anywhere he can go. Is there anything anyone can do? I couldn't find anything. (Left home)

And he was attacking me with things, and I was calling the police. He sprayed some de-icer into my eyes, and I had to go to the cottage hospital, and he was with me, and he was rocking backwards and forwards and punching himself in the head, saying, 'I want to die, I want to die', while my eyes were being swilled out. And the doctor then did say, 'Is he all right, does he need any help?' And I said, 'Yes, he does need help but I can't find any help. This is us, this is how we are.' (Left home)

Adopters reported that if young people would not engage, the offer of a service was withdrawn. Adopters accepted this decision; although from the accounts we were given, some of the young people did not seem to be well enough to have made an informed decision. Children refusing a service appeared to be a way by which agencies could avoid their responsibilities. Many adopters stated that over the years they had become well informed about the causes of their child's difficulties but the interventions they were offered were often ineffective. For example, one father said:

They would help us to understand all about attachment, and why he was doing what he was doing . . . we understood all of that but we'd always come out of there and we'd think, 'Well that's really helped, but what the hell do we do? How do we change his behaviour? What is the best help?' (At home)

Adoptive parents became more and more desperate in their attempts to get help. Some became angry with professionals and "fell out" with those who were meant to be supporting them. They thought they were seen by professionals as demanding and pushy, and got the impression that their phone calls for help were avoided. One parent said:

I always felt judged; always felt that we were failing. They never worked in partnership with us, it was always them versus us, and that was the worst time of all . . . I think I'm traumatised by that. I think even now when I'm talking about it I could cry because I was so hurt by their lack of sensitivity, their lack of recognition that she was our daughter and that we were fighting to hold on to her . . . This little girl who is behaving barbarically, we're not blaming her, but we can't do it in this way any more. And that was a terrible time . . . it was as if I had become the abusive mother. (Left home)

However, from parents' accounts, there were professionals who also felt overwhelmed by the extent of the young person's difficulties and did not know how to help. A parent said that a therapist sadly told her, 'I don't know how to help you'. As difficulties escalated, some young people told their adoptive parents that they no longer wanted to live with them and would prefer to become looked after again. The stress and tensions in the family home were too great for both young people and their parents. The response from services was to try and keep the family together, but many young people ran away, refused to engage with support services, and put themselves and others at great risk. Adoptive parents reported behaviours that showed that many of the young people were out of control, unsafe and very vulnerable.

We were just fire-fighting. It was catastrophic, what was going on, drugs, criminal activity, incredible violence . . . If I took him to school, he would run away. And I needed someone to say to me at that point, 'This is an extreme situation, it's the first time this has happened to you but not the first time it has happened, actually the child needs extra help'. But I was given nothing. All they kept saying was, 'You're doing a great job in the circumstances. I don't know how you are managing this'. And it just kept being pushed back into the family. (Left home)

I didn't know that there could have been a possibility that Simon could have gone into a therapeutic community at the age of 14 years to try and stop all this . . . to where we are now. Which is an extreme place. No-one ever told me that. They should have looked at the situation and thought, 'My God, this is really bad.' But they didn't. (Left home)

There was a great reluctance to intervene and to consider residential care to stabilise the situation and ensure the safety of the young person and other members of the family.

During the interview, parents described their attempts to get help for their child. Forty-two per cent of parents were satisfied with the support that they had received from the adoption agencies but many were angry and frustrated at the professional response. However, it was clear that the behaviours the children were exhibiting had challenged parents and many professionals. Lack of targeted support left parents feeling hopeless and blamed. In the next chapter, we examine how the move out of home occurred for the 35 young people who had left.

Summary

- At the time of wanting post-adoption support, 71 per cent of parents in the "Left home" group and 49 per cent in the "At home" group had lost touch with the agency that had approved them.
- The majority of the parents were dissatisfied with the overall response from support agencies, citing difficulty in accessing services, arguments over funding and eligibility criteria that excluded adopted children.
- The majority (83%) of parents had received some support from local authority post-adoption services. One-quarter of those who received services rated input from social workers as the most helpful of all the interventions they had received.
- Parents spoke positively about social workers who were consistent and who understood the challenges. Parents particularly appreciated social work support combined with a package of therapeutic support.
- Parents were critical of social workers who kept telling them that they were doing a good job without providing help to address the child's challenging behaviour, or who repeatedly offered the same intervention as difficulties in family life escalated. Agencies were often not flexible enough to consider offering or sourcing support other than that which they routinely provided.

- Lack of appropriate intervention was also apparent in the delivery of Child and Adolescent Mental Health Services. Families who were able to access CAMHS were usually offered only what the local team provided and not necessarily what was needed. In two cases, the local CAMHS staff refused to work with children who had disclosed sexual abuse, as they did not have the training or skills to deal with it. In another family, a child was admitted to hospital because there were no CAMHS staff available at night.
- Specialist Tier 4 CAMHS services were generally rated highly by adoptive parents, as were adoption support agencies such as Chrysalis, Catchpoint, the Post-Adoption Centre, and Family Futures.
- There were a few accounts of excellent life story work provided by social workers that parents thought had made a real difference to the young person. However, some parents attributed their child's escalating difficulties to poor life story and direct work.
- Respite care was often used as a last ditch attempt to keep the family together and was rarely used proactively. Parents complained that access to respite was often only through making their child "looked after" once again and that the system was inflexible and did not meet the needs of the family.
- Parents reported unhelpful responses from the emergency duty teams. The usual advice from the team was for the adopter to phone the police. Adoptive parents used the police as a support agency.
- For most children, their difficulties were apparent in school. Twenty-six (37%) of the children had a statement of special educational needs. About half of the parents stated that they had received good support from educational professionals, such as teachers, teaching assistants and educational psychologists.
- Although parents reported helpful support from individual educational professionals, they also complained that, generally, schools had little understanding of the needs of adopted children. Elements of the curriculum caused distress to their child. Some had had to fight, including taking legal action, to get the right school place for their child.

- Parents described feeling blamed by professionals who themselves often expressed their powerlessness to help the family.
- Some parents desperately tried to get help for their child. About half of the parents had paid for private therapy and nearly one-third had been in touch with their MP. Many read widely on the subjects of attachment disorder, foetal alcohol spectrum disorder and developmental trauma. Although they understood the theory behind the difficulties, they struggled to find effective interventions.

11 Events leading up to disruption and the aftermath

In this chapter, we focus on the 35 children who had left their adoptive home prematurely: the reasons why they left, the support that the families received at the time of the crisis, and events since the disruption. Most young people had left home about three years before the interview with their parents. Six disruptions had occurred within the previous year.

Most of the 35 children (20 boys and 15 girls) who had left home had been late-placed for adoption (mode six years old) and four children had been aged eight years or older. They had left home on average at 14 years old (range 10–17 years, SD 2.2).

The cumulative stress on adoptive parents, often exacerbated by the young person's violent and unpredictable behaviour, led to the majority (63%) of disruptions. In 13 families (37%), a specific incident ultimately triggered the move. The incident was usually in the form of an argument that had got out of hand or involved an assault by the child on a family member, or both. The police were often involved at this time. One young person had to flee his adoptive home to avoid drug dealers who were looking for him. Another disruption occurred shortly after it became known that the young person had been sexually abusing a much younger child outside the family. In 28 of the 35 families, child to parent or child to sibling violence had either triggered or contributed significantly to the disruption.

Violence was not a contributory factor to the disruption in seven families. All these families had a female child and five of the seven disruptions had been child-led, with the young person wanting to leave home. For these families, it was a combination of factors that had brought about the move out of home. These included a wish by young people to find or return to birth family, ongoing child–parent relationship difficulties, serious mental health problems, behavioural and cognitive difficulties associated with foetal alcohol spectrum disorder, problems at school, and extreme jealousy and rivalry between siblings.

In the months leading up to the disruption, most of the young people were out of parental control. Typically, the young people were defiant and oppositional, refused to be parented and had withdrawn from family life. One mother recalled a conversation with her son, shortly before the adoption disrupted:

> He was genuinely out of control ... He said to me, 'If you didn't care so much, Mum, and you just let me get on and do what I need to do, what I want to do, then everything will be fine. So just stop caring about me.' He meant, 'Don't care for me because it messes me up inside; just let me get on and be who I am, then everything's fine. Let me run riot, set fires, play truant and it will be all right.' He genuinely believed that. (Left home)

Shortly before moving out of home, 15 (43%) of the young people were regularly running away or going missing, sometimes for days at a time. There were instances of young people sleeping on park benches, in woods and graveyards. Several were known to have been exploited by adults who they met outside the home, and parents described how they were unable to keep their child safe. Some young people escaped from home via first or second floor bedroom windows, only adding to parents' fears for their safety.

For those young people still in compulsory education, problems at school had usually escalated shortly before their move out of home. Young people were disruptive and unco-operative in class and others were truanting or refusing to go to school. Several young people had been excluded in the months leading up to the disruption, placing greater pressure on adoptive family life, as the child spent more of their day at home. For eight young people, behavioural difficulties were exacerbated by their abuse of alcohol and/or drugs and at least three others were behaving in ways consistent with an emerging serious mental illness (evidenced, for example, by dissociative and catatonic states, visual and auditory hallucinations).

For about one-quarter of the young people, the physical or

psychological presence of the birth family was thought by adoptive parents to have contributed to the young people's difficulties. Some young people were in direct contact with birth family members shortly before or soon after the adoption disrupted. One mother believed that her daughter, then aged 14, had manipulated her return to care as a way to re-establish contact with her birth family. She explained:

> *I do have a theory, which is that Bethany needed to leave here in order to get back to her family . . . I think to a certain extent, she found it difficult to think that she could do that from here, partly out of loyalty maybe, or respect, I don't know, but she just felt that she couldn't really have the freedom to get back with her family unless she left. I feel the whole project about leaving was all about getting back to her mum, which she did in the end.* (Left home)

According to parents, a few children had been ambivalent about their adoption from the start. They had loyalties and significant attachments to their birth family, whom they had not wanted to leave. One mother, for example, explained that, even before the adoption order had been made, her son (aged nine) had stated clearly that he did not want to be adopted. The adopters were persuaded by social workers to press ahead with the adoption order on the basis that: a) it might help him to settle b) it might upset him if they adopted only his younger sister; and c) without the adoption order, his birth family would be allowed contact with him. The child had a long-standing allegiance to his birth mother and never called his adoptive parents Mum or Dad. Another child, placed for adoption at 11 years of age, had maintained contact with birth family members. The birth mother arrived unannounced at the adoptive home when the child was aged 14 and the child became embroiled in birth family life. At around the same time, she started staying out at night and drinking alcohol, she was sexually active and became physically and verbally abusive to her adoptive mother. At the age of 16, she announced that she was returning to her birth family:

> *She said, 'I am leaving after I have done my exams [GCSEs] and*

going back to my maternal grandparents and back to my biological family'. (Left home)

The support for families on the verge of disruption

Many parents described how they had fought for help when the difficulties at home escalated. Typically, however, appropriate support was not forthcoming or was simply insufficient. That is not to say that the families were not known to the support agencies – in fact, several families had many professionals involved in their lives. It was often children's social workers (and sometime crisis team staff) rather than adoption team workers who were the most involved with families in the months leading up to the disruption. A few parents described helpful social work interventions at this time, including good examples of family work. Much more commonly, however, parents reported that professionals refused to acknowledge the gravity of the situation or thought that they were simply out of their depth. Some parents were sure that support had been denied due to budgetary constraints rather than a decision based on an assessment of the family's needs.

Parents described the mismatch between the support they needed and the interventions that were offered in the period leading up to the disruption. Several parents thought that there was a real reluctance by professionals to address the violence shown by the young people. Many parents were desperate for help in keeping family members safe and some wanted respite care to put space between their child and other family members. One father, for example, described living in fear of his son, who was defiant, out of parental control and extremely violent and who had threatened family members with knives. He was advised by the social worker to start a sticker chart to help reward good behaviour. Another mother, whose 15-year-old drug-misusing son ransacked the house, stole from her, was in trouble with the police, was harassed by drug dealers, and went missing for days at a time, was sent on a parenting teenagers course where she was advised to try sitting down and having a chat with her son over a meal.

At the point that families were on the verge of disruption, and often pleading with professionals for help, a number of parents unexpectedly found themselves subjected to or threatened with a child protection investigation, usually on the grounds that they did not appear to be showing their child sufficient emotional warmth, were being neglectful in their care or were not protecting siblings sufficiently. Allegations and child protection investigations are discussed in Chapter 8.

The move out of home

More than two-thirds (68%) of the young people had left home as a result of action taken by their parents. Adopters described how they had become worn down and worn out by the chaos and disruption caused to family life by parenting distressed, confused and angry young people. Parents often described feeling frightened and many knew that the situation at home had reached the point at which they were unable to keep everyone (including the child) in the family safe. The following accounts illustrate the desperate situations that families faced shortly before their children moved out:

> He'd pick up a knife and just look at it and look at you, and then put it down, choosing to put it down – hugely threatening and I didn't feel safe . . . Our post-adoption social worker had come out and said, 'Start practising safe parenting. Put the boys in separate bedrooms.' I thought he'd kill us, I really thought he'd kill us . . . he punched [husband] in the back of the head and I just said, 'I can't do this any more, I can't carry on like this'.

> We were just worn out . . . All of our resources were going into Danny and we didn't feel that his siblings were getting what they needed . . . He threatened me with a knife . . . He would come into the house with a half-brick, which he threatened his sibling with. We were scared physically for the other children that things could get out of hand, starting to worry about his size, aggression, teenage hormones kicking in. Was it physically safe for the rest of us? And also, my ability to cope with his outbursts

and tantrums had got so low. I was concerned that I was going to thump him or something.

In contrast, 10 young people (29%) left home of their own accord – they initiated the move out of home. Nine of the young people had already been voting with their feet and had been running away. Some had been reported to the police as a missing person before the move. A few young people, mainly girls, were self-harming at this time. Some young people told their parents that they just needed to get out of the family. As one mother explained:

She [daughter] said, 'I want to move away from home, I don't want to be part of this family any more, I don't want you as my parents, and I especially don't want you as my mum'. So we said, 'Well, you know we'll always listen to you and we will always try and get help but this is going to be down to social services – they might not agree to it', and she said, 'You tell social services, if they don't find me foster care, next time I run away you won't find me and the police won't find me and nor will the social workers, no-one will ever find me again, and I'll make sure of it'.

Another mother described how her daughter had orchestrated her move out of home by making an allegation against her father. Although an investigation found in favour of her father, the young person remained in care at her request. Her mother explained:

She was 13 when she left. She made an allegation [against husband]. She called the police and then she didn't come back. Prior to that, she had been saying for quite a few months that she didn't want to live with us and she needed to find a way out and she didn't know what to do. Then she found it ... but she'd had several periods before that ... of getting herself into hospital and that was almost like a respite for her.

Only one young person's move out of home was initiated by social workers. The child was constantly running away from home, often for days at a time and was vulnerable. Both the police and children's services were regularly involved in returning him to his adoptive home. When his parents contacted children's services to report him missing on yet another occasion, the social worker said that the situation could not continue and that he would be accommodated. His parents agreed.

Preparation and planning for young people's return to care

We asked adopters about the arrangements for the young people's return to care. In most instances, the moves were made hastily with little sensitive planning. Several parents described how the opportunity for a more timely and considered response by the local authority had been missed. Most parents had been asking for help for weeks or months before the disruption. In feeling that their request for help had been brushed aside by the local authority, parents sometimes took desperate measures to get the response they needed. As two mothers explained:

> I am afraid to say I packed a bag, because we had been desperately asking for help from social services. Could they give us some respite or could we please have some help? They wouldn't give us any. One of the people I spoke to said, 'We haven't got any places, we've only got emergency places and that's for children who get put out on to the street'. So we were waiting with his bag when he came off the school bus, which was awful.

> We phoned social services, they said adamantly, 'We will not take Ethan into care'... I phoned my post-adoption social worker and she said, 'You can't carry on, you're not safe, and if it means abandoning Ethan at social services offices with a suitcase, that's what you have to do – I'd get legal advice'. I got the name of an adoption lawyer who charged £300 an hour, who helped me draft an email to get him accommodated under section 20. A marvellous solicitor, amazing solicitor, without her I think I'd have jumped off a bridge or something probably. And

we went to social services with it. They phoned that afternoon and he went in the next day.

Just four parents spoke positively about the arrangements made for their child's move out of home. Three young people were given the opportunity to visit the foster carers and their home shortly before the move. One father described the consideration given to the move:

His new social worker drove him there. She had wanted to pick him up from school, but twice in the past he had gone to school in the morning and been picked up by a social worker and taken to a new placement. We didn't want to repeat that. School is hard enough for him as it is, and he was showing a huge amount of separation anxiety going to school. So that wasn't going to happen. She came here to the house and picked him up.

The best example of good practice was a local authority that funded a specialist foster placement, where the move was made *between* crises in the adoptive family. The adoptive parents, social workers and CAMHS team liaised with one another in the weeks preceding the young person's move. His parents were able to plan when, how and who would tell the young person about his move. The parents had even rehearsed with social workers how to respond to a range of possible reactions that he might display. The young person's belongings were carefully packed in suitcases and storage boxes that had been bought for him. Although a desperately difficult situation for everyone involved, the parents thought that the move out of home had been planned and managed in the most sensitive and least traumatic way possible for their son.

Where young people first went upon leaving home

Table 11.1 sets out where young people first lived after leaving the adoptive family home. Ten young people first went to live with the family of friends or other adults. Two of these young people were under the age of 16 and had moved into a friend's house at the behest of social workers. However, both placements were short-lived – one

Table 11.1
Where the young people first went to live on leaving their adoptive home

First placement/accommodation after the disruption	
Foster care	16
Family of friends/other adults	10
Local authority residential care	2
Supported lodgings	2
Therapeutic residential school	1
Hostel (homeless and vulnerable)	1
Extended adoptive family (grandparents)	1
Independent living	1
Squat	1
Total	**35**

young person soon moved in to foster care and the other moved to a local authority residential unit. Eight older young people (16/17-year-olds) moved in with either the family of friends or other adults, although some of these people were hardly known to the young person. One 16-year-old girl, for example, went to live with a much older man she had met in a pub the previous night while another moved in with the family of a new boyfriend. Several parents described how they had involved the police or children's services to help bring their child home, but were told that as the young people were not staying away against their will, no action would be taken.

Two young people initially presented to the housing department as homeless. One was accommodated in a hostel for homeless and vulnerable young people, and the other young person moved into supported accommodation. One other moved directly to a bedsit close to her birth family. One other young person moved into a squat after his mother had tried unsuccessfully to secure respite care. She explained:

I asked for a Section 20 meeting because he was coming up to 16 and [I feared] they would wash their hands of him, so I thought I've got to get in there quickly before he's 16. So we organised a meeting, we had an argument where [children's services] said, 'Of course we won't abandon you when he's 16', and I said, 'Of course you will . . . he needs help now, he's on drugs, he's going to hurt himself'. I wanted to get respite care and I wanted him to get help with his drug addiction. Anyway, it didn't happen. So he started to live in a squat. He couldn't live at home. He owed that much drug money in town that he couldn't go out of the house.

In total, 26 of the 35 young people (74%) returned to care upon, or soon after leaving their adoptive home.

The movement of children after leaving their adoptive home

At the time of the interview, four young people had only recently moved out of their adoptive home into foster care, so the stability of these placements over time could not yet be determined. However, only three of the 20 young people who had returned to care more than six months previously were still in their original placement. More than half had had three or more different placements since leaving home (excluding the planned moves that were to be expected, such as the transition for older teenagers from foster care to supported lodgings). This included three young people who had passed through at least 10 placements since the adoption had disrupted.

Some young people had been moved on from an emergency foster care placement, or had needed to leave units that were closing or which had failed an Ofsted inspection. However, most often the moves came about because foster carers or residential staff could not cope with the young person's behaviours or could not keep them safe. The young people usually moved between foster carers or local authority children's homes, although a few also passed through residential units managed by health or education. One mother recalled her daughter's experience:

> *She was taken into a foster placement . . . and she never came back. She moved round and round. It wasn't like she had moved to a foster placement and then all of a sudden her life was calm; it carried on escalating. The first foster placement was 12 weeks and she basically ran away, on a two-day bender, and the police were out looking for her. She was just a week before her 14th birthday actually. Then she moved to another temporary foster placement for about six weeks. That broke down because of her behaviour and then she was moved to a residential placement for about a year. That was mayhem, there were no boundaries or rules there, she ran riot, but that closed down and then she moved to another residential one for about eight weeks – more secure. She wouldn't comply or co-operate with anything and they threatened to move her on if she didn't co-operate, and she said she wouldn't co-operate so they did move her on. So then she moved to her final one, which she was at for about 18 months, another residential unit. This was the most secure but without it being a secure unit, so alarmed doors, one to one, and it only housed two other children. She's just left there. She's a care leaver now [aged 17] so she's now living in a flat on her own. It's an independent flat but she is labelled as a care leaver . . . she's got a keyworker three times a week; for five hours a week she's supported, the rest of the time she's independent. Quite a journey.*

Parents were not always satisfied with the placement arranged by the local authority. Several adopters expressed reservations, fearing for the safety of the young person or for those around them. Some parents said that their fears had been realised. Three mothers reported that their daughters had been raped or sexually assaulted whilst under local authority care. Parents described how their concerns about the appropriateness of placements were dismissed. As two mothers recalled:

I wanted her to move into a residential therapeutic placement, but they [children's services] didn't feel that she needed it. They felt that a foster carer would suffice. I didn't agree, but they found a foster carer ... It lasted, I think, two weeks before she had a complete meltdown. She had one of her rages. The foster carer completely gave up just like that, and took her to social services offices with her clothes in black bags, and everything I had wanted to avoid had happened. I was fuming that we'd hung on for seven bloody years and now within two weeks, exactly what I didn't want to happen [was happening] – she was going through the care system.

Rebecca then went to live with the foster carers. We warned them ... but we were told it [the foster placement] was going to happen and that we needed to be less negative about it. So we said, 'We'll always be positive in front of Rebecca, but I'm telling you now that it's not going to work' ... The placement ended last year when she menaced the family with a lighter and nearly killed them all. The police then arrested her for assault and for attempted arson, and for criminal damage, because she completely wrecked the house. But the worst part of that was that she spent the weekend in the [police] cells ... because social services would not fund a secure placement for her and they said that the cells were a secure place for her to stay. On the Monday, the phone call came through that they were placing her in a children's home and I lost it, I just howled down the phone. I was so angry that they had done this.

Four young people were known to have been held in police cells after their placement broke down and before appropriate alternative accommodation could be found. One mother explained how her daughter had been held overnight in the police cells because children's services did not have the staff to deal with the situation. Another mother described how her son, then aged 12, spent two days in police cells:

He attacked a pregnant care worker, he barricaded himself in a room, and caused chaos, things got absolutely horrendous. The police were involved all the time, and they decided that they couldn't think of anywhere for him to go. So he was placed in a cell for two days and then he was transferred to [next placement].

The living arrangements for the 11 young people who did not become looked after were also unstable. At the time of the interview, none of the young people were living in the accommodation that they had first found on moving out of home – arguments, violence, drinking or other crises had caused the young person to move on. A few young people sought help from the housing department or adult services to find accommodation and were usually then provided with a place in hostels or supported housing. Three young people returned to their adoptive homes for a brief period before moving out again. Four young people had tried living with or near birth family members, but the arrangements had not worked out. Two young people had spent time in prison or a young offender's institution. In recalling the movement of her son since leaving home, one mother described a fairly typical scenario:

He went to live with a friend of his [aged 16]. They were happy for him to live there for four months and then they kicked him out because he was violent and he put his fist through the ceiling and he was drinking. Then he went to live in a hostel geared up for 16- to 21-year-olds and he got into a fracas there and he put a policewoman in a neck brace. Then we had a phone call from social services saying, 'Could we [adopters] have him back?' and I said, 'You're joking?' . . . so he was rehomed [supported lodgings] . . . He'll be 18 next month. He's got a social worker now and he said he gets on well with him.

Table 11.2 shows where the young people were living at the time parents were interviewed. Nine young people were living independently, although some were reliant on financial support from parents. Two adopters were acting as guarantors for their child's tenancy agreement; others were paying bills or buying food for their children to help sustain independent living. Eleven young people were in foster or residential care and a further seven were in supported accommodation. Two others, both of whom had had many placements since moving out of home, were in secure units. Two young people were homeless at the time of the interview, one of whom was thought to be living in the local woods. The whereabouts of two other young men were unknown.

Table 11.2
Living arrangements of the young people at the time of the interview

Where the young people were living at the time of the interview	
Independent living	9
Foster care	8
Supported lodgings	7
Local authority residential care	3
Homeless	2
Unknown	2
LA secure unit	1
NHS secure mental health unit[47]	1
Friends	1
Bed and breakfast accommodation	1
Total	**35**

The impact of the disruption on family members

We asked parents how they thought their child had felt on leaving home. Just over half (54%) thought that the young person had been either pleased or relieved to be leaving the family, whilst one-quarter were thought to have been upset or troubled by it. The remaining

---

47 Young person sectioned under the Mental Health Act.

young people were thought to have had mixed feelings or parents did not know how they had felt about leaving home.

We also asked parents how they had felt at the time that their child left home. About half of the parents said that their main emotion was one of relief and the other half said that they were devastated, sad, and bereft. One mother recalled:

> *It broke our hearts and I have never been the same, none of us have, since the loss of Erin. The day she moved out something died for all of us.*

According to parents, just over half of the young person's siblings were pleased or relieved that their brother or sister had moved out of home. Parents reported that many had become exhausted and frightened by the chaos and violence within the family. Parents often reported that siblings had felt angry with the young person and some had chosen to sever all contact. Siblings sometimes blamed the young people for "ruining" their lives. One mother recalled a recent conversation with her daughter, the study child's sibling:

> *I tried to talk to her the other day. [I said] 'You must have some good memories, Charlotte, because you used to love your brother so much'. She said, 'I can't remember them'. She can't bear him now and doesn't want to ever see him again. She says he's upset her, frightened her, scared her, and hurt her.*

About one-third of siblings were described by parents as having been upset or troubled by the young person's move out of home and parents recognised that it had raised a range of painful issues for them. Two parents explained how siblings became very unsettled after the disruption, unsure as to whether or not they would also be moving out. The disruption reawakened feelings of loss. As two mothers explained:

> *He says he never wants anything to do with her again. He has lost everybody now in his birth family. He probably doesn't want any contact with her to protect himself from more hurt.*

When we finally cut through all the emotion, [birth son] said to me, 'You have to remember, Mum, you gave me a sister and then you took her away and that's the sadness'.

In three of the 35 families, a second adopted young person had also moved out of home prematurely. Parents described how the original disruption had triggered an escalation of difficulties with another child. Two parents reported that the "perks" that the young person attracted after returning to care had strongly influenced their second child's desire to leave the adoptive home. The ease with which young people left their families on the promise of a few pounds highlights the fragility of relationships and lack of belonging in their adoptive families. As one parent explained:

Alfie went to a residential unit, like an assessment unit, and really enjoyed himself there. He texted [sibling] about how much money he got, and he got £50 as soon as he arrived because it was his birthday. He said, 'Well, you can please yourself here'. So [sibling] wanted to go and he said to me not long after Alfie had gone in, 'I want to go back into care'.

Several parents wanted to draw attention to the lack of interest or concern that they thought professionals had shown to their other (usually adopted) children both immediately before and after the disruption. As one parent explained:

Matthew [sibling] was really struggling with Erin's escalating behaviour and had been for quite a while . . . He couldn't cope, he just couldn't cope with her, the "push me pull me" effect . . . she adores you and is so intense that you can't breathe, and then she hates you and all this venom comes at you. I always struggled to get anybody to understand that Matthew was a child too. No-one ever considered Matthew except me and my husband, ever, in the midst of this; it was always focused on Erin.

Adopters' views on the finality of the disruption

At the time of the disruption, most (66%) parents thought that their child's move out of home would be a permanent arrangement, whilst one-quarter (26%) were not sure, or felt that a decision about the situation had been outside of their control. Only three of the 35 parents had thought that the separation would be temporary.

Missed opportunities for reunification

A few parents said that once the young person had been taken into care, there had been no effort by professionals to work with the child or family on the issues that had triggered the disruption. Little consideration had been given to the possibility of reunification. One mother, who sought legal advice to get what she thought would be respite care, explained:

> They said, 'We will give you three weeks respite'... she went for respite, and there she stayed. No-one has ever said, 'Let's try and get this family back together, let's deal with it'. No-one has ever asked me what I want. I genuinely thought they would give us some help... I dropped her off [at the foster placement]... I managed to get back into the car before I just burst into tears. But my actual feeling was, it's only for three weeks and they have to assess her now there are knives [involved], they've got to see what's going on for this girl. She needs help.

Two mothers thought that their daughters had not known how to re-establish relationships with family members after having made unfounded allegations against them. The mothers thought that social workers too readily assumed that a "disruption" was the end of an adoption. Another mother, in describing her experience of social work intervention, reflected on what she thought would have been a more helpful response from the social worker:

> Social workers add to the adversarial nature of the child–parent relationship. That is what I felt should have happened. Once Hazel went into care, the social workers needed to champion

us as parents, because there isn't anything wrong with the parenting in our family. They needed to be saying to our child, 'These people are the right people for you, they're the best people there are, don't mess it up, try and make it work, let me help you make it work, let's find a way'.

Parental involvement in care planning

About two-fifths of parents said that they had been minimally involved in decisions about their child's care since the disruption, whilst a similar proportion reported some involvement. Only five adopters considered that they had been wholly involved in decisions about their child since they moved out of home.

Occasionally parents had been happy to hand over responsibility to children's services and did not want to contribute to future decision-making. Much more commonly, however, parents had wanted more involvement, but had felt excluded by social workers. Some parents described how they struggled to find out if their young person had settled in placement; others had not been invited to meetings, or invited but with so little notice that it was impossible to attend. There were also instances of parents being barred from meetings at the behest of the young person. Several parents pointed out that, even though their child was in care, they still retained parental responsibility.

Parents often described feeling very much maligned by professionals. They felt that they were being judged, blamed and punished for their perceived "failings" by social workers, residential staff, and even foster carers. Some parents thought that others did not quite know how to relate to a parent who wanted to remain actively involved in the decisions made with and for their child. Professionals were also thought to have "taken sides". There was a failure to recognise that the best chance for the young person's future was to work towards improving family relationships. Instead, social work efforts went into preparation for independent living. One father summed up his experience with the social worker involved in his son's return to care:

[Looked after team social worker] was always implying that it was our fault, and all we wanted was some help, but she just wouldn't listen to our opinions, didn't even want to hear what we had to say. She had no interest in us whatsoever – she was acting only on behalf of Connor. It was all our fault and there was no help for us as a family, the only help that was available now was for Connor.

Current parent and child relationships

We asked parents about the current state of relationships. Several parents observed that they had a different type of relationship now with their child and that a comparison with the relationship pre-disruption was impossible. These adopters usually said that they were no longer actively parenting and this had changed the dynamics of their relationship. Thirteen parents (37%) said that their relationship continued to be strained or had deteriorated further. This included most of the families where the disruption had occurred recently. In six families, parents and the young person were currently estranged.

Encouragingly, 16 parents (46%) reported that relationships had improved since the young person had left home. The passage of time was a key factor, with those parents where disruptions had occurred some years ago tending to report better relationships.

After leaving their adoptive family, four young people had tried to live with or near their birth family but had felt let down or rejected by them. This had led to a re-evaluation of their lives. Some had moved back to the area where their adoptive family lived and others were back in their adoptive family in a psychological sense, as they sought out their adoptive parents for support, comfort and advice. In three instances, the birth or imminent birth of the young person's baby had helped adoptive parents to forge a closer and more mutually satisfying relationship with their child.

Disruption had been a traumatic event for parents, young people and siblings. It was not the end of the adoption journey but the beginning of a new phase. Nearly half the parents had established relationships that were more positive and were able to parent the young person at a distance. In the next chapter, we report on parents' reflections on their adoption journey and think ahead to what adoptive life might be like in five years' time.

Summary

- The average age of the young person on leaving their adoptive home was 14 years old. Most young people had been late placed into their adoptive families.
- In 80 per cent of the families, child to parent or child to sibling violence had been a key factor in the young person's move out of home. In the months leading up to the disruption, young people were out of parental control, defiant, oppositional, refused to be parented and had withdrawn from family life. Fifteen children (43%) had been regularly running away.
- The physical or psychological presence of birth family was thought by adoptive parents to have contributed to the difficulties shown by several children around the time that they moved out of home.
- For children still in compulsory education, difficulties at school had usually escalated in the months preceding the disruption – children were disruptive and unco-operative in class. Some truanted or refused to go to school, others had been excluded.
- In seven families (all with girls) where violence did not feature, a combination of other matters brought about the move out of home. These included ongoing attachment difficulties, serious mental health problems, difficulties associated with foetal alcohol spectrum disorder and a desire to reconnect with birth family.
- Many families were in contact with children's services in the months preceding the disruption. Parents typically described a lack of appropriate support at this time. Disruptions are rare events and parents reported that social workers were unprepared and lacked skills.
- Just over two-thirds of the moves out of home were instigated by adoptive parents. Parents described feeling worn down and worn out by the chaos and disruption to family life. Many were frightened by the violence that they endured and felt unable to keep everyone

in the family (including the child) safe. Ten young people led their move out of home. Some could not cope any longer with family life, others left in search of their birth family. Just one disruption was initiated by a social worker.

- Twenty-six young people returned to care after the disruption. Most went immediately to a foster placement; others moved into residential care or supported lodgings. A few went to live with friends or relatives for a short period before becoming looked after. Those young people who did not return to care usually first went to live with friends or other adults.

- Most young people's return to care was hastily arranged. Several parents thought that there had been missed opportunities for a more timely and considered response by children's services.

- On returning to care, the young people's placements were not stable. More than half of those young people who had been looked after for more than six months had had at least three different placements. Placements usually broke down because foster carers or residential staff could not cope with the young people's behaviour. Young people who did not become looked after also tended to move accommodation often.

- A few parents had expressed reservations about the suitability of placements, but their concerns were dismissed. Four young people had been held in police cells before appropriate accommodation was found.

- At the time of the research interview, 13 young people were living in foster care or a residential unit (two of whom were in secure accommodation), nine were living independently, and seven were in supported lodgings. Two young people were homeless, one was living with friends, and another was in bed and breakfast accommodation. The whereabouts of two young men were unknown.

- In the main, young people were thought to have been pleased or relieved by their move out of home. One-quarter were considered upset or troubled by it. About half of parents were upset or devastated by the disruption; two in five reported feeling overwhelmingly relieved. Most siblings seemed pleased or relieved that the child had moved out of home. Some felt angry with their brother or sister. One in three siblings were upset or troubled by the move and for some it raised painful issues.

- Two-thirds of parents believed that the move out of home would be a permanent arrangement, whilst just over one-quarter did not know what to expect. Only three parents thought that the separation would be temporary. Several parents described missed opportunities for reunification and little interest by professionals in addressing the issues that triggered the disruption.

- Most parents had wanted to be more involved in decision-making. Parents described feeling excluded by social workers, judged, and blamed for their perceived failings as parents. Parents reported that information on their child was withheld.

- At the time of the interview, 13 parents (37%) said that their relationship with the young person continued to be strained or had deteriorated further. Encouragingly, more parents (n = 16, 46%) reported that the relationship had improved. Relationships tended to improve with the passage of time.

- Nearly half of the parents had established more positive relationships and were able to parent the young person at a distance.

12 Looking back and looking forwards

In this chapter, we report on parents' reflections of the adoption process – whether they or agencies could have behaved differently to facilitate better outcomes and what, from a parent's perspective, were the positive and negative aspects of their adoption experiences. Adopters were also encouraged to look forward and to consider what family life might be like in five years' time. At the time of the interview most of the children who were the focus of the interview were adolescents or young adults (average age 16 years, range 12–22 years SD 2.5).

Adoptive parents' reflections on their adoption journey

Parents were asked, 'Looking back, is there anything that you would have done differently?' Only two adoptive parents thought that they would not have done anything differently. Most adopters talked about wishing they had sought support sooner, fought harder for services, or gone with their instincts about what was right for their child.

Seven adopters said that they should not have adopted their child and wished that they had refused the match. One of the parents responded to the question about whether they would have done anything differently as follows:

> *Not adopted her. I should have insisted on an older child . . . I should have relied more on my instincts than being swayed by other people. I would have insisted on liking the child and knowing the child before adopting . . . they do not make it easy for you to meet any child. They find a child, they match the child, they say, 'This is the child for you'.* (At home)

Five parents questioned the wisdom of placing siblings together and thought that more searching questions should have been asked about placing siblings together or apart. Three parents of sibling groups wished that they had sent the children to different schools and one of the parents said:

> *I think it would have been useful to have split them up into different schools. I don't know what else I could have done to have shouted louder, to get these blessed statements. I think I should have gone to my MP. I don't know what else.* (Left home)

Some parents, although recognising the difficulties, were still pleased that they had adopted siblings. As one parent said:

> *Do I wish anything else had been different? I don't really wish we'd only adopted one child; although it's been difficult I am glad we've got a pair.* (At home)

Parents also wondered if they were at fault in some way, for example, some admitted that they had asked themselves whether they were to blame because of some personal deficiency, such as a lack of patience or self-awareness, or because they lacked the right kinds of skills. Parents said:

> *I would like to have been more relaxed and less stressed with him . . . Ideally, I would have liked to have been a full-time mum really, stay at home. And I think I'd like to have been a bit more patient with him and perhaps tried to maybe do more things together. I think I should have developed more the family support around him . . . I don't know what else one can do really. You do the best you can, and you're only human, and sometimes you do lose it.* (At home)

> *I don't think we had the skills to do anything differently really.* (Left home)

Over the years, parents had educated themselves on the needs of traumatised children. A sentiment frequently expressed was the wish to have known then what they know now. For example, parents said:

> *Well, I wish I'd known then what I know now ... known more about therapeutic parenting. I've often thought about this.* (At home)

> *I wouldn't have tried to mother her; I would have been her carer, which isn't adoption in my concept of adoption. I would have just been like a foster carer and tried to be a helpful friend.* (Left home)

Conversely, other adopters were beginning to see that their efforts had had some positive effects:

> *I guess we would have tweaked things here and there but I don't know if there's anything fundamental that we could have done differently to be honest, even with the knowledge we've got now. I think what we did was done with the best intentions and it seems to have stood them in good stead at the moment.* (Left home)

Parents also talked about how they wished that they had challenged the views of professionals and not been so trusting.

> *We were too polite, too compliant, we just assumed things ... we would make assumptions and I think that's where we've gone wrong.* (At home)

> *We've always been on the back hoof ... we've been one beat behind, and I think if we'd have known what we now under-stand ... we would have been on people's cases much sooner, and we wouldn't be where we are now. He's 14½, we're running out of time to crack this problem really ... We would have trod on people's toes a lot sooner ... we are a pain now, and the last meeting I went to with the disability team – I'm not a rude person, but boy was I rude. I was incredibly rude. My daughter said to me, 'Mum, that was embarrassing'. I've never been rude*

to people I meet, and now I feel as the Americans say, "kick ass", because now is the time. Do you know what, I've nothing to lose. That's how I feel. (At home)

Trusting that the professionals knew what was right had led a few parents to go against their instincts, for example, several parents said that they wished they had not sent the child to school so soon after placement, but kept the child at home so that relationships could be established. On the other hand, some parents wished that they had listened to social workers and not sought more face-to-face contact with the birth mother than originally agreed, or had made more efforts to ensure that the whole family was committed to adoption before proceeding. Many parents wished that they had sought support sooner, although some commented that it was difficult to know what support was available:

I would have got different help for him if I'd have known it existed. I didn't know it existed, so I couldn't do it. (Left home)

Adoptive parents' reflections on adoption support services

Parents were also asked if there was anything that the support services could have done differently to support the family. Three of the parents whose children were at home and one parent whose child had left stated that they could think of nothing else that agencies might have done because of the state of knowledge at the time they adopted, or because they were happy with the support provided by their LA/VAA. For example, one of the parents said:

I think they were really good, really supportive, very helpful, and having that written agreement I had was very helpful. (At home)

The majority of parents were very critical of the service that they had received. Parents stated that, at the time of the placement, professionals had known and recorded that their children were likely to be challenging but agencies had not matched that assessment with appropriate support services. Many parents talked about being on their own with nothing in place at the time of the order. Parents complained about the lack of information at the start of the placement, a lack of honesty from professionals, and being unprepared for parenting children with relationship difficulties. Four of the children had a diagnosis of reactive attachment disorder (RAD), but parents complained that there was a great reluctance to consider RAD as a possibility. Parents believed that an assessment of attachment difficulties would have led to more appropriate services being implemented.

Adoptive parents wanted a service that respected their views, that acknowledged that adopted children were likely to need support at some point in their lives, and a service that was delivered by specialists who understood the complex and overlapping difficulties of adopted children. Many parents spoke about feeling as though professionals did not believe their accounts or treated them as though they were abusive parents. For example:

> I think an absolute understanding from day one that developmental trauma in the early years is a lifelong disability, which then impacts on healthcare, CAMHS provision, education. I should never have had to sit in meeting after meeting at school telling them again and again and again why he's doing what he's doing when you're putting trauma trigger behaviours in front of him, I shouldn't have to do that time and time again. (At home)

> I think that they could have given us the help we needed, which would have been specialist help. I am not talking about the sort of help, which they're going to give us now, the odd social worker with generic experience who doesn't understand adoption issues. I'm talking about really there should be specialists like the Post-Adoption Centre, they're lovely ... as soon as we had those two assessments, I felt relieved because she understood, she knew what was going on, and I've never felt that with the

local authority. Even their post-adoption team have no idea. So I think it does need specialist help who understand about adoption. (At home)

Parental accounts of battles to get appropriate services were common. Parents wanted services that were delivered quickly, of the right intensity and matched to children's needs – not those that were simply available. Parents complained:

It's been a battle to get help really. We're able to afford that and some people can't. We're articulate, middle-class, middle-aged people who know how to get help and we found it difficult, so goodness knows what it's like if you're not in our situation. (At home)

Some parents responded to a question about how adoption agencies could have better delivered services by suggesting specific improvements:

I think that really what they could do is they could contact all adoptive parents after three years, after five years, or as their children hit their teens, just to say, 'Hey, is everything all right?' And I do realise that a lot of adoptive parents don't want anything to do with social services, and I can understand that as well, but I think that would help. (At home)

There should be some sort of practical handbook written in collaboration with adoptive parents and that is a bit like the rough guide to adoption . . . if this starts happening you can call in this – signposting. It's all very ad hoc, some sort of overall guide would be a really good thing, more than a handout but not a great big thick book, a sort of reference, an A to Z of what do you do if this happens, like most frequently asked questions type thing. That would be useful. And updated – so you've got people's phone numbers and email addresses and that type of thing. (At home)

Other parents suggested more training for adoptive parents focused on developmental stages, especially puberty. Several parents wanted practical help at the start and respite care delivered later in ways that did not change the status of children to a looked after child and might be for the day or for a weekend. One parent suggested that therapy should be part of looked after children's lives so that it was normalised. Another parent, whose child had left home, thought that all parents who experienced a disruption should be given a questionnaire and an appointment made automatically to help with the aftermath of a disruption. She said:

> *There should be a questionnaire, because it's safe to do a questionnaire. You could do it in your own time, there's no pressure, and that asks, 'How do you think you're coping? What can we do? Do you think this might be helpful? We've made a routine appointment for you and you can leave it or cancel it.' That would be bloody brilliant.* (Left home)

Again, parents emphasised that support needed to be delivered by those with the appropriate skills and knowledge. One parent said:

> *They didn't have the knowledge ... I could have been better prepared. I needed more information about Simon and his daily parenting. I needed to build a relationship with the foster carer instead of this prejudice that somehow we would be mortal enemies. I needed financial support so ... that I could work part-time and be there for him at the start and at the end of the day – just for the first couple of years until he built up the security within him that he doesn't have to keep checking that I'm there. He used to go to school, I'd drop him off, come back, he'd be on the doorstep [saying to me], 'I was worried that something might happen to you, or the house might burn down'. To have support groups, which they did do but it was very limited and very early days. To offer training. I did go to the training that they did, but it was a bit rare and sporadic. The best thing that I ever did was going to an AUK conference and hearing this chap*

called Greg Keck, this American therapist, talk about his adopted children. (At home)

A father, reflecting on how he felt that the dominance of females in social work and CAMHS led to men's needs being ignored, said:

Most of the focus is on the mum because she is in the thick of it but . . . everyone we saw was female. [They were] working with my wife and understood her situation and probably didn't understand how difficult it was for me. If you read books about parenting traumatised children, it's almost exclusively about the mum's relationship.

There's nothing about the dad's relationship . . . I missed out on support because no-one understood. (Left home)

The best and worst aspects of the adoptive experience

Parents were asked, 'Looking back over your whole adoption experience, what has been the best thing to come out of it all?' Four parents could not identify anything positive that had come out of their experience, and these were all parents whose child was still living at home. In these families, parents were just waiting for the young person to be old enough to leave home without fear of prosecution. One parent who had been subjected to years of violent attacks said:

The best thing? The fact that they're coming to be adults and I can release myself from the responsibility and that's awful, but I can finally say, 'No, enough is enough' . . . Nobody should have to be treated like this for 13 years. (At home)

The best
Parents whose children had recently left home were saddened by their current poor relationship. They looked back with fondness at their early years as an adoptive family and said:

I had such lovely years with him. That was somebody who was a

227

wonderful little boy to bring up. And I can remember when the kids were little, saying, 'I'm so glad I couldn't have my own children because I wouldn't have had them'. It was just total adoration – that was up to two–three years ago. The last three years have been so horrendous . . . I can't go through that again. (Left home)

Despite all the difficulties, most parents talked about their love for their children, the importance of family (even if they described it as dysfunctional) and the strength of most of their marital relationships. Parents talked about 'my child' and their love for their children:

I'm amazed by how much love I feel for a kid who is incredibly rude, and at times makes my life a misery, but he's lovely as well. I love the relationship we have built up together and his sense of humour. There's so much about him that I adore and I find it fascinating, that whole journey. (At home)

When we have our days out . . . when we're just like a normal mother and child. I still love him no matter what he's done. (Left home)

Some parents talked about their pride in seeing their child develop and pride in their own achievements. For example, one parent said:

Us three together – we've turned Mike's life around. (At home)

Parents were pleased that they had been able to make a difference and that young people's lives were going to be better than if they had remained looked after children. Parents talked about young people having had a good education, a family life, learning new skills, and having a set of values that would stand them in good stead in the future. For example, parents said:

They do know how to experience happiness . . . I feel now that my children will get through life one way or another. (Left home)

To all intents and purposes, we did give him a sound childhood. He's chosen not to embrace it, but clearly, he's taken away certain values with him. So I think ultimately he will be OK. (Left home)

Other parents talked about the privilege of having parented adopted children and of having the opportunity to do things that they would never have done if they had remained childless. For example, one parent said:

We've ended up with two boys who are full of energy and we're probably doing things that we wouldn't be doing otherwise . . . outdoor things like sailing and kayaking, camping a lot . . . I really enjoy being outdoors. That's been good. (At home)

A few parents responded to the question by reflecting on how both they and the children had changed as a result of the adoption:

He's changed us, we were very quiet . . . I wouldn't have said boo to a goose. I certainly wouldn't have argued with a professional. (At home)

I think it has been about knowing Terry . . . and one of the things is that he's made me completely who I am. I wouldn't be who I am if I didn't know him. It's been a growing together . . . He's made me a much braver person, a much stronger person. (At home)

Parents thought that reducing expectations, taking pleasure from small things, accepting children for who they were, and accepting that the effects of early trauma could not be removed were important learning points in their own adoption journeys. For example, a parent reflecting on her own journey said:

Actually recognising that you've done the best you can, even when it's gone tits up because you can't control your kids. You can't make life better, you can't repair the past, you can only do the best that you can. (Left home)

The worst

Parents were asked what the worst part of their adoption experience had been. Many parents described the previous few years as "hell on earth", painful, and being hard work, leaving them feeling exhausted, inadequate and helpless. Often parents said that the worst thing was the physical and verbal aggression they had suffered:

It has stretched me to breaking point and it still continues to do so . . . it is all-consuming . . . my thoughts are always about him. (At home)

I'm not safe in my own house. I can't breathe. I can't relax. (At home)

Parents talked of wasted years and of lives being ruined and blighted – not only their own lives but also those of their partners and other children in the household who had been adversely affected by the ongoing violence and aggression. One mother said:

Six years of my life. It's a waste. She's just gone. She's not interested. She won't give me a second glance. (Left home)

Other parents thought that perhaps the worst was yet to come and they feared that the young person would die because of the way that their life was spinning out of control or that the young person would return and kill them, as they still felt very vulnerable in their own home. One mother said:

Even now I still care about him and I do worry, I think about him every day, I have nightmares about him every night, I can hear him coming in and getting us. I cannot be in this house on my own without having all the windows locked, the gates locked. (Left home)

Parents talked about how the child's behaviour had made them socially isolated and shamed. Those who had been subject to allegations of maltreatment or threatened with child protection investigations thought that that had been the worst possible experience. Two parents thought that the child's return to the birth family was hurtful and others talked about how they were frightened for their child when the running away had begun, as they did not know where they were. Parents' responses to the question, 'What has been the worst part of your adoption experience?', replied:

Ten years ago if you had said to me that these are the things you will go through: police, sexting, psychiatric assessments, suicide . . . I would have thought, what? They were things I had no experience of. (At home)

When he went back to his birth mum. That was an absolute kick in the teeth and he got hold of his adoption certificate and he ripped it in half in front of me. That was horrible. (Left home)

Having your heart broken. (Left home)

Other parents said that the worst thing was that their child was unable to live with them at the present and they had to live with the loss and guilt.

The worst part was having to say, 'This is it . . . enough is enough'. In the back of your mind, you're thinking, 'Could we have done more? Could we have kept going longer?' (Left home)

Some parents said that the worst aspect was knowing that their child would always struggle through life and that they had not been able to help them or get the appropriate support:

The worst part of it all is seeing them struggle with things that an ordinary child from a normal family would do, and knowing that this family is not normal and it never will be and it never could be. But I didn't know that would be a possibility when I adopted them. (Left home)

Being a parent

Parents were asked if they thought that their son or daughter still thought of them as "mum and dad" and whether they also thought of themselves in this way. The words "mum" and "dad" were very emotive and parents paused to reflect on what being a "mum" or "dad" actually meant and the distinction between biological and adoptive parenting.

Some parents were unequivocal in replying that they were still absolutely mum and dad: 'Oh, God, YES!' This group of parents talked about their commitment to the child:

> Yes, that will always be there . . . what I committed to at the beginning . . . and was why I wanted to adopt. So OK, it's not gone happy families but he's still alive. At one point, I thought he'd be in prison or dead by now. (Left home)

> He's our son for better or worse. (Left home)

Other parents were less certain of their role, partly because their child called them by their first name and/or because their son or daughter's conception of what a "mother" or "father" should be like was different from the norm. Some parents also wondered if it meant that they were not loved if young people did not use the words "mum" and "dad" and others were aware that the withdrawal of the words was used as a tool by the child to hurt or punish them. Parents answered the question, 'Do you think (child) thinks of you as mum and dad?' in the following ways:

> She calls us "You guys": 'When are you guys coming down?' And she wants us to come down and paint the flat she is living in. (Left home)

> Yes I do . . . I think his perceptions of those words are different from most people's . . . I don't think "mum" has quite the same feeling that it might do to you or I. He's had a lot of different mums along the way and I'm one of them and I'm the one who's still there. I'm the one who's got a chequebook and a

purse and remembers birthdays and Christmases . . . I'm not the mum he would like to have . . . so his concept is different. (Left home)

Parents also reported that a few young people were also struggling with how to hold two families in mind. One adoptive mother said that the young person referred to both her and their birth mother as "mum". Some young people were said by their parents to deny the existence of a birth family, while others longed for their birth mother, and yet others had chosen to refer to only their adoptive mother as "mum". Parents described the following scenarios:

[Sibling living with birth mother] said something like, 'Mum would like to meet you one day'. and [young person] replied, 'I'm seeing my [adoptive] mum tomorrow'. (Left home)

He doesn't know what to call me and he's very confused at the moment. (Left home)

I was talking to her about [family] this morning . . . we had had a row . . . and she was starting to look a bit tearful, which is a bit unusual for her, and I was saying, 'We are your only family, there's no other family out there waiting for you. So don't treat us as though you can throw us away, because we're your family and we are here for you every day.' (At home)

Five mothers replied that they no longer thought of themselves as "mum" and that social services were now the parent. Most of these were parents whose child had left home, and who responded to the question, 'Do you still think of yourself as mum?' in the following ways:

No, not really . . . that's a weird question because yes you are, but I don't have any control . . . I don't have any dealings with him. Maybe in the future. But I think I fell out of love with him . . . he put us through so much and there's only so much you can take. (Left home)

Haven't got a clue. I know I was his mum. I'd love to be his mum and I'd love him to want me to be his mum, but at the minute, I'm not his mum. (Left home)

Impact of living with a child with challenging behaviour

Adoptive parents were asked about how the challenging behaviour of their child had affected them. Parents talked about the adverse impact in seven main areas of their lives, with the impact often involving repeated experiences of loss (Table 12.1).

Table 12.1
Parent reported negative impact on self of child's challenging behaviours

Negative impact	At home		Left home	
	(n)	%	(n)	%
Mental health	22	63	28	80
Partner relationship	18	51	15	43
Social life	16	46	22	63
Employment	15	43	20	57
Daily living	10	29	22	63
Physical health	9	26	13	27
Financial situation	4	11	8	23

Impact on mental health

The majority of adoptive parents thought that their adoption experiences had adversely affected their own mental health. Parents talked about having had low mood, difficulty sleeping, panic attacks, needing medication, and counselling. Poor mental health was attributed to coping with challenging behaviour; not being able to relax and being constantly alert for the next flashpoint; dealing with the impact of allegations; battling to get support; feeling a failure; and difficulties in marital and other relationships.

Examining parents' responses, it was clear that some parents had had brief episodes of low mood and depression but had quite quickly bounced back. Parents talked about the importance of having a supportive network of family and friends, the benefits of physical exercise, and having coping skills that had been taught as part of their professional role (e.g. training as a therapist or an A&E nurse). Over time, some parents had found a kind of equilibrium by learning to accept the child for who they were and not seeing the lack of improvement as a personal failure. For example:

I would say we've learnt to switch off, and we've learnt to take pleasure in smaller things, and I think that's really helped. And I think we have stopped blaming ourselves. (At home)

I became very hard to live with because I was very obsessed with her, and I just used to keep thinking . . . I'm missing something. If only I could just work out what it is I need to do. Actually, what I needed to do was to stop doing things, and just let it be. When she became 16 that was a bit of a turning point. I thought, I can't have any say in anything any more, so why not try to just wait and see what happens. (At home)

Other adoptive parents, after years of managing very challenging behaviour, were from their own descriptions showing signs of secondary trauma:[48]

They've brought me to breaking point. If someone asked me to describe myself, I would say . . . a very placid, level-headed, sensible person. But I have actually wished myself dead. (At home)

When she's home you have to tread very carefully, you can't be

---

48 Until recently, it was thought that trauma was only experienced by those directly exposed to the trauma. Now, it is recognised that adoptive parents and foster carers and those clinicians and professionals who work closely with traumatised children are also at risk of developing the same symptoms. See www.childtraumaacademy.com.

normal in case you upset her, and then she'll blow up and it's worse then. But you don't know what's going to set her off, so it's like walking on eggshells. (At home)

Mostly parents talked about the impact on their own health, but some also chose to talk about the impact on their other children, and this was often especially hard to bear. Parents described how siblings had been physically attacked and/or sexually abused by their brother or sister, and, because of their sibling's difficulties, found their own mental health, school life and friendship groups adversely affected.

Loss and grief

Parents thought that their adoption experiences had involved many losses: loss of employment or promotions, friendships, social life, self-esteem, and financial loss. Parents also spoke about the loss of their dreams and hopes of adoptive family life, an imagined family life that was in stark contrast to the reality. For example:

I have been incredibly upset. I feel really disappointed because I haven't got the family I wanted. I've been making mistakes at work, I've lost weight ... I have a lovely relationship with my own mum and I just wanted half of that with my daughter. I might get it, you never know, it may come, but it's not here at the moment. (Left home)

Whenever I think of Alice I always have this heartbreak about it really, the fact that I've not managed to make her happy, give her happiness. (Left home)

Most employers were reported to be very understanding of the situation and had given parents time off to deal with crises. Schools would often ring and expect a parent to go to the school immediately to be with the child, or their child's needs were such that working became very difficult. Parents thought that they had missed out on promotions, as they now had different priorities. One mother said:

I would have continued up the career ladder but because of the fact that even now he doesn't sleep every night of the week . . . I'm 50-odd and I need sleep. So when I'm woken up two or three times a night, I can't do a job, let alone have a career. (At home)

Other parents treated work as a refuge, away from the chaos at home and a place where relationships were good and predictable. One parent said:

When I go into work it is a real oasis for me, because I go into work, I can be cheerful, polite, people listen to me, they do what I ask, and then I come home . . . So I'm walking home and . . . I'm feeling sick. What else can I do other than go home? I don't want to walk into that house. (At home)

The child's challenging behaviour often resulted in families becoming more insular, finding it difficult to have holidays or socialise with other families. Even a trip to the shops had to be carefully managed, as in this example:

*I can't even go shopping with her because she'll swear at me in the middle of a supermarket or whatever, and the last time was because I wouldn't buy her socks that weren't allowed at school, and she just said, 'Just go to the f****** till and pay for them then, or I'll punch you'.* (Left home)

Parents whose children had left some years ago commented that the feelings of grief and loss did ease. As one mother explained: 'It does get better, because the loss isn't so acute,' and some parents had decided to channel their energies into advocating on behalf of other adoptive parents. For example, one mother said:

I don't want anyone to go through what we've been through, and when I meet parents in a similar situation . . . I want to do what I can to get this right. I can't let what happened to us happen to anyone else. (Left home)

The impact on parents' lives of their child's difficulties was not unexpected, given the severity of the behaviours they had described. What was unexpected was how many talked about the impact of their loss of faith in the professionals in whom they had placed their trust. Loss of trust and subsequent sense of betrayal was a common theme in the interviews, as one parent explained:

> *All those dreams, all those hopes, all those lies ... part of the grief is losing faith in people who you believed in and you feel a mug for believing ... all those things are really important and the loss of that belief and faith in professionals is a separate grief.* (Left home)

Looking forwards

Parents were asked to look forward and think where they and their child would be in five year' time. Parents said:

> *Oh my God, that's what really worries me, that's the thing that keeps me awake at night, if I'm honest. I have no idea. Just pray to God he's not a prisoner.* (Left home)

Some parents talked about history repeating itself, fearing that their children would link up with abusive partners and have children that would become looked after. The vulnerability of their child to sexual exploitation and further abuse was also of great concern. Parents were fearful for their child's future:

> *The best scenario would be living in some form of sheltered housing and the worst would be she's dead or she's in Broadmoor having murdered somebody.* (Left home)

> *I'd like to think she's matured ... and that we can get on and have a normal family life together, but where I think she'll be is in prison.* (At home)

Some parents whose child had left home hoped that the move away would be cathartic and that without intense battles, relationships would improve. Parents hoped that with the young person's increasing maturity would come a new understanding of what they had provided and that relationships could be renewed:

I hope he will somehow wake up and realise he's got to make a living for himself ... Wherever he is, we want him to know that we're always here for him. (At home)

I hope we get some level of forgiveness and some understanding. We would like them back in our lives at some point but without the behaviour. (Left home)

Two adoptive mothers hoped that good relationships would be re-established and that they would become grandmothers. One mother said:

We've always kept the doors open and he knows that ... and believes it. I hope to be a grandma. (Left home)

Three parents hoped that life at university would bring great benefits for their children, and other parents hoped that college courses would have been completed and that their children would be in employment. Interestingly, the parents of three of the six girls who had had children of their own or who were pregnant reported that the pregnancy had had a positive impact on their children's lives. The girls enjoyed the attention that was focused on them and the fact that, for once, the attention was positive.

A couple of parents thought that their child would go in search of birth parents and that they would only come back to their adoptive home for material things. They did not expect to be playing a big part in the child's life. However, this was a minority view – the majority of parents hoped that they would be playing a part in the young person's life, as one parent said:

And I hope that she'll stay perhaps attached, maybe at arm's length where she feels comfortable. But I hope she always thinks that we're her adoptive parents and always her friends. (Left home)

Seven parents thought that their child would never be able to live independently and they were worried about the future and the transition to adult services. One family caring for a young person with foetal alcohol syndrome remarked that it would be manageable while both parents were alive, but were concerned about what would happen when they died. They did not want the responsibility to pass to their birth child.

Advice to prospective adopters

Parents were asked what advice they would give to prospective adoptive parents. Adoption was described as not for the fainthearted. Many parents said their advice would be 'Don't do it'. However, despite their own experiences, not all were completely against adoption, as one parent said:

But then if I said, 'Don't do it', I'd be denying someone the joy of having a child who comes back from a weekend away saying, 'I missed you', which is what I got this morning, and Mary said she missed me. And that's the first time she said she missed me. There are ups and downs. But yes, my bottom line would be don't do it. Unless the world of adoption changes significantly, don't do it. (At home)

The importance of receiving skilled specialist support was a point made by the vast majority of adopters. One parent said:

We're setting up people to fail . . . you can make adoption sound lovely and "happily ever after", but the children who are coming into care now have had such serious trauma and neglect and abuse and it's more than most families can cope with. And placing two/three children together, it's something that I think a whole team of people would struggle with, never mind one working parent. It's going to blow up in their faces unless there is proper funded help . . . And it annoys me when all the Government does is put a sticking plaster on the top, and we don't look at how it's all come about. (Left home)

Parents' advice to anyone considering adoption was to become well informed and not be afraid to ask basic questions. Getting experience of traumatised children (e.g. through fostering) was recommended and parents were keen to let prospective adopters know that they should not assume that they would not have difficulties. Parents said that they had been too ready to discount the difficulties they had heard about at the adoption preparation groups and think that it could not happen to them.

Basically, go for it and just keep yourself really well educated on all the latest issues, parenting techniques, get the information into the school about what they can do to help, build a bit of a good support network around you, even if it's not family. Just make sure you've got the right people, safety net in place ready for any event. (Left home)

Most parents thought that their advice to prospective adopters would be to adopt one child and as young as possible, to not depend on support from family and friends and to be sure that both prospective adopters were equally sure and committed.

Do not expect your family and friends to understand and continue supporting what turn out to be extremely difficult children. Instead, cultivate buddies with either experienced foster carers or experienced adopters. (Left home)

One father, parenting on his own after his wife had left, said:

Don't assume that you're going to do it together, look long and hard in your partner's eyes, and decide whether you will be able to put up with the good times, but also possibly the bad times, and if you can't do that, don't adopt, just don't go there. (Left home)

Adopters also emphasised the importance of developing a thick skin, to ensure that parents had time for themselves and to seek support when needed:

Cease to be embarrassed about anything that will happen to you in public, or in private. Reserve a chunk of time for yourself, absolutely every week, and take it. (Left home)

Not to be afraid (because I kept this under my hat for a while) that she was self-harming and things. I could see she was getting low, and I think you just have to say hang on, I don't know everything . . . And it's nothing to feel guilty about (which is what I was thinking), Oh God, I must be able to cope with this, I must be able to manage this on my own. But I think there gets a point where you can't. And going to that GP for the first time, I came out and thought what a big weight was off my shoulders. I told somebody about this, and now we're going to get some help, and share the difficulties. (At home)

There was a general view that adoptive parents had to learn to accept children for who they were. One parent's advice to prospective adopters was, 'Don't expect miracles', and another pointed out that it was unrealistic to expect that children would change simply because of the experiences, stimulation and love they would be given in an adoptive family. One parent said:

So you might have all this love, but they don't want it, you have to find a different way . . . But it's really rewarding. (At home)

Several parents thought that their children had grown up to be more like their birth parents than their adoptive parents. One mother said:

What I had no understanding of was the generational nature of neglect and abuse, and how that rings through each generation, and that my children will be much more like their birth family than they are like our family, even though they've lived most of their lives with us. So things like undiagnosed mental health problems, undiagnosed autism, the fact that these kids have not had enough nutrition in the womb, all of those things compound so much into modern adoption. (Left home)

Parents also described their adoption journey as remarkable, rewarding and life-changing. One parent summed up the feelings of many of those interviewed when she said:

Read as much as you can and understand as much as you can about things like attachment, how you will cope with them if they become difficult. Be very open and honest about your own expectations, because if you think it's going to be a normal family life, 99 per cent of the time you're mistaken. These children don't fit into moulds, and like my girls, she will look in the mirror and she'll go, 'I don't look like you, Mum', and it's always there ... But you have to ask yourself some really searching questions about what can I really realistically deal with, because the strain it puts on a marriage or a partnership or any relationship is massive, and lots of husbands walk. Are you then going to be able to cope with bringing this child or children up on your own? You've got to ask yourself so many very searching questions, and if at the end of that you still think you will be able to do it, then do it. But it's a massive life change. (At home)

Summary

- Thinking back over the course of the adoption, all but two adoptive parents could identify something that they would have done differently. Seventeen per cent wished that they had turned down the match.
- Some parents wondered whether they had been partly to blame for

their child's difficulties. They questioned their own personal qualities and their parenting style.

- Many parents wished that they had sought help earlier and had been more assertive and less trusting in their dealings with professionals. However, it was very difficult to find out what support services were available.

- The majority of parents were critical of the support provided, of unhelpful advice, and of the failure to provide appropriate services when needed. Parents were frustrated by professionals who did not treat them as reliable and credible informants. Parents wanted a service delivered by professionals who understood the complex and overlapping difficulties shown by adopted children.

- In describing the best thing to have come out of their adoption experience, some parents fondly remembered the time spent with their child when younger. Many talked about the love for their child and the importance of family. Some parents described feeling pleased to know that their child's life would be better than it would have been, had they remained in care.

- The worst part of parents' adoptive experiences was often the physical and verbal aggression shown by their child. Others described feeling socially isolated and shamed by their child's behaviour. For a few parents, the rejection by their child had been hard to bear.

- Most adopters considered themselves their child's parent and thought that their children too saw them as their parents. Some children's understanding of what was commonly meant by the words "mother" and "father" differed from the norm. Parents had had to adjust their own expectations accordingly.

- The children's challenging behaviours had had an impact on many aspects of parents' lives. Parents described their own behaviours changing, sometimes for the better. There had also been losses, including loss of friendships, intimate relationships, social lives, self-esteem and employment opportunities. Parents also described a loss of the family they had once imagined. In addition, parents had lost trust and faith in the professionals who they had believed would be on hand to support them if needed.

- Most of the parents would not recommend adoption to others, unless adoption support services were significantly improved. Nevertheless, many parents described their adoption journey as remarkable, rewarding and life-changing.

13   The well-being of children and parents

Before being interviewed, the 70 parents were asked to complete standardised measures on: 1) their child's emotional and behavioural development; and 2) their own well-being and parenting. One parent in the "Left home" group and one in the "At home" group refused to complete the information about their child, whilst two parents in the "Left home" group refused to complete it about themselves. To provide a comparison and calibration of the measures, 35 parents who had responded to the LA survey, stating that the adoption was going well with no or few difficulties, were contacted and were asked to complete well-being measures on their child. The "Going well" group were not interviewed.

First, we examined whether the children in the three groups – the "Left home", the challenging "At home" and the "Going well" groups – differed. There were no statistical differences in the proportions of boys and girls between the groups. However, the children in the "Left home" group were significantly older at the time of the adoption order compared with the children in the other two groups (Table 13.1). The "Left home" group, because their placement had disrupted, had lived with their families for a shorter time (average eight years), compared with the "At home" and "Going well" groups (average 11 years).

Table 13.1
Children's age at the time of the adoption order

Type	Mean	n	SD
Going well[49]	2.97	33	2.271
At home (challenging)	4.23	35	2.296
Left home	6.24	35	2.613
Total	**4.42**	**101**	**2.844**

49 The child's age at the time of the adoption order had not been completed on the survey for two children.

The children's measures

Details of the two measures used in the questionnaire are provided in Appendix B. The Strengths and Difficulties Questionnaire (SDQ) is a widely used screening measure of common emotional and behavioural problems, and of a child's peer relationships and their kind and helpful behaviour. It is highly predictive of psychiatric disorders (Goodman and Goodman, 2011). The Assessment Checklist for Adolescents (ACA) covers some of the same ground, but with many more items on difficulties rare in the general population, but more common in adopted and fostered children (Tarren-Sweeney, 2013).

Analyses of the measures

The analyses[50] were completed without any knowledge of the findings from the interview data. It is as well to consider at the outset how to interpret these comparisons of the measures, because the samples were taken from a survey where the return rate (34%) was modest (although typical for such approaches when tracing families who adopted more than 10 years ago), and because we do not know the representativeness of the sample. However, the proportion of parents who were finding parenting very challenging was similar in the LA and AUK surveys, although the sampling and time periods differed. The proportion who reported a disruption in the surveys was similar to that found in previous adoption research (Appendix A). In addition, it should be remembered that the groups were defined on the basis of the parents' own evaluations of how the adoptions were faring. There was no other way to do this, since agencies do not routinely monitor the outcomes of adoptive placements. Most of the "Left home" group of parents had experienced disruptions some time previously (77% over two years ago), so the rawness of their immediate feelings may have diminished, allowing for more reflective judgements.

The intention behind using measures was not to give prevalence

---

50 Analyses completed by Emeritus Professor David Quinton, who had no knowledge of the interviews or the findings.

rates of difficulties in adopted children, but rather to understand which behaviours parents found most challenging and whether there were systematic patterns that differentiated the groups.

The Strengths and Difficulties Questionnaire

The 25 items in the SDQ comprise five scales of five items each. The scales are: emotional symptoms, conduct (behaviour) problems, hyperactivity, peer problems, and pro-social behaviours (e.g. kind and helpful behaviours). For each of the five scales, the scores can range from 0–10. To calculate the total score, the pro-social scale is excluded and the four scales are summed; the total score can range from 0–40. An abnormal total score is 17 or above. In the general population, about 10 per cent of children would have scores indicating mental health difficulties within the clinical range. However, in unrelated foster care, abnormal scores have been found in 45–74 per cent, depending on the sample taken (e.g. Meltzer *et al*, 2000, 2003; Minnis *et al*, 2001; Ford *et al*, 2007). Abnormal scores for the individual scales are emotion (5–10), conduct (4–10), hyperactivity (7–10), peer (4–10) and pro-social (0–4). The comparisons of the SDQ scores can be approached through using the cut-off points for abnormal scores, indicating problems within the clinical range, and through examining the means for each scale. The latter analyses are more sensitive to differences, but the former are useful in giving an easy-to-understand look at the data.

Table 13.2 shows the proportion of children in each group whose scores were in the abnormal range. The majority (77%) of the "Going well" group did not have scores in the abnormal range. There were no statistical significant differences when comparing the "Left home" and "At home" groups except for "behaviour problems". This was the only scale where the entire "Left home" group had abnormal scores. Table 13.3 compares the mean scores for each of the SDQ scales.

Analyses of variance[51] using the mean scores repeated the overall differences from the analyses of the total scores. Analyses confined to

---

51 Anova is a statistical test of whether the means of several groups are equal.

Table 13.2
Percentage of children in the abnormal SDQ range based on the cut-offs

SDQ problems	Going well n = 35 %	Challenging but at home n = 34 %	Left home n = 34 %	Statistical significance Chi Square
Total score	23.0	82.4	97.1	0.000
Emotional	11.4	55.9	58.8	0.000
Behaviour	22.9	82.4	100.0	0.000
Hyperactivity/ inattention	25.7	55.9	70.6	0.001
Peer problems	25.7	73.5	76.5	0.000
Pro-social behaviour	17.1	50.0	52.9	0.001

the "At home" and "Left home" groups confirmed the significant differences on problems in behaviour[52] and was close to significance on the total score.[53] The analyses of means showed no significant differences between the "At home" and "Left home" children on emotional, peer problems, hyperactivity, or pro-social behaviour.

Summary and interpretation of the SDQ findings

The most striking feature of these findings is the extraordinarily high level of social, emotional, and behavioural difficulties in the "At home" and "Left home" groups. The two groups had more similarities than differences. Given the lack of difference between the two groups on the SDQ, the "At home" group may essentially be disruptions waiting to happen, but this pessimistic conclusion would be premature before the findings from the ACA and, more importantly, the interviews have been considered. In addition, their placements had already lasted for longer. The adopters' contribution to this was revealing, with most placements expected to continue (see Chapter 9). The exceptionally

---

52 F 6.259 p = 0.015
53 F 3.891, p = 0.053

Table 13.3
Mean scores of children on the SDQ total and sub-scales

SDQ problems	Going well	Challenging but at home	Left home	Statistical significance
	n = 35	n = 34	n = 34	
	means	means	means	
	SD	SD	SD	Anova
Total score	10.43	22.59	25.91	0.000
	7.84	6.42	5.62	
Emotional	1.91	5.12	5.12	0.000
	2.39	2.65	3.13	
Behaviour	2.31	6.00	7.47	0.000
	2.35	2.44	1.96	
Hyperactivity inattention	3.86	6.79	7.74	0.000
	3.44	2.29	2.17	
Peer problems	2.31	4.62	5.44	0.000
	2.31	2.10	2.23	
Pro-social behaviour	6.91	4.44	4.18	0.000
	2.63	2.18	2.33	

high rates of disorder in these two groups preclude finding any more subtle differences between them using the SDQ, but we can consider what the implications are of these very disturbing figures for estimates of child psychiatric disorders overall. The SDQ is a highly reliable and well-validated screening instrument and shows a strong predictive relationship between high SDQ total scores and psychiatric disorder, as assessed through a clinically validated interview measure (Goodman and Goodman, 2012). Figure 13.1 shows the relationship between an individual SDQ total score and the probability that the score indicates that the child has a psychiatric disorder. The vertical bars show the 95 per cent confidence interval for each score. Five out of seven of the "Going well" children, who were above the SDQ abnormal threshold, are well above it, scoring a 23 or higher; 26 of the challenging "At home" group are above this threshold; and all but two of the "Left home" group.

Figure 13.1
Probability of parent-rated SDQ scores indicating child psychiatric disorders at the individual level

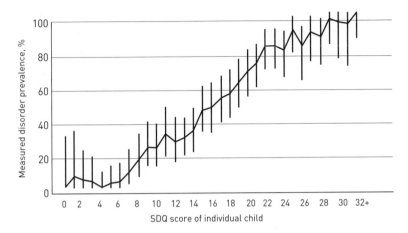

Reproduced with permission from: Goodman A and Goodman R (2012) 'Strengths and Difficulties Questionnaire scores and mental health in looked after children', *British Journal of Psychiatry*, 200, pp 426–42.

Figure 13.2 shows the estimate of the prevalence of psychiatric disorders for sub-populations of children in different family circumstances. The black dots at the left of the line give the estimates according to increasing levels of social disadvantage in children living at home divided into fifths based on the small area deprivation indices (Office of the Deputy Prime Minister, 2004). The square markers give the estimated prevalence for (in ascending order) kinship care, foster care, children looked after but with parents, and residential care. If we use the data from Table 13.3 and compare it to the estimates of prevalence, the mean score of the "Going well" group (10.43) was similar to that of a general population disadvantaged sample (9.7). The "At home" group (22.59) and the "Left home" group (25.91) were higher than the mean scores of the most poorly functioning group – those in residential care. The problems are, indeed, substantial. Even when adoptions are going well, many of the children have a residue of difficulties that take a long time to subside and make the parenting task challenging.

Figure 13.2
Estimating the prevalence of child psychiatric disorders from sub-population scores for different family circumstances

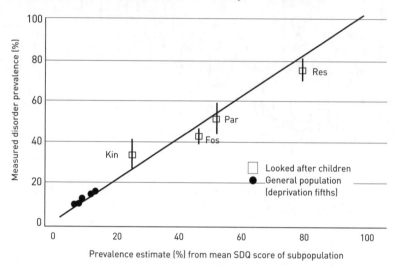

Reproduced with permission from Goodman A and Goodman R (2012) 'Strengths and Difficulties Questionnaire scores and mental health in looked after children', *British Journal of Psychiatry*, 200, pp 426–427

The Assessment Checklist for Adolescents (ACA-SF)

The availability of the large-sample population data for the SDQ was invaluable for understanding and interpreting our SDQ data. However, as previously observed, these very high levels of disturbance allow little scope for teasing out differences between the groups on those feelings and behaviours that are reasonably common in looked after and adopted children but rarer in general population samples. For this reason, we also used the Assessment Checklist for Adolescents (ACA-SF) in order to consider more subtle differences between our groups. The psychometric properties of this scale are well established (Tarren-Sweeny, 2014). As yet, population data are not available, although clinical cut-offs for the probability of clinically significant difficulties are. The ACA-SF has 37 items, making up six scales using a three point (0–3) response (does not apply, applies somewhat, certainly applies). Details of the ACA measure, including an explanation of the items in each scale, can be found in Appendix B. Table 13.4 shows the percentage of children who were above the borderline clinical range. In brackets is the proportion that was at the higher end of the scale in the marked range.

Overall, the findings parallel those from the SDQ, with the "Going well" group showing significantly lower scores than the other two groups. The differences between the "At home" and the "Left home" groups are substantial at the "marked" level and, indeed, comparison of the frequency at which they reached this level showed that the two

Table 13.4
ACA: Proportion of children at the "Indicated" (bold type) and "Marked" level (brackets)

Clinical level ACA sub-scale	Items	Going well % n = 35	Challenging at home % n = 34	Left home % n = 34	Statistical significance (Chi sq)
Non-reciprocal	6	**28.5** (11.4)	**85.3** (55.9)	**97.0** (79.4)	0.000
Social instability	8	**34.3** (20.0)	**76.5** (50.0)	**97.0** (79.4)	0.000
Emotional disregulation, distorted social cognition	6	**42.9** (14.3)	**88.3** (82.4)	**100.0** (93.9)	0.000
Dissociation/trauma	6	**5.8** (2.9)	**38.2** (20.6)	**66.7** (36.4)	0.000
Food maintenance	5	**2.8** (2.8)	**17.6** (14.7)	**29.4** (17.6)	0.001
Sexual behaviour	5	**5.6** (0.0)	**26.4** (11.7)	**29.4** (17.6)	0.000

attachment-related scales were elevated in the "Left home" group, significantly so for "social instability"[54] and approaching significance for "non-reciprocal behaviour";[55] that is, the "Left home" and "At home" groups show markedly elevated levels of attachment-related difficulties compared with the "Going well" group, but many of the latter show raised levels of attachment problems according to the clinical cut-offs.

Table 13.5
Mean ACA sub-scale scores for the three groups

Clinical level ACA sub-scale	Items	Going well n = 35 mean SD	Challenging at home n = 34 mean SD	Left home n = 34 mean SD	Statistical significance Anova
Non-reciprocal	6	2.06 2.27	5.88 3.16	8.18 2.87	0.000
Social instability	8	3.83 3.23	7.65 3.54	9.85 2.78	0.000
Disregulation, distorted social cognition	7	2.43 2.35	7.59 3.39	9.24 3.27	0.000
Dissociation/trauma	6	0.83 1.38	2.74 2.66	4.64 3.30	0.000
Food maintenance	5	0.91 1.87	3.18 3.14	3.85 3.33	0.000
Sexual behaviour	5	0.23 0.84	1.79 2.55	2.35 3.08	0.001

The same comparisons based on the mean score for each scale are given in Table 13.5. The picture of progressively elevated sub-scale scores across the groups is even more apparent for the first four scales on the comparison of means. In addition, "food maintenance" and "sexual behaviour", which were much rarer problems, were

54 2 sided exact probability = 0.021
55 2 sided exact probability = 0.068

significantly higher for the "At home" and "Left home" groups than for the "Going well" group.

Additional statistical tests found significant differences between the groups, as expected, but they also exposed the significant differences between the "At home" and "Left home" groups. There were significant differences between the "Left home" and "At home" groups on three scales: non-reciprocal behaviour (p = 0.004); social instability (p = 0.007); and dissociation/trauma (p = 0.029).

Predicting membership of the "Left home" and "At home" groups

This study was concerned with understanding disruptions in adoptive placements. The SDQ analyses show that the "Left home" and "At home" groups contained children with very challenging behaviour. There was little difference between the groups and so a series of logistic regression analyses were performed to see if there were significant predictors of group membership ("Left home" or "At home"). The final model included the SDQ total, age at the time of the adoption order, and two ACA scales (non-reciprocal behaviours and social instability). Age at the time of the order and the social instability scale had some predictive power, resulting in a model with 77.9 per cent correct classification (Table 13.6).

The relationship with age at the time of the order was not unexpected, since nearly all studies of adoption show older age at

Table 13.6
Predictor of "Left home" or "At home" group membership

	B	S.E.	Wald	Df	Sig.	Exp (B)
Step 1ª SDQ total	.011	.060	.035	1	.853	1.011
ACA sub 1	.135	.112	1.439	1	.230	1.144
ACA sub 2	.238	.104	5.248	1	.022	1.269
Age	.356	.136	6.845	1	.009	1.427
Constant	5.148	1.596	10.406	1	.001	.006

a. Variable(s) entered on step 1: SDQ total, ACAsub2, ACAsub2, Age.

placement to be a risk. Nor is it surprising to see indiscriminate forms of attachment difficulties coming through in the multivariate analyses. The social instability scale covers a combination of unstable, attachment-associated difficulties in social relatedness, involving craving affection; relating to strangers as if they were family; being too friendly with strangers; impulsivity; talking or behaving like an adult; preferring to be with adults or older children; and trying too hard to please other young people. The lack of any other significant predictors of disruption is not unexpected, given that the "At home" and "Left home" groups were very similar in so many ways, both showing very high levels of emotional and behavioural disturbance.

Looking at it the other way around, the "Left home" group is significantly different from the "Going well" group on *all* the SDQ and ACA sub-scales, pointing to the exceptionally high levels of difficulties encountered by these children and their parents. The "At home" children were not far behind in their difficulties, but their adoptions had already lasted longer and were not necessarily destined to disrupt. The contribution of the adopters in maintaining these placements cannot be overestimated. It is also clear that the parents of children in the "Going well" group were often facing substantial parenting challenges, over and above the issues surrounding adoption itself.

In order to illustrate the extent of difficulties for many children in all three groups, Tables 13.7 a, b and c show the formal diagnoses given to the children in each of our three groups – many of which are recorded in the Diagnostic and Statistical Manual of Mental Disorders (DSM-5). Adoptive parents were asked to list the diagnoses that their child had received: 29 per cent of the parents in the "Going well" group, 76 per cent of the "At home" group and 68 per cent of those whose child had "Left home" recorded conditions. Each row represents one child, with the diagnoses in the order they were made. Some children had multiple diagnoses.

Abbreviations

ADD   Attention Deficit Disorder
ADHD   Attention Deficit Hyperactive Disorder

BESD   Behavioural, Emotional and Social Difficulties
FASD   Foetal Alcohol Spectrum Disorder
OCD   Obsessive Compulsive Disorder
PTSD   Post-traumatic Stress Disorder
RAD   Reactive Attachment Disorder

Table 13.7a
Adopters' reports of diagnosed conditions

Going well: 10 of the 35 children had a diagnosed condition

RAD, ADHD, Asperger's syndrome
Attachment disorder, PTSD, ADHD
Speech delay
Attachment disorder, moderate learning difficulties
Attachment disorder
Learning difficulties
FASD, dyspraxia, dyscalculia
Hearing loss
Learning difficulties
Tourette's syndrome, learning difficulties

Table 13.7b
Child has left home: 23 of the 34 children had a diagnosed condition

RAD
Asperger's syndrome, Tourette's syndrome
Asperger's syndrome
OCD
Attachment disorder
Motor co-ordination, eating disorder
PTSD
Attachment disorder
Neurofibromatosis type 1

Attachment disorder
RAD, hyperactive
Attachment disorder, Semantic pragmatic disorder, Asperger's syndrome
FASD, PTSD, hyperkinetic personality disorder
Developmental delay, trauma, lower borderline functioning, abnormal brain activity in the frontal lobe, ASD
ADHD, attachment disorder
ADHD, FASD, attachment disorder
ADHD, conduct disorder, personality disorder
Attachment disorder, PTSD with dissociative amnesia, atypical autism, emerging personality disorder, ADHD, semantic pragmatic difficulties, developmental delay
RAD, PTSD, dissociative disorder, sleep disorder
Attachment disorder, anxiety
Attachment disorder, speech and language difficulties, impairment in receptive language, hyperkinetic conduct disorder, oppositional defiant disorder, ADHD, PTSD, developmental trauma
Dyslexia audio and visual

Table 13.7c
Challenging but child at home: 26 of the 34 children had a diagnosed condition

Severe attachment disorder
Dyslexia
Depression, ADHD
ADD/ADHD, Asperger's/ASD, social and general anxiety disorder, conduct disorder, early childhood truma
Attachment disorder, OCD, ADHD, ASD, BESD, bipolar body dysmorphic
ADHD, attachment disorder
Dyslexia
Depression
Learning difficulties

Dyslexia, depression, hyper-vigilance, dyspraxia, FASD
Delayed speech
Moderate learning difficulties, attachment disorder, depression
Sensory integration disorder, attachment disorder, executive functioning disorder, dyspraxia
ADHD
ADHD, shaken baby syndrome
ADHD, ASD
Attachment disorder, selective mutism, Asperger's syndrome
Atypical ASD, FASD, ASD
Dyscalculia, dyslexia
ADHD
RAD, ASD traits, conduct disorder
Attachment disorder
Developmental delay
Memory deficits – brain damage
Oppositional defiant disorder
Dyslexia

The adoptive parents' measures

Standardised measures of well-being and parenting were completed by 68 of the parents who were interviewed. Two parents in the "Left home" group refused to complete questionnaires about themselves. Questionnaire measures were also completed by the 35 parents in the "Going well" group; the "Going well" group was not interviewed.

We were interested in several dimensions of well-being, especially adopters' satisfaction with their parenting role; feelings about their own competence; their levels of anxiety, depression and trauma-related symptoms; and whether the challenges they had faced had resulted in any personal growth.

Sense of competence and satisfaction with parenting

Parental sense of competence is a broad way of describing an individual's feelings and beliefs about being a parent. It reflects a parent's perception of their parenting skills and satisfaction with the role of parent. The theory underpinning the measure is that parental satisfaction and self-efficacy moderates child and parent relationships and the ability to cope effectively with difficult child behaviours (e.g. Stoiber and Houghton, 1993).

Usually, as parents gain experience of raising children, their parental self-efficacy increases, but persistence of difficult behaviour can erode parents' assessments of their abilities (Maniadaki *et al*, 2005). Unsurprisingly, parents who report lower parental self-efficacy experience greater levels of stress related to parenting; are less able to put parenting knowledge into action; experience high levels of emotional arousal in challenging parenting situations; and do not show persistence in parenting tasks (Mash and Johnston, 1983; Grusec *et al*, 1994). Additionally, parents who feel that they are less able to control or influence their children's behaviour are more likely to use coercive or abusive parenting strategies in challenging situations (e.g. Teti and Gelfand, 1991).

We wanted to use a measure that would tap into these two domains of parental efficacy and satisfaction, as we were interested in understanding how parenting children with such high levels of difficulties might have affected parents' belief in their competence. To do this, we used the *Parenting Sense of Competence Measure* (Gibaud-Wallston, 1978). It produces two sub-scales: a) efficacy – knowledge and skills; and b) satisfaction – a sense of being comfortable and satisfied with the parenting role. Example questions are 'My mother/father was a better mother/father than I am', 'A difficult problem in being an adoptive parent is not knowing whether you are doing a good job or a bad job', 'I meet my own personal expectations for expertise in caring for this child'. The questions were altered slightly to ensure that each statement referred to "adoptive parent". Higher scores indicate greater confidence and satisfaction (Table 13.8). The maximum score is 42 on the efficacy scale and 54 on the satisfaction scale.

Table 13.8
Adopters' knowledge and skills (efficacy) and satisfaction in parenting their child

	Going well		At home		Left home	
	mean	SD	mean	SD	mean	SD
Efficacy scale	35.69	6.5	26.94	5.8	27.00	6.6
Satisfaction scale	40.00	7.7	31.03	6.1	34.48	6.3
Total	**75.77**	**13.29**	**57.97**	**8.83**	**61.40**	**10.54**

Unsurprisingly, the "Going well" group had scores that were significantly higher than the other two groups on both scales, indicating that they were confident in, and satisfied with their adoptive parenting role. More surprising was that the "Left home" group of parents had significantly higher scores on the parenting satisfaction scale[56] compared with the "At home" group of parents. There could be several explanations for this result. Perhaps the "Left home" group had recovered some of their belief in their own parenting abilities over time – 77 per cent of the children had left home two or more years ago. Time may have provided opportunity to reflect, but it also may have confirmed parents' views that the difficulties the family had faced were not simply the result of the way they had parented – children often had further placement breakdowns after leaving their adoptive home. Another explanation is that in some families, parent–child relationships had improved and adoptive parents were feeling that they had achieved some success in parenting their child, even if small. Many of the "At home" group of parents were in the midst of managing their child's challenging behaviour and some were struggling, which could have reduced their sense of satisfaction.

Anxiety and depression

The measure used to assess parental anxiety and depression was the *Hospital Anxiety and Depression Scale* (HADS). It is a 14-item scale, with higher scores representing more distress (maximum score is

---

56 Mann Whitney *U* 400.000 *z*-2.18 *p*<.029

21 on each scale). The measure asks about feelings in the previous week. It focuses on identifying treatable depression and omits concepts such as low self-esteem, hopelessness and guilt. Crawford and colleagues (2001)[57] established norms for the scale and we chose to use their cut-offs (Tables 13.9 and 13.10), identifying moderate and severe symptoms, as well as more common milder symptoms experienced by many people in the general population.

Table 13.9
Adoptive parents and symptoms of anxiety

Anxiety symptoms	General population n = 1,972 %	Going well n = 35 %	At home n = 35 %	Left home n = 33 %
Normal score 0–7	67	86	34	42
Mild score 8–10	20	9	34	33
Moderate score 11–15	10	6	23	9
Severe score 16–21	3	0	9	15

Table 13.10
Adoptive parents and symptoms of depression

Depression symptoms	General population n = 1,972 %	Going well n = 35 %	At home n = 35 %	Left home n = 33 %
Normal score 0–7	87	80	57	52
Mild score 8–10	9	9	26	24
Moderate score 11–15	3	11	14	21
Severe score 16–21	1	0	3	3

It was surprising to find that the adoptive parents in the "Going well" group were, on average, less anxious than most people in the general

---

57 Norms established on an Australian population.

population, but had more symptoms of depression. This group of parents were not interviewed and therefore we do not know if symptoms of depression related to their adoption experiences or to other events in their lives such as bereavement or work-related issues. It should be remembered that 23 per cent of the "Going well" group were caring for children with scores on the SDQ indicating mental health problems within the clinical range. Indeed, the scores on the HADS and SDQ were correlated – higher scores on the children's SDQ were associated with higher scores on the parental depression scale.[58]

For the parents in the "At home" and "Left home" groups, the tables of symptoms of anxiety and depression show some interesting differences. Three-quarters of the parents whose children had "Left home" had normal or mild levels of anxiety, which we assumed was because the source of the anxiety was no longer present. In contrast, one-third of the parents whose children were "At home" had moderate or severe symptoms of anxiety. High levels of anxiety were associated with high children's SDQ scores.[59] Although the "Left home" group of parents showed less anxiety, nearly one-quarter had moderate or severe symptoms of depression. The same was true for 17 per cent of parents in the "At home" group.

Trauma

Adoptive parents often used the word "trauma" during the research interview to describe the impact on the child of their early life experiences and to describe *their own response* to living with this distress. Measuring the impact of trauma is complex because until recently the *Diagnostic and Statistical Manual of Mental Disorders* (DSM)[60] criteria for post-traumatic stress disorder (PTSD) demanded a single specific

---

58 Kruskal-Wallis: 73.979, df2 *p*<.000
59 Kruskal-Wallis: 43.000, df2 *p*<.000
60 *DSM* is the handbook used by healthcare professionals in the US and much of the world as the authoritative guide to the diagnosis of mental disorders. *DSM* contains descriptions, symptoms and other criteria for diagnosing mental disorders. It provides a common language for clinicians to communicate about their patients and for researchers to study the criteria for potential future revisions and to aid in the development of medications and other interventions.

traumatic incident. Many traumatic events (e.g. car accidents, natural disasters) are of time-limited duration, but some people experience chronic trauma that continues or repeats for months or years (e.g. women living with domestic violence). DSM-5 has moved PTSD from an anxiety disorder to a new category, which includes a range of trauma and stress-related disorders (the new category also includes attachment disorders) and acknowledges that repeated exposure to stressful events can result in PTSD.

DSM-5 pays more attention to the behavioural symptoms that accompany PTSD and proposes four distinct diagnostic clusters instead of three. They are described as:

- Re-experiencing the event, e.g. spontaneous memories of the traumatic event, recurrent dreams related to it, flashbacks, or other intense or prolonged psychological distress.
- Heightened arousal, e.g. aggressive, reckless or self-destructive behaviour, sleep disturbances, hyper-vigilance or related problems, flight or fight reactions.
- Avoidance, e.g. distressing memories, thoughts, feelings, or external reminders of the event.
- Negative thoughts and moods or feelings, e.g. a persistent and distorted sense of blame of self or others, to estrangement from others or markedly diminished interest in activities, to an inability to remember key aspects of the event.

Adoptive parents in the "Left home" group completed the *Impact of Event Scale – revised* (Weiss and Marmar, 1997), a screening tool for PTSD. It has 22 items, which are rated on a scale of 0 (not at all) to 4 (extremely). Questions ask about feelings in the last seven days; examples are: 'Any reminder brought back feelings about it. I felt as if it hadn't happened or wasn't real'. 'I thought about it when I didn't mean to'. The questions were completed only by the "Left home" group of parents. We had assumed that the measure was only suitable for the "Left home" group, as they had experienced a specific event, and we had not expected the "At home" group to be experiencing repeated exposure to traumatic events. In hindsight, the measure

Table 13.11
**Parents who had experienced a disruption: symptoms of PTSD
(n = 33)**

Symptoms	Mean	SD
Intrusion	13.64	9.11
Avoidance	9.45	7.29
Hyper-arousal	8.09	7.40
Total	**31.18**	**22.03**

could also have been used with the "At home" group (Table 13.11).

Thirteen parents had scores totalling more than 33 (range 36–73), suggesting that they had PTSD, and 11 other parents had some symptoms. Only nine parents were symptom-free. Most often, parents had problems with intrusion. Items on this scale include being preoccupied with the events, thoughts and pictures popping up in the mind, waves of strong feelings, difficulty sleeping, and dreaming about the events. All bar one of the 13 parents at the high end of the scale also had symptoms of moderate to severe anxiety on the HADS measure. However, other parents' symptoms were less severe and these may indicate that they were engaged in an internal struggle to rebuild their lives. The symptoms may be a sign of post-traumatic growth and not of a disorder (Joseph and Butler, 2010). There is a tendency to focus only on negative outcomes when researching events that are assumed to have had a negative impact; however, developments in positive psychology emphasise that growth and change can be the flip side of traumatic experiences. Therefore, we added two scales to the questionnaire measures that examined satisfaction with life and personal growth.

Satisfaction with life and personal growth

The first scale, the *Satisfaction with Life Scale* (Diener *et al*, 1985), was designed to measure a person's subjective opinion of their overall satisfaction with life. It focuses on cognitive judgements and considers each respondent's perspective on their own life. It is brief, and on a scale of 17, respondents are asked about the extent to which they agree with the following statements: *In most ways my life is close to ideal; The conditions of my life are excellent; I am satisfied with my life; So far I have got the important things I want in life; If I could live my life over, I would change almost nothing.* The possible range of scores is 5–35, with a score of 20 representing a neutral point on the scale. Scores between 5–9 indicate the respondent is extremely dissatisfied with life, whereas scores between 31–35 indicate the respondent is extremely satisfied.

As expected, 94 per cent of the "Going well" group reported that they were satisfied with their lives and 77 per cent scored at the higher end of the scale, being highly or extremely satisfied. Just over half (51%) of the "At home" group were satisfied with their lives, with one-quarter scoring in the highly/extremely satisfied range. The "Left home" group of parents scored similarly (Table 13.12). Just over half of the "Left home" and "At home" adoptive parents reported that they were currently satisfied or very satisfied with life.

Previous research (e.g. Diener *et al*, 1999) has found that people who score at the high end of the scale tend to have close and supportive family and friends, gain satisfaction from their employment or role, such as being a parent, and are satisfied with their personal worth, such as satisfaction with their spiritual life or leisure activities. The high scores do not mean that life is "perfect" but that life is going well and they may draw motivation from any areas of dissatisfaction.

People who score in the average range are generally satisfied but have one or two areas of life where they would like to see some improvement. Low scores indicate substantial dissatisfaction with life

Table 13.12
Parents' overall satisfaction with life

Extent of satisfaction with life	Going well (n = 35) %	At home (n = 35) %	Left home (n = 33) %
Unsatisfied	6	49	46
Satisfied	17	26	27
Highly/extremely satisfied	77	25	27

indicating a need for support or professional help. Examining individual items on the scale, the lowest mean score for the "Going well" parents was in disagreement with the statement *If I could live my life over, I would change almost nothing*. For the "At home" and "Left home" parents, the lowest mean score was on the statement *In most ways my life is close to my ideal*.

The second measure was the short form of the *Post Traumatic Growth Inventory* (Cann *et al*, 2010). This was only completed by the "At home" and "Left home" group of parents, as we assumed that the "Going well" group had not experienced an adoption-related traumatic event. Parents were asked to indicate the degree (five being a maximum score for each item) to which certain changes (e.g. *I established a new path for my life* or *I know I can better handle difficulties*) occurred in their life, as a result of their adoption experiences. The two groups of parents had very similar scores. The mean score for the parents whose children had "Left home" was 22 (SD 11.1) and was 20 (SD 9.6) for those whose child was still "At home". Parents reported very little positive change on most of the items on the inventory. Adopters showed no or little change in the domains of developing closer relationships with family, friends, or neighbours or in enhanced spiritual beliefs. Positive changes was seen in two areas: recognising their own inner strength and a changed set of goals and priorities in life.

Overall, the "Going well" group were confident and satisfied in their role as adoptive parents, pleased with the way their life was going and had fewer symptoms of anxiety compared with adults in the general population. They did have raised levels of depression and this may be because about one in five were parenting a child with significant difficulties.

The "At home" group of parents were less satisfied with their parenting and had more symptoms of anxiety than did the parents in the "Left home" or the "Going well" groups. Most were still actively trying to find a way of managing their child's challenging behaviours. However, half of the "At home" group of parents were satisfied with their life and had seen some positive changes in themselves and their goals in life. Fewer parents had symptoms of moderate or severe depression compared with the parents in the "Left home" group.

The "Left home" group of parents had higher scores on parental satisfaction compared with the parents whose children were still at home, and were freer of symptoms of anxiety. However, nearly one-quarter had moderate to severe symptoms of depression and 13 (37%) parents had symptoms suggesting that they had PTSD. Many of the parents who had experienced a disruption were bothered by intrusive thoughts and feelings. Nevertheless, about half of the parents were satisfied with their lives and had changed their priorities in life.

Summary

- The well-being of children and their parents were compared using standardised measures.
- Thirty-five parents whose child had "Left home" prematurely, 35 parents who were finding parenting very difficult ("At home"), and 35 parents who reported all was "Going well" completed a questionnaire.
- There were similar proportions of boys and girls in the three groups. There were no age differences between the groups at the time of the study.
- There were extraordinarily high levels of social, emotional and behavioural difficulties in the "At home" and "Left home" groups on the SDQ. The majority (97%) of children who had "Left home" and 82 per cent of the children who were "At home" had scores in the clinical range. Even 23 per cent of the "Going well" group were above the cut-off that indicates problems within the clinical range, which would make parenting more challenging.
- Parents reported that the majority of children in the "Left home" and the "At home" groups had had specific conditions diagnosed and many had multiple diagnoses. Ten of the children in the "Going well" group had also received a professional diagnosis.
- Comparing the SDQ scores of the three groups of adopted children to Goodman and Goodman's findings (2011) in large population studies, we found the SDQ mean score of the "Going well" group

was similar to that of Goodman's disadvantaged population sample. The mean scores of the "At home" and "Left home" groups were higher than the mean scores of Goodman and Goodman's residential care sample.

- Findings on the ACA paralleled those of the SDQ, with the "Going well" group having significantly lower scores on all the sub-scales compared with the other two groups.
- The "Left home" children differed from the "Going well" group on every sub-scale of the SDQ and the ACA. The scores of the "At home" group were not far behind. This makes it difficult to differentiate between the "Left home" and the "At home" groups. Both groups of children had abnormal scores on most points.
- The "Left home" group differed from the "At home" group in two respects. First, they were older at the time of the adoption order, and second, they were statistically more likely to have scores above the cut-off in the clinical range of attachment-related difficulties.
- On a measure of parenting confidence and satisfaction, the "Going well" group had significantly higher scores than the other parents. They were confident in and satisfied with their adoptive parenting role. The "Left home" group of parents had significantly higher parental satisfaction scores compared with the "At home" parents.
- Nearly one-quarter of the "Left home" group of parents had symptoms of moderate to severe depression and anxiety at the time of the interview. Thirteen of the parents in the "Left home" group had symptoms that indicated they were likely to have PTSD. Parents of children who were still "At home" had higher levels of anxiety (32%) and lower levels of depression (17%).
- The "Going well" group had fewer symptoms of anxiety compared with the other parents in the study or even parents in the general population. However, the "Going well" group had slightly more depression than would be expected. Higher scores on the parental depression scale were correlated with higher children's SDQ scores.
- The majority of parents (94%) in the "Going well" group reported that they were very or highly satisfied with their lives. Even though parents were or had been managing very challenging behaviours,

half of the "At home" and "Left home" parents were also satisfied with their lives.

- Parents in the "Left home" and "At home" groups reported some positive growth in their lives, as a consequence of their adoption experiences. Growth had occurred in two areas: a change of priorities in life and recognition that they had greater inner strength.

14 Talking to young people about adoption disruption

Twelve young people (six males and six females) who had experienced an adoption disruption were interviewed. At the time of the interview, the young people were on average 18 years old. Most had left their adoptive home during adolescence (Table 14.1). Five of the young people's adoptive parents had been interviewed as part of the research study. Seven other young people had agreed to take part after hearing about the study: we had no information on or from their adoptive parents.

Young people's current circumstances

Many of the young people talked about wanting to settle down, organise and take control of their own lives, partly because they were getting older and needed to be in employment to pay rent, and partly because they were thinking ahead to having children of their own. One young woman was pregnant and another young person already had a child. At the time of the interview, one young man had recently

Table 14.1
Gender and age of the young people interviewed

	Boys (n = 6)	Girls (n = 6)
Age at adoption	Mean 6 years (range 4–8 years)	Mean 6 years (range 4–9 years)
Age when left adoptive family home	Mean 14 years (range 11–16 years)	Mean 14 years (range 10–6 years)
Years since leaving home	Mean 5 years (range 1–11 years)	Mean 4 years (range 1–8 years)
Current age	Mean 19 years (range 16–23 years)	Mean 18 years (range 15–20 years)

returned to live with his adoptive family and had started an apprentice-ship with the intention of setting up his own business.

Accommodation

Nine of the 12 young people had moved around since leaving their adoptive families, having several foster and residential placements or lodgings. Young people talked about how placement/accommodation instability had left them feeling very isolated and lonely, and some were currently living a long way from friends. The young woman who was pregnant said:

> I'm very aware now that when it comes to the time in your life when you have your own children . . . you probably have . . . your closest friends around you and stuff like that . . . Although I have made friends here, I'm aware that they are people who I've only known a year or so. They're not the people that I went to school with or anything like that. And I feel not very settled here . . . So I feel a bit floaty at the moment.

One teenager was in a settled foster placement and another young man was in a specialist (an alternative to custody) foster placement. He hoped to move to independent living soon. It was apparent that many of the young people were either already living independently or the plan was for that to occur soon.

Four of the 12 young people remained unsettled. They were not in college or in paid employment and had no stable accommodation. One of the young women said:

> I was in supported lodgings but things went downhill and they decided to kick me out at such short notice that my friend's brother and sister-in-law took me in. College? I've just quit college because I got a disciplinary for something I didn't do. I'm going to take this year out of college and then go back and try and sort things out.

Education

There was recognition from four young people that they needed to catch up on missed education. For example, one young man who had not attended school since he was 15 years old said:

> I've started college and doing English once a week 9.00am-12.00pm. It's for adults. I'm trying to turn my life around because I left with no GCSEs and I've been finding it really, really difficult.

However, criminal records were affecting employment and training opportunities for three young men. One, who had committed a serious offence, found that no college would accept him and, although intelligent, he was spending much of his day in his room playing video games, unable to take his GCSEs. Two other young men, who had been prosecuted for offences whilst they lived in residential care, found that the enhanced criminal records bureau[61] (CRB) check meant that they were excluded from courses that would have qualified them to work in social care. Both of the young men wanted to work with looked after children.

Another young man with a criminal record was attending college two days a week to study building maintenance and wanted to settle down. He had a young son and wanted his child's life to be different to his own. He said:

> I've always wanted my independence, because I've grown up quite quick. You have to when you live in care, you have to develop quickly. Since I had this nine months of straight and narrow . . . it's sorted me out and now I've got a son. You don't let the things that happened to you as a baby happen to your son. You do as much as you can to give him the best life you can give him.

Two young women were living independently – one working and one in college. Both also aspired to work in health and social care. One

---

61 Now known as the Disclosure and Barring Service.

young woman was very positive about her life:

> I've been working since I left school at 16 years and I really want to work with young children. I'm now out of care, renting a room in a shared house. I've got a great boyfriend.

However, neither was entitled to leaving care services and both were concerned that they could not afford to go to university.

The youngest person was in a settled foster care placement but wished to return home:

> I'm at school, the last year, doing my GCSEs. To be honest, I don't feel like people understand what it's like being in care, especially my friends.

Health

Young people were not asked specifically about their health, but some spoke about the difficulties they were having with depression, self-harm, suicidal thoughts, and eating disorders:

> I can't pay for the prescription . . . and can't get to the GP . . . I just feel so crap I can't be bothered.

> I've lost my emotion to cry . . . no matter what I do a tear won't leave my eye. I've got no emotions.

> I don't go out. Only time I go out is to sign on, go to Tesco or college. I have no family here, no friends. I have nothing. Sometimes I think, what's the point? My [birth] mum doesn't want me; my [birth] dad doesn't want me.

Two young people (one female and one male) were trying to extricate themselves from violent and controlling partners. One said:

> He still texts me, he still harasses me, he still gets into my head, making me feel like I need him. He's already tried to stop me going to college. He breaks me down, tells me I'm stupid, disgusting . . . he stole my house keys so I can't get home. He sent me a letter written in blood.

The other had multiple scars from the cigarette burns inflicted by his female partner.

Adoptive family life – the early years

All the young people had been late placed with their adoptive family. They were asked how they had settled in during the first few years with their adoptive family. Four young people took the opportunity to talk about their time in care *prior* to adoption. One young person had had 10 foster placements before being placed for adoption, aged four. Others talked about their experiences in their birth families.

> I know why we were taken from them, because they used to physically and mentally abuse us. They used to take certain types of drugs that used to make them do stupid things. They used to starve us so we had to go and rob from the old people's home across the road, and this was when I was five or six. My brother had to go to supermarkets, he was about seven or eight, and rob food for us to eat. We slept on the stairs and we were barely clothed. We had one pillow between the three of us.

> I was in and out of care from day one, home, care, home, care, and they finally got a freeing order, and she obviously lost and we were put into care. I had lots of nightmares about being in a dark room. I don't know what that was about, but there were things about neglect on my files.

Thinking back to when they first moved into their adoptive home, young people talked about not understanding what was happening and not being asked if they wanted to be adopted. Some said that they had wanted to stay with their birth mothers, although they now recognised that would not have been possible. One young man said:

> I never wanted to be adopted . . . ever . . . I was adopted with my older brother and older sister. Before it went to court, I got sat down with social workers and told what was going to happen. But I was too young [about seven years], but I was behind and I

didn't understand . . . I wanted to be with my real parents, but I know for a fact now that it would never have been achievable.

When you have to go to court and they say, 'Do you want them to be your new mummy and daddy?' I can always remember that day. I couldn't say 'Yes' and I couldn't say 'No'. My brother and sister said 'Yes'. I went blank, but I had this teddy in my hands and I was shaking it to say 'No' . . . but they just thought I was playing with it.

Another young man, who had many placements in care, described the day he moved to his adoptive family. He knew very little about what was happening and said:

It's scary moving into a new family . . . when I was in care [before adoption] . . . I came to the top of the stairs and I remember all the bags packed and a strange man [the social worker] saying, 'Come on, you're moving'. So when I got moved . . . it's affected me . . . still does, I never feel settled.

Four young people said they had always felt as if they did not fit in with their adoptive family or felt blamed for everything that went wrong. Two young people described adoptive mothers who had their own mental health problems, such as depression and bulimia, or who were very controlling. Comments included:

I still had strange feelings about where I came from and not fitting in.

But when I was growing up, I was always told I was different because I was adopted and the others weren't. In the family, there were three birth children . . . and I was the youngest. I didn't get on at all with my sister but I do now! Me and my brothers always got on . . . Growing up and even now, everything was my fault . . . just by my mum, it's always my mum. She's, like, wrapped up in her own world.

Just four of the 12 young people described early adoptive family life positively and said that they had been happy in the first few years. More often, the young people said that they were struggling with feelings of loyalty to their birth mothers and a deep desire and longing to be with them and know more about them. They explained:

I had life story books full of stuff about her. I started running away at about nine years old. They treated me differently than my brothers so I used to try and run away. I thought they gave them more attention and were kinder to them. She [birth mother] wouldn't have been able to look after me because she was depressed and had a breakdown when we were took off her . . . but I wanted to find her and be with her . . . That was my instinct then . . . be with her.

When I first got adopted I was too young to know what was going on, what with my dyslexia, I thought it was just a holiday . . . and I was slower than other people . . . because of all the bad things in the past, but after a while I started thinking, 'What would it be like living with my birth family?'

Young people also recognised that their own behaviour was difficult for adoptive parents to manage. For example, one young woman, who had never felt close to her adoptive mother, said about the first few years of her adoptive placement:

Things were tough then. I'd been to see play therapists and had emotional detachment . . . disorder and those sorts of things, which my mum and dad tried to recover me from. Things were still difficult.

Bullying

Six of the 12 young people said that they had been bullied at school because of their adoptive status. Two young people became school refusers and most of the others had truanted. In talking about bullying, they said:

I didn't tell people [I was adopted] because I was frightened of being treated differently . . . teachers knew . . . I was excluded in one of the lessons in front of everyone: 'Go to learning support' . . . Everyone was looking and saying, 'Why does he get to go?' And the teacher said, 'Because this lesson is sensitive'. I didn't have a clue what the lesson was about, I just walked out and they were laughing [the lesson was on child abuse and foster care]. I had loads of people coming up to me saying, 'If I had a kid I'd sell them on ebay', and I got angry and stormed out to the other side of school and cried and felt horrible. It went all around school . . . people would come and say, 'Oh you're adopted . . . you're different . . . you're not one of us. You're the kid nobody ever wanted.' Even closest friends if they fell out [with me] would use it against me and it hurt . . . I just gave up and ignored it and went quiet and it started affecting me at home.

It was quite horrible, it was really nasty, and it got to the point where I was self-harming.

When I went to secondary school and that's when my insomnia started too. Threatening, attacking, knives to my throat, putting a gun to my head, and more . . . very bad.

Reasons for leaving the adoptive family

Young people were asked about the reason that led to them leaving their adoptive homes. Six young people believed that the reasons for the disruption lay in their early history. One young man, reflecting on his move out of home, said:

Nothing to do with my adopted parents, it was me, because I was adopted at four. As a baby I had a rough four years out of my life . . . I had issues as a kid, so up to 11 I think I grew a bit too quickly, and wanted my own ways of life and that . . . I weren't the best behaved kid . . . I've done a lot of things. But I have got to say it's nothing to do with my mum and dad, because we've had such bad upbringings before they adopted us. There's nothing they could have done. I've been challenging since probably the day ... well, since I was about four years old, but it's because of what I went through, and you just can't turn back time, you just have to deal with it, knock it on the chin.

Early abuse and neglect had a negative impact on the building of relationships. Young people commented on their limited capacity to tolerate intimacy, their feelings about mothers, and their lack of trust in others. One young person, in describing herself, said:

If people describe me they would probably say I'm like a bubbly person, I'm always happy and smiling, but I may not necessarily be happy underneath ... I have this fake smile ... I find it difficult to express my feelings and talk about it because I've never done it before. There was no-one to talk to, and I just learnt to smile. I was taught to smile for the camera, so I was probably doing a lot of smiling ... not letting my emotions out and bottling them up to the point where I suddenly just break and it just comes out, like a volcano when it erupts.

Another young person, using the same simile of being "like a volcano" said:

I have mother issues ... if anybody tried to mummy me I got angry. I punched walls ... With my mum I never used to physically hurt her but I used to mentally hurt her on purpose. I used to find satisfaction in seeing her crying. It sounds sick and twisted ... but I used to think it was funny.

Interviewer: *'Where did that anger come from?'*

It had been boiling for years. It's still there; it's boiling and boiling and boiling like a volcano. At the back of my head I thought, 'I'm going to find my [birth] parents and when I do, it will be all right'.

One young person's adoptive mother became ill, which resulted in him (but not his siblings) returning to care. He expressed no feelings of rejection and spoke about how becoming looked after had been the best solution for the family:

> She got really poorly and I was the younger one so I was a bit more hard work . . . and I was stressing her out. So her and my dad had a discussion, and they thought because I was younger it would be easier for me to possibly go back into care, because I would be able to settle quicker than my older brother . . . We had that brotherly relationship that we literally hated each other. We were always at each other's throats, we were always arguing, whatever my mum could do, we never seemed to get on, ever. I was quite naughty at school, and I had lack of concentration. I couldn't concentrate on anything, and stuff like this. I was expelled and then I was suspended a couple of times from my high school. So it was very difficult.

Oppositional behaviour in school led to some young people being excluded. Exclusions added to the pressures felt in families, which, in turn, contributed to the young person's move out of home. One young man said:

> Basically it all started with me having trouble at school, kept getting excluded and out of stress and anger . . . I wasn't hitting, I was verbally shouting.

Two young people thought that when difficulties arose, their adoptive parents had been too ready to accept the adult version of events and had not supported them. They had wanted their adoptive parents to "stick up" for them and fight their corner, but they had lost trust in their parents, saying:

> They [adoptive parents] didn't understand me. They would always agree with other adults, other teachers . . . they wouldn't stand up for me . . . she never listened to me about what really happened.

Five young people talked about being angry and aggressive in their adoptive home. One young man said:

> *They found out that I keep weapons beside my bed. It wasn't just a metal pole, I had a BB gun, had my . . . knife, they found out that I'm quite defensive, I've got intense anger issues, got OCD. Everyone has got two different sides, but my sides are completely different.*

Most of the young people said that there had been many heated, angry family arguments and that they had wanted more independence than they were allowed. Some young people thought that their parents were over-protective and that they were treated more harshly than their peers because their parents were older and from a different generation. Three young people thought that because of their early lives, they had had to "grow up quick" and they resented the rules and restrictions. One young person said:

> *Just arguments really, me and Mum clashing, me and Dad clashing, which in turn made Mum and Dad clash. [Arguments were about the] times I was out and what I was doing, not telling Mum and Dad where I was going or what I was doing, I still don't do that, it's none of their business. I'm not going out doing anything troublesome, that's all they need to know. They were too pushy and . . . it was like a cat on a mouse, if that's a good way to describe it. Always over you, in a way, wanting to try and find out what you're doing or kind of catch you out and kind of places like that and all kinds of stuff.*

Three young people thought that their behaviour was normal teenage stroppiness and that there had been an over-reaction because post-adoption support services were already involved, as one described:

> *I turned into a very stroppy 13-year-old basically, as everybody does. I suppose because there was more intervention going on, just because I had been adopted and there were adoption workers in and out anyway. It was maybe noticed a little bit more.*

Relationships with siblings were also problematic. For three young people, an older sibling had already left the adoptive family home. In another family, the young person became distressed when his older sibling left care and they lost contact. More frequently though, young people talked about fights and arguments with siblings where they felt that they were always the one blamed by their parents, as one of them explained:

> Usually Isobel [sibling] would do something, and she used to be a real pain in the backside, she used to scream out, 'Ouch, that hurts', and they [parents] used to go 'What's happening?' And sometimes they think maybe I'm hitting Isobel or something, I'm not even hitting her, she's making it up . . . and then I used to get in trouble. 'Go to your room', 'I didn't do nothing', and then they go, 'Oh yes you did, we heard Isobel'. And then she would smirk at me, which made it more irritating. My sister used to always wind me up, because she'd know what buttons to press.

Unlike the other 11 interviews where the reason for leaving was the young person's challenging behaviour, one young person left after the abuse she had suffered for years in her adoptive placement was finally investigated. She said:

> My adoptive family were abusive the whole time I was with them . . . She used to hit us . . . used food as a sanction . . . It wasn't even the hitting that really upset us. It was the mental stuff . . . telling us we were worthless and no-one would ever love us and we'd be useless. She used to spit in my face and not let me wipe it away and everything like that. That's still haunting us and I've needed counselling to get over it. One night it got really bad and it was worse than it had ever been. I ended up getting a black eye and I went into school. There was a safeguarding alert, police [were called] . . . and I couldn't go back home and I ended up in foster care, and that was it, adoption over. It was a relief and it was scary because although they hit,

scratch, and spat at us a lot, they were a family at the end of the day and I was leaving the family security.

Five young people had run away frequently from their adoptive families. These young people also had other difficulties, such as self-harming, setting fires, and one teenage boy was becoming alcohol-dependent. Two young people explained how they came to leave their families:

I used to run away quite a lot and they [adoptive parents] thought they couldn't look after me any more. I wanted to be with my birth mum and I used to try and run away and try to find her. They [adoptive parents] said they couldn't do it any more and took me into care for my own safety.

When I was running away [I ran away 16 times in two months] about 30 times all together. When I was 14/15, before I disappeared... in the end I got so fed up... I waited until they were asleep and I packed my bag and nearly burned the whole house down on purpose. At the time I made out that I didn't care about anything, when I did.

Some young people thought that going into foster care might be easier than remaining at home, especially when relationships were fraught and arguments were a frequent occurrence. When foster care became a possibility, it seemed a way to get out of the situation, as for this young person:

He [social worker] asked the question to me, 'Do you want to go into foster care?' And I said, 'Yes'. So I just made it easy.

For some young people, the move out of their adoptive home came as a relief from the intense arguments.

The move away from home

Not all the young people became looked after when they first left their adoptive home. One young person moved in with a member of the extended adoptive family, another first stayed at a friend's house, and two young people, who ran away in an attempt to find their birth families, stayed anywhere they could find. Two young men said:

> When I disappeared for good, I ended up living in a house party for nearly a year, as I was homeless. That's when I started slipping up, as if I didn't take any alcohol or drugs I'd have got kicked out on the street – it was pressure. I just took sniff and stuff... My brother came for the night and slept on their floor and when he woke up, he was like stone ice. He'd drunk a quarter of a bottle of whisky and he couldn't move and I had to carry him. And then a short while later I moved to his house and... he had a friend there who had also been in foster care. I stayed there a while until I got told how to get to my birth mum's.

> I saw my real mum for the first time. It was set up by SSD... I was 15... Made my feelings worse, after I'd seen her; it brought back memories I never knew. I went to talk to my adoptive parents [but we weren't getting on] and I physically needed someone that day... but I never got that... I got, 'Go to your room'. So, I kicked off and was gone. I told my dad, 'I've got to do this... Go off the radar.' He gave me a hug and he was shaking... he turned round crying and he never saw me again for a year.

In contrast to the three young people who ran away and did not return, three young people who became looked after were taken to their foster placement by their adoptive parents. They were pleased that this had happened; one young man said:

> I didn't really know what was going on... I kind of knew it was for the best. They came with me and settled me into the foster placement.

One young person, whose adoptive mother was ill, described a gradual introduction to the carers, beginning with short periods of shared care until he eventually moved in permanently:

> Mum was with me the first time, and she took me a couple of times for the respite and to pick me up, so I always knew she would come back. And she was in the car and she said, 'I love you, and you know I'll always be there for you', and all this lot. And then I think after about six months I went to live with this foster family, and it just went on from there ... So it was gradually done. I wasn't just plonked there and dealt with, it was gradual, so it was alright.

Not all the young people had felt so prepared. Two young people were shocked that they were going into foster care. They stated that "care" had been used as a threat by their parents but they had never expected it to happen and described their feelings of rejection and fear:

> Came as a complete shock. I was out in the back garden having a cigarette and [mother] and me had an argument 'cos I had been excluded ... but I'd done nothing wrong ... and I said, 'You know what, you're a f****** bitch' ... It was mixed emotions: I was scared, I didn't know what to feel ... Other kids get to look around but I never did ... [mother] didn't come with me, she stayed at home, she didn't want anything to do with me, she didn't care about me.

> When I got moved away it was really upsetting for me, but the thing is, to be honest, I wasn't really, really upset, it was numbing. I thought it would be a worst nightmare to go into care, and suddenly it's happening. To be honest, if I'm really honest, it was too quick to actually feel any emotion. I was more worried about what's it going to be like? Where am I going? I was crying when I left because I was really upset and gave them a hug and everything, I felt angry at them at the same time, but really upset with them. I didn't know which to feel, I was just, 'Why are you doing this, don't you love me?' It was really upsetting.

Living away from home

Three young people had settled in foster care and one young woman described the settling-in period:

> Well, it was a bit awkward at first, to be honest, coming and living with people you don't know at all. It's a bit of pressure. It's more awkward because you have to get on with them. You're going to live with them so you have to get on with them, you have to adjust to their house rules, and how they live and everything. They are very nice and welcoming. But it's just weird. I'm really settled and I can have a laugh. It's good. I feel a bit more relaxed here than at home, because at home I feel much more tense. I can be myself but not exactly because I don't know if it's turning into an argument or something.

Two of the young people wanted to return home but the "short break" had now stretched to over a year and it was difficult for them to find a way back. The "short break" seemed to be becoming permanent and they were unsure of how they could return home. One young woman said:

> It was brilliant the first couple of months, because I got away with a lot more stuff than you do when you [are living with parents]. It was a bit like a holiday, to be honest, and then it was harder to go back then. It was at that point I thought that it had all been ruined already, even though, to be honest with you, I would have wanted to probably go home at that point.

There seemed to have been missed opportunities for reunification. One young man said:

> When I wanted to go back, everyone [professionals] was against it, no-one wanted me to go back. Me and my mum wanted each other back, but everyone was against it, saying 'No'.

Five of the young people did not make positive relationships with their foster carers and placements quickly disrupted. All five had had multiple foster and residential placements. One young man described the next disruption:

> *It was weird at first . . . I was room-bound; you would see me on the Xbox just not participating with the family. It was like I was a houseguest, just staying, as if it was a hotel, staying in my room, don't even talk to them. Then things started going from bad to worse, like basically I kept staying up late and not being able to sleep, waking up, going downstairs having midnight snacks. I've got OCD so I get obsessed with all my possessions, and they tried to take them away from me . . . I started shouting and screaming at the foster people.*

Another young man described some of the eight placements he had had since leaving his adoptive family:

> *One I was too old for, the other one, yes, I had a lot of fights there, because I just didn't like it there, and then the other one I just went into foster care. My aunt took me on because we did a lot of criminal damage there and it was either that or they pressed charges if I didn't move out straight away, so that's why I had a full care order put on me and moved.*

Two young women did not receive any post-adoption services at the time they left their adoptive families (aged 15 and 16). They came to the attention of children's services through safeguarding or housing services. One was placed directly into supported housing and the other in a self-contained flat on her own. They described the detrimental impact of these placements:

> *They put me in supported housing in a hostel full of drugs, violence, the worst you can think of, everything you can think of. I was around kinds of people . . . people who would steal off you, people who would hurt you, psychologically abuse you . . . and because I was vulnerable [I still am very vulnerable] and get very lonely . . . people take advantage. I saw things I had never seen in my whole life. I didn't get any choice of going into care. I*

didn't get any help, just got put straight into the hostel, as they said I was homeless.

I was put in a self-contained flat on my own ... Going from having adoptive parents constantly on my back saying I couldn't go out, to having no controls, no boundaries. I got into things I shouldn't have ... alcohol, drugs, skiving school, going out with friends, men – very dangerous. I put myself in very dangerous situations. They tried to force me into sex but I didn't and I don't know how I survived that. I went on an ecstasy binge and I was snorting MDMA. I overdosed and I was rushed into hospital and my heart stopped for two minutes.

Young people who left their adoptive families were very vulnerable. Three young people who had tried to find their birth parents found that the reality did not match their fantasy. All three were rejected again by their birth mothers and instead ended up being targeted by gangs or individuals who wanted to take advantage of their vulnerability, and they were subjected to further abuse. Recollections included:

Then I went to a hostel and got in with the wrong crowd – thieving and drugs – but I was lucky not to get caught. I was scared of this [older] guy – he preyed on people in the hostel. He befriended me, he forced drugs on me, amphetamines, coke, and then he wanted me to go out robbing. He'd go out scouting during the day and then he would come back and tell me exactly where he wanted me to go and if I didn't do it he threatened to kick my head in. So I was scared and I couldn't report it. 'If you do report me, you're dead.' But then I told him to get lost and he beat me up. My social worker dragged me into the police station to make a statement, but I was so scared. Then they moved me to another hostel to get away but I met similar people in the next hostel ... got kicked out of that hostel ... moved back with my adoptive parents but it only lasted four weeks, and then shared accommodation but I didn't like that ... I felt like an outsider, I shouldn't be there. Who am I?

*At the time I felt like I had a place there [at her birth mothers']
but when I look back now but I just wanted to know what it would
feel like to be there, see what they were really like, when there
were no social workers around. Were they different inside? After
a while, things started changing and they started showing who
they actually are, what they are really like. It took a while for me
to realise . . . Where I've been so abused in the past, even when I
was with my adoptive parents I got abused by other people who
they still don't know about . . . But you get used to things; I
thought this is a natural thing . . . basically an everyday thing.*

Social workers did recognise that independent living was disastrous
for one young person and moved her to supported lodgings – a
placement that she thought had saved her. Being treated as one of the
family, being cooked for and eating together were very important for
her. She said:

*They found me supported lodgings living in a family's home and
I moved in. They cooked for me. It was weird, being in someone's
house, seeing people in the morning in their dressing gowns; I
hadn't lived with anyone for so long. But I tell you what, they
were the BEST people. I love them so much, I'm seeing them
later. They were perfect . . . there were some boundaries, but
not enough for me to hate them. I got used to it . . . and they had
kids same sort of age as me and I got on really well with the
daughter. And they were a family and . . . they called me their
bonus daughter. She was German and bonus means step! It was
really nice and absolutely brilliant and I didn't want to leave. I
liked the way they cooked for me and we all ate together around
the table and that is so important to me. If I have kids, I'm going
to make sure that happens.*

All but one of the nine young people who had become looked after
were able to identify benefits of being in care. One young man
compared his life to that of his previous friends who went to school
and lived at home. He said:

I live in a nicer area. I ride motorbikes on a daily basis, I get £50 a week, and I've got a tattoo now . . . I've got more friends than I ever had. I have a lot more links and I know where they can get me [drugs, weapons, alcohol]. I'm more independent, I'm looking for jobs, and I'm looking for courses. I wouldn't be doing that if I was living with my adoptive parents, granted I would be in college, but I wouldn't be looking for jobs on my own, I wouldn't be on my own, I would still be, 'Mum, can you cook this for me?' But now, I'm cooking for myself, I'm fending for myself, so granted, this has advantages.

The young woman who had left abusive adoptive parents said:

I'm glad I left. When I was there, they had marked out my future for me . . . you are going to do A levels in these subjects, go to this university. I was being bullied at school because I was adopted and timid. Because my adoptive parents were SO controlling I was never able to have the social life the rest of them had . . . going to parties . . . I was never allowed out after school, I had no social life, so I couldn't build those friendship connections. So [other kids] bullied me because I was different. It was no wonder I bunked off school a lot . . . there was no escape. When I did go back, I was a completely different person. I plucked up courage, I'd redone my hair, and I started saying, 'You can't say that to me'. I became a lot stronger person. I should have been this person all my life. I shouldn't have been held back. I wasn't allowed to speak when I wanted to, express an opinion.

Other young people thought that being in care had brought more opportunities. One young man had been given the opportunity to shadow the local MP, had been a delegate to the United Nations (UN), and had spoken at conferences about children in care. He said:

I think I gained most of my skills and knowledge and experiences from being with my adoptive family, who have taught me knowledge, emotions, street smart and being part of a family.

And then going back into care taught me different skills, and so I've more skills from the two.

A few young people were also complimentary about the quality of social work support, for example, saying:

But the best person was my leaving care worker, he has been inspiring ... They did get me counselling and I opened up more than I had ever done to anybody and he was great and he said to my social worker that he was worried about my mental state. I was on the verge of a breakdown.

Support

Young people were asked about the support that they or their parents had received before they had left home. Eight of the young people thought that they or their parents should have been given more support and that this might have meant that they would have been able to stay within their families. Young people said:

My mum and dad asked for social services help a lot for six years ... but the social services turned them away and said, 'It's your kid, deal with it' ... [They needed] support and strategies. I wasn't your average toddler or kid, I had issues, and I had big problems because of what happened earlier in life.

There was a school counsellor, didn't really do much, I used it as an excuse to get out of lessons ... Social services actually doing stuff that would have helped, instead of just sitting around ... they just did nothing about it, they didn't even suggest things like a foster placement, etc. Financial help as well.

Other young people had been offered therapy and either refused it or thought that it made the situation worse:

I never had any support in school, I was referred to a counsellor in school, but she made it worse. She didn't understand where I was trying to come from and most people don't get that about me.

If I'd more help in coping with my emotions, there was no-one I could explain to. One of the schools tried but the person stopped working there and I got angry.

The capacity to make use of therapy was also affected by early adverse experiences, as one young person explained:

We went to see family therapy and different types of therapy but in the therapies I felt like I couldn't say what I wanted to say . . . I was seen on my own but I thought if I said something they would tell . . . I couldn't trust. It's affected me in later years because I couldn't trust. It's affected all my relationships, as soon as I get close to someone I push the people I love away. Then as soon as I get to that intimate point . . . I think I don't like this.

Other young people thought that post-adoption support was entirely for their parents, and that they were forgotten. They thought that there should have been two workers, one for the young person and one for the parents. One young person observed that, while she had only been able to have a support worker for six weeks, her parents were able to have ongoing support. She said:

There was also a social worker working with my mum but she was always shouting at me and telling me off . . . for upsetting my mum. She was biased on my mum's side and the social worker was for my mum, not for me. I was made to feel that everything was my fault – just like now I'm made to feel everything is my fault.

Two of the young people, who had had very unstable early lives, thought that they should have been removed from their adoptive families much earlier. They did not prioritise stability in the same way that social workers or other professionals did. One young person, when asked what could have happened (at the time of the disruption) to improve matters, said:

> Put me back in care . . . Get me out . . . I wouldn't have minded that. I was used to that . . . I don't like being in one place.

The young person who had been abused by her adoptive parents was asked if she had tried to tell or get help. She expressed her fear of what might have happened if she had told and said:

> I opened up to one of my friends once but she didn't know what to do. She wasn't mature enough to deal with it. She was 13 and had lived quite a sheltered life . . . and she laughed about it. I wasn't able to put across what was happening in a way that people could understand. I couldn't describe . . . I didn't have words. There was a counsellor [in school] . . . I opened up to her. There was only so much she could do. I was scared about what would happen . . . if I wasn't taken away and I was sent back . . . what would happen when they found out I had told someone? I did try to use ChildLine – they basically gave me no support. There was an advert on TV when I was younger with the desks that were stopping parents getting to their children . . . so I phoned them up and they said, 'Why don't you phone the police?' That would have made things worse. Once I ran away and the police took me back and it was SO bad that night, I don't want to go back there again.

Talking and thinking about adoption and adoptive parents

Young people were asked what they liked and disliked about being adopted. Five of the 12 young people liked being adopted and could not think of anything they disliked. They said:

> It's cool, strange, you're special from everyone else, and if they take the mick out of you because of it . . . You get a thump.

> My family, I suppose, that's the best part about it.

I like being adopted; I haven't got anything bad to say about it really.

If I'd stayed with the people who gave birth to me, I don't know whether I would be here.

It's such a positive thing to be adopted rather than be in care . . . even if someone is a little bit older, like I was. It's been such a positive thing that I was adopted rather than just carried on being in care my whole life. It's better to have a stable family than be in care and seeing your mum every now and again, it's just . . . and I've had both experiences and I think that it's just a lot better to be – I just think adoption is good.

Most of the young people could think of things they liked and disliked about adoption. While some liked the way that the adoption marked them out as different, others found that to be what they disliked most, saying it was "weird". Young people also disliked not feeling connected to their adoptive family, being prevented from having contact with their birth family, and having adoption often in their thoughts. For example, one young man, who thought that what he most liked about adoption was the security, especially because his house had glass that could not be smashed for "someone to get in", also said that what he disliked was:

At first when I was younger, and I turned the wrong way, it did bother me. I didn't want to be adopted. A lot of other people still had their families and I wanted to be like them. But now it doesn't bother me.

Two young women chose to comment on their physical similarity or dissimilarity from their adoptive mother. One young woman was proud that they looked so much alike and that people outside the family never questioned their relationship. She said:

I look a lot like my adopted mum, a lot like her, and I went into a midwife appointment with her the other day and said, 'This is my mum', and she said, 'Well, yes obviously'.

Another young woman, who often had adoption in her thoughts, wondered what others made of her situation when she looked so dissimilar to her adoptive parents. She did not like the strangeness of adoption and said:

> But being adopted, it's weird, like parents' evening and stuff. It's mainly people saying, 'You don't look alike', that's the thing that really annoys me. And you go round . . . school, look around the community, wherever you go you always see parents and you know [they and their children] look alike. Me and my brother, we look the same, probably got the same nose and face, it's nice.

Describing adoptive mothers and fathers

Young people were asked which adjectives they would use to describe their adoptive parents. Most young people described their adoptive mothers using only positive adjectives such as lovely, kind, generous, fun, and caring. Three young people used positive and negative words, saying, on the one hand, "caring" and "loving", but also "lacking in understanding" and "controlling". Two young people used only negative words to describe their adoptive mothers, describing them as "controlling", "manipulative", "judgemental", "critical" and "abusive".

Adoptive fathers were mainly described as "nice", "very lovable", "easygoing", "funny", and "caring". Their negative qualities for five young people were usually in relation to how they allowed their wives to dominate and control and they were described as "weak", "distant", "unable to show he cares", but also "stroppy" and "annoying".

Young people were asked about their current relationship with their adoptive parents: whether they thought of them as mum and dad and whether they had any contact with them. Four young people's relationships had improved since they had left home, including one young man who was hoping to be moved much closer to his adoptive family. He said that it was important for him to have his mum close and said:

> I'm moving to be near them, I'm my mum's boy! My dad is just as good. To be fair, I don't know what to say about him, he's fun to be around. It's nice to be this age where I can just go and knock

about with my dad and just have laughs. I'm making up for lost time here . . . we've got the best relationship we've ever had. We've kept it alive; they will always be my parents now, no matter what happened they will always be my mum and dad . . . I appreciate what my mum and dad have done, because they gave me a second chance.

The young pregnant woman, when asked if anyone would be with her during her labour, said:

Yes, my mum, because . . . I've realised that the only person who makes me feel better is my mum, just how it is with everyone I suppose. So I think that she's the only person who could relatively calm me down when I'm in labour.

Most young people were not hoping to return to live with their adoptive parents. They were already (or planning to be) living independently, but they were often being supported by their adoptive parents financially and emotionally. Parents were acting as guarantors on flats for four young people. One young person described the support he still got from his parents:

I never went back, but she only lives round the corner, and I still call them Mum and Dad, so I do still go and see Mum and Dad. They are still family, they still give me birthday presents, they still give me Christmas presents, they still take me shopping and they still are Mum and Dad . . . They never ever said, 'You can't come back'. They never said, 'We don't want anything to do with you any more, you're not our son'. They've always been there for me if I've needed anything, always been there for me.

Interviewer: *In what ways have they been there for you?*

If I was unwell, 'Come and stay here', like I stay for Christmas and my birthday they let me go down, they always get me things. They're there if I need to talk to them about anything . . . They come here, they actually helped me move in here. They brought me quite a lot of things in here.

Three young people had decided to stop calling their adoptive parents mum and dad from the day they went back into care. They were angry and felt rejected. They thought that no matter what they had done, their parents should not have given up on them. However, only two young people had no contact with their adoptive parents and most were having regular contact, although relationships were still fragile. They said:

> Things started off bad, then we started building bridges, and it's gone downhill again.

> Yes, I still go up and see them, Christmas and birthdays, but it has taken a very long time to get to this point.

The young person abused by her adoptive parents referred to them by their first names and was having some contact with them but on her terms. She said:

> Since I left, I've been in contact with them a little bit . . . I've made one call every three–six months. At the end of the day I still care, although I might not love them any more . . . I would never go back to my adoptive parents or make them a big part of my life like if I get married . . . I wouldn't have them involved in my life.

Four of the young people regretted their previous actions, saying that they wished they had not been aggressive, or got into trouble, or run away. Two of them said:

> Looking back, I respect everything they did for us and if it wasn't for them I wouldn't be who I am now.

> I regret some of the stuff I've done to my adopted parents, but you got to learn.

Talking and thinking about birth families

The young people were asked whether they had been able to talk about their birth families with their adoptive parents. Two young people stated that, although their adoptive parents had always been very open in talking about their birth families, it had not always satisfied their thirst for information. One young person said:

> Brilliant, they've always been really forward . . . with informa-
> tion, and just wanting to talk to me about it and stuff. I did
> ask a couple of times, but there's a lot of things they didn't know
> about . . . but there was quite big things that they didn't
> know about.

Another young person could remember nothing of his early life and found out he was adopted at the age of seven when he came across papers connected with his adoption. His adoptive mother told him that she had intended to tell him when he was older. She had not known how to tell such a young child about the severe abuse he had suffered. He said:

> I found my life story work, and when I read it when I was seven,
> it messed me up a bit . . . I just saw paperwork with my name. So
> I ran up to my room with it, and read it myself without anyone
> knowing. Then my mum found out and she tried to sit down and
> explain, but I wasn't having it, because then I realised you're not
> my mum. It's not what you want to hear, that two strangers are
> looking after you, not given birth to you. But I see my mum as my
> biological mum now; I have done for years, and my dad.

Other young people said that the topic of birth family was a hard subject to raise, as one of them described:

> No, it was never talked about, and when I was 14 I wanted to
> know more and what I found out from her was a load of lies.
> They lied about [sister] and said she was hurt in my real mum's
> stomach. I found out from my best friend's mum that [sister]
> was seriously hurt when she was three weeks old. My real mum
> and five others picked her up and she threw her and she had
> traumatic brain injury.

Two young people had had regular face-to-face contact with birth relatives during their childhood. One young man had seen his birth father every six weeks, which he enjoyed, and another young woman had had contact with grandparents. These arrangements were said to have worked well for birth and adoptive families. One of the young people said:

It's weird because people say that you don't usually get contact [with birth family] when you're adopted, but I do with my grandmas. It's really nice actually, to talk to somebody who you're actually related to.

However, it was not easy for most young people to talk about their birth mothers with their adoptive mothers. Even when the adoption was considered an "open adoption", communication about birth mothers was described as awkward and difficult, as in the following example:

Talking about my mum to her, I felt like she will feel bad, because she knows she's not my real mum and it will remind her.

Some young people did not want to think or talk about birth parents. Two young people had chosen (after being given the option to meet) to have no contact with birth parents or with siblings who had not lived in the same adoptive family. They said:

I'd rather not think about it, to be honest. It makes me angry. She was 16 when she had me, and we had three dads so it just makes me angry to think about it.

There's just one person I never want to see until the day I die and that's my birth dad.

Other young people were thinking about birth families and about what life might have been like had they remained with their birth parents. These thoughts occurred particularly when young people were in conflict with their adoptive parents. As one young woman said:

> Sometimes, when I used to have arguments with them I used to always think (you know one of those thoughts that you don't think out loud), would my mum have treated me better than this? Would my mum have treated me worse than this? Would my birth family have treated me any differently to this, any nicer? Would it be different to this?

After having left their adoptive home, five of the young people had traced birth family members. Three young people had always wanted to find their birth parents to see what it would be like to live with them, but they had either been rejected again or found that they were not what they had hoped. Young people explained what had happened when they made contact:

> When I left at 15 years and went to XX, my real parents came round, and they, like, used me as a weapon against each other. I'd be standing in the middle of a room and they would literally pull me from side to side . . . 'Sit next to me' . . . 'No, sit next to me' . . . I asked them: 'Why did you hurt me?' They blamed each other: 'It's your dad's fault', 'It's your mum's fault'. I got angry and told them to take full responsibility for their own actions. I asked them questions about things I could remember.

> She [birth mother] rejected me . . . saying she didn't have room for me. She said, 'I can't give you what you need'. I said, 'All I need is love and, if you can't give me that, I'm not in the right place'.

> I see one of them [brothers] all the time. I got in contact with my birth mum at about 16 years. I asked my social worker if she could find her and it went from there. Mum has been able to keep one of the six other children she had . . . and she is getting there. [With birth father] we have an on-and-off relationship and we are not speaking currently.

The young people who had traced birth family members had made choices about whom they were going to stay in touch with. Only one young person described her relationship with her birth mother as good. One young man wanted to stay in touch with a sister he had recently contacted but described what had happened when his birth mother rang asking if she could see him on his birthday:

> She [birth mother] called up yesterday and she wanted to see me on my birthday but I've already got my [adoptive] parents coming up.

Three of the young people still had hopes of tracing siblings who had been born after they had been placed for adoption or of rebuilding relationships with siblings from whom they had been separated. One young person said:

> I think me and my brother were too old. We told them that we did not want to be adopted but they thought it was the best thing for us. And we were separated from our other two brothers and we are trying to build those bridges back again but it's so hard. I've missed so much of their lives . . . my brother is, like, 'Do you remember when . . . ?' I go 'No, I wasn't there'.

However, there were more concerns about the lack of contact with siblings who still lived with the adoptive family. Although young people described arguments and fights whilst they lived together, they also admitted missing siblings now that they had left. One of the young people was very angry that her adoptive mother was limiting her contact with her sister and said:

> You can't split sisters up . . . and I only have contact with my sister once a week for an hour but that is down to [mother]. I'm now 17 and I can't see her Christmas or New Year or on my 18th birthday and I have got a solicitor involved.

Young people's advice to prospective adoptive parents

Young people were asked what advice they would give to prospective adoptive parents. They said:

- *Show them the same love as if it was a kid who was actually their own.*
- *Wait for the child to come to you. Treat them as your own. Work out what they need. Some kids need to be told, 'You are beautiful'.*
- *Children will turn into teenagers one day. Make sure you're in the right place, you've thought about every option. Make sure you've got a lot of support, because if they have come from a bad place, they could be quite challenging, and adopt babies not toddlers, I would.*
- *Take the time to know the person you are adopting and tell them in depth when they are 14 or so why they were adopted, filling in the gaps.*
- *Make sure you really, really want the child . . . and don't give up at the first sign of trouble. That's what my parents did. They gave up on me.*
- *To understand what you are taking on. To understand that it's not going to be just like having your own baby, there's probably a little bit more that you need to deal with and maybe a little bit more that you need to prepare yourself for and make sure that you're the type of person that can do that. Because if you're not, then you're going to have a hard time and so is the kid.*
- *If the child tries, let them see their birth family more often but not too much, as it might break the bond. But if they don't see them enough, that might break the bond and then there's no trust.*
- *Be ready to deal with all people and be sensitive and understanding, and listen to them. The most important thing is to listen and just be ready for anything and just get to know them before you actually assume things and decide what's best for them and decide what they like and what they don't like.*
- *Make sure you pick wisely. Be prepared to look after everything that they will need and everything, sometimes they will have stuff like I*

have, or apparently I've got anxiety stuff and all that kind of thing, separation issues. Make sure you're actually able to become a parent in a way. Make sure you're ready to be a parent.

Young people's advice to a child about to be adopted

Young people were also asked what advice they would give to a child who was about to be adopted. The young people found this question much harder to answer and wanted to know the age of the child. The question was often re-phrased to ask what could have been said to them at the time they were adopted:

- *I really don't know, say if I was about seven and someone asked me that, I needed support, I needed help, the right help, and the right people should have stepped up and gave it to me. But they didn't, and there was only my mum and dad in the family and they was trying so hard.*
- *Don't be afraid to talk about it . . . if anything happens, you have to address it. You can't keep thinking it will go away – it will catch up with you. I went on for eight–nine years thinking one day I would wake up and it would all have changed.*
- *If you're in trouble, ring this number. Give them a pack . . . have a children in care council for adopted children . . . have mentors.*
- *These people are going to take good care of you and make you part of the family.*
- *Don't get yourself labelled; it's nothing to be ashamed of.*
- *Try and just accept it, just go with the flow, go with what is going on and it should work out OK.*
- *Give them a chance . . . because my parents, they're really nice and I'm glad I call them a family now and I'm glad. I'm happy with them and I'm happy where I am, and met loads of nice friends and teachers and people and everybody. The main thing is give them a chance, get to know them before you decide whether you want to live with them or not, because mine turned out to be really good, so I'm happy about that, so I can say yes. I could say, 'Look where I am now, it's a really good place'.*

Other comments

Young people were asked if there was anything else they wanted to say at the end of the interview, and wanted the following recorded:

- Young people thought that they were often not listened to and not believed, especially in relation to adoption. They wanted to have a voice in adoption and thought that any child over four years should have to agree to adoption. They also thought that there should be more in-depth investigations if they made a complaint about a social worker.
- There was a suggestion that all adopted children should have an appointment to see a social worker once a year, away from home, and be seen on their own.

Summary

- Twelve young people who had experienced an adoption disruption were interviewed. They were aged 15–23 years old and all had been placed for adoption over the age of three years old. Since leaving their adoptive family, most of the young people had had unstable accommodation and had moved around placements or flats/squats, but at the time of the interview, young people wanted to get their lives back on a stable track.
- Pregnancy or the birth of a child had made two young people reassess their lives and strengthen their connections with their adoptive family. One young person had recently returned to his adoptive home and another was moving to live closer to his adoptive parents. The remaining young people were living in foster care, supported lodgings or independently. Only one young person had no contact with his adoptive family.
- Criminal records were adversely affecting the employment and education of three young men. Four young people were not in education, employment or training (NEET), while the rest were in college or employment.
- Three of the young people had been placed directly into hostels/independent flats when they left their adoptive home, as the LA had

treated them as homeless. This left them open to further abuse and being targeted by those who prey on vulnerable young people. They had not been eligible for leaving care services, were struggling financially, and could not see a way of being able to attend a university full time.

- Young people were vulnerable and spoke about depression, loneliness and self-harm. Two of the young people were trying to escape violent partners.

- Most of the young people said that at the time they were adopted nobody had really asked them if they wanted to be adopted. They stated that they had not wanted adoption and some had wanted to stay with their birth mothers. After they had left their adoptive families, four of them had traced their birth families but found that the reality did not match their fantasy and were rejected again.

- Before being placed for adoption, most of the young people had experienced neglect and abuse, many moves in foster care, and failed reunifications. As young adults, they had come to understand that this had affected their capacity to trust (including their ability to make use of therapeutic interventions) and make relationships (with their adoptive parents and now in their intimate relationships) and made them vulnerable to further abuse. They had difficulty feeling they belonged anywhere.

- Half of the young people had been bullied at school because of their adoptive status.

- Young people had left home generally because relationships had become too difficult. Some of the young people said that their early abuse and neglect had negatively affected the way they felt about mothers; others described themselves as volcanoes with rage burning inside; and others were desperate to find their birth mothers and had run away. Exclusions and difficulties in school had also put more pressure on the families and young people. One young person had been abused by her adoptive parents.

- Three of the adoptive parents were described as having significant mental health problems of their own. Young people also described feeling that other children in the family were favoured more than them.

- Most young people stated that they had difficulty living in a family, kicked against firm boundaries and discipline, and had had problems in their relationships. Some now regretted their behaviour and wished they could turn the clock back.
- Young people wanted more support for their adoptive parents and for themselves. They would have liked their own social worker when relationships had been difficult at home.
- Four of the young people were saddened that they had become looked after and that their parents had not stuck with them. However, two other young people thought that they should have been removed much earlier and that social workers were too keen on preserving the family. All but one of the nine young people who had become looked after identified benefits of being in care.
- Some young people readily agreed to going into foster care, as they saw it as relief from the intense arguments. However, there seemed to have been little work done on reunification. Young people thought that sometimes social workers had blamed their adoptive parents for the disruption and had wanted to "punish" them.

15 Providing post-adoption support – the views of adoption managers

We now turn to the views of adoption managers from our sample local authorities, 12 of whom were interviewed on the provision of adoption support services. All the local authorities (LAs) had volunteered to be part of the study and therefore may not be representative of adoption services in England.

Adoption services in our sample LAs ranged from those whose adoption services had been assessed by Ofsted as outstanding to those which were thought to be under-performing. The variation could be seen on two indicators of LA performance on the 2012 adoption scorecards (DfE, 2012). The indicators showed that, in the sample LAs, the proportion of children who had waited less than 21 months between entering care and moving in with their adoptive family varied from 5–80 per cent. On another indicator, between 5–25 per cent of children leaving care in the LAs had been adopted. In 2012, the number of children adopted from our sample of LAs ranged from less than 100 to more than 460 children.

Structure of services

The 12 LAs had structured their adoption services in different ways: five had a single adoption team that recruited prospective adoptive parents, matched and placed children and provided support; whilst the other seven LAs had separate teams for recruitment/placement and post-adoption support.

Managers (n = 5) with a single adoption team thought there were advantages to this structure, as it provided an opportunity for continuity of worker through the different stages. It also enabled workers to develop professional skills in all aspects of adoption work.

Managers (n = 7) with a separate team that provided post-adoption support often provided support to other kinds of placements too. For example, post-order support was provided to those with special guardianship or residence orders or to looked after children generally.

There was also variation in whether the LA provided birth parent and access to records counselling, as most had commissioned this out to VAAs. All mentioned the large and growing workload related to contact services and there seemed to be some successful letterbox and direct contact services. For example, in one LA, birth parents were encouraged to meet with the adoptive parents and the adoption social worker, to ensure that contact arrangements were firmly established.

Some managers commented on the support for their service from elected members, which had resulted in investment beyond that provided by the adoption reform grant. Adoption services were being expanded. More commonly, however, managers reported small cuts to their services. Some managers were concerned that they were likely to face significant cuts in their budgets in 2015. There was concern that innovations supported by the Adoption Reform Grant might not be able to continue.

Staffing and skill set of adoption teams

The adoption workforce was generally said to be very stable with little turnover of staff. There were three models of service provision.

Model A – social work teams

In these LAs, the adoption team/s comprised qualified social workers, qualified and/or unqualified family support/resource workers, and administrators. Some adoption agencies had a noticeable imbalance between the large number of social workers in the recruitment/placing teams who found adoptive families for many children and the small post-adoption team.

Model B – social work plus

In this model, the adoption team/s comprised qualified social workers, unqualified family support workers and administrators, plus trained counsellors and/or a clinical or educational psychologist or psychotherapist who joined the team for one or two days a week. Psychologists were able to provide consultations for staff and/or adoptive parents, for example, a clinical psychologist was in one team for two days a week, providing consultation for staff and a link to the local CAMHS. The manager explained that one of the benefits of having a psychologist in the team was that: 'She can help us do referrals so they hit the right spot and she can talk to people. She will be able to point us in the right direction.' In another LA, the psychologist saw adoptive parents prior to them being matched with an older child or with a child with specific needs and then saw the family again, post-placement.

Having therapists and psychologists based in the team brought many additional benefits. Managers spoke about how much they and the team had learnt about child development and attachment from close contact with other professionals. Psychologists/therapists brought students with them and some students had contributed to adoption support services, for example, by running groups for girls whilst they were on placement.

Model C – multi-disciplinary
In a few LAs, post-adoption support was provided by a multidisciplinary service staffed by full-time clinical psychologists, therapists, such as family or art therapists, and social workers. These teams also tended to provide support to children in other types of permanent placements or to looked after children more generally.

Skills
Adoption managers were very proud of their services and the high level of skills in their teams. It was very noticeable that all of the teams had developed skills in therapeutic interventions based on attachment theory. The most popular type of training for staff was Dyadic Developmental Psychotherapy (DDP),[62] with many post-adoption support workers trained at least to Level 1. Teams were also skilled in Theraplay and filial therapy. In one LA, a member of staff was trained

---

62 http://www.dyadicdevelopmentalpsychotherapy.org/

in Non-Violent Resistance – an approach to work with aggressive and violent young people.[63] The approach was also being piloted in another authority. This is an important development, as violent behaviour was a key factor in many adoption disruptions in this study.

DDP was widespread and a preferred way of working for many. It was particularly liked by adoption workers because it provided a way of making sense of the complex and sometimes contradictory behaviours that children displayed. DDP also offered practical ways of working with adoptive parents and was thought by the managers to be liked by adoptive parents as it "made sense" and did not apportion blame. Many managers stated that the principles of DDP were embedded in their team's approach to adoption support. In some LAs, those working in the recruitment team had also been trained in DDP so that they could examine an adopter's reflective capacity, while other social workers used the Attachment Style Interview (Bifulco, 2012)[64] in their assessments of prospective adopters.

A few LAs were widening training beyond the adoption teams, in the belief that it was important for frontline workers to understand the basics of work based on attachment theory. For example, in one LA, staff across children's services had been trained in Theraplay, since this was one of the attachment-based therapies forming a cornerstone of specialist CAMHS provision for adoptive families. This had resulted in a range of childcare professionals working in partnership to provide appropriate intervention for adoptive and foster families. In another LA, therapists from the Institute of Theraplay had been commissioned to train 30 frontline workers. The intention behind this investment was for those workers to become the "permanency champions" within the department.

Managers wanted to ensure that training in their teams stayed up to date and that skills were developed. New staff needed to be trained and managers wanted to ensure that those who were qualified at DDP Level 1 could achieve Levels 2 or 3. However, there was currently little

---

63 www.partnershipprojectsuk.com/info-for-pros.html
64 www.attachmentstyleinterview.com/pdf%20files/ASI_for_Adoption_summary.
pdf

opportunity for advanced training. Some workers had paid for their own training.

Having staff working in a therapeutic way with adoptive parents did not always fit easily within children's services. One manager explained:

The social work model of supervision is about safeguarding, accountability and care planning rather than people's internal world. We are often sitting with people in acute crisis . . . we are being bombarded by trauma, sadness, disappointment and then go away into our own families and just carry that.

Another manager thought that there was a cultural resistance within social work to clinical supervision. When such supervision had been requested, the response had been to remind staff that they were social workers and not therapists. In challenging this assertion, this manager said:

I say look at the work they are doing! There are workers who do the most amazing work and one of them pays regularly (for supervision) out of her own pocket. That is the work of adoption support, unless you are just going to do assessments and tick boxes and then say, 'but we can't provide it'. Adoption support is therapeutic, there's a bit that's practical but virtually everything has a therapeutic base. We need a shift to recognise that.

One LA held group supervision sessions four times a year where the team came together to reflect and consider each other's cases. Elsewhere, a new two-hour forum (led by a service manager) was being planned where cases could be brought for discussion – the first hour was focused on the child's history and the second was spent on planning. Both these innovations had been well received.

Placements out of area
Most of the adoption managers said that notifications from other LAs of children placed in their area had improved. Notifications were received more frequently at the time of placement but were often

forgotten at the time of the adoption order. If notified of an adoptive family living in their area, managers stated that families were contacted and asked if they wanted to join the agency's mailing list. Some managers also requested a copy of the support plan at the time of the notification. However, managers commented that some LAs were still failing to give any notifications and they were unaware of some families until an adoptive parent rang in crisis. Only one of the LAs was proactive in notifying another LA when the three-year period was up, unless support services were already being provided or agreed at the time of the placement. Some managers thought that they would need adoptive parents' permission to contact other LAs and that it would be too resource intensive. Yet in one LA, about half the families on the caseload of the post-adoption support team concerned children placed into that county by other local authorities. Post-adoption support was often being provided to children who the LA had not placed and to adopters they had not assessed or approved.

Placing children out of area was mainly a concern because of the unavailability of CAMHS in some areas for adopted children. There was concern that perhaps the family and child were being set up to fail, particularly when it was expected that the child would need therapeutic support. The rule stating that, for the first three years, the placing authority is responsible for funding support services and then financial responsibility shifts to the receiving authority was unpopular. One manager said:

> The three-year rule is nonsense, as there is a lack of clarity. Take therapy: is this a health or an adoption support responsibility? There are children we've placed in a London borough where there is a CAMHS and specialist worker and after the three years, they say it is our [the manager's authority's] responsibility because it is a health need. But there are other children. First of all CAMHS say, 'There is nothing for you to buy anyway, you'll have to buy it privately and if you do start paying for it, it will remain your responsibility'! It doesn't make sense. I think we should establish that therapy is a health need and that

*responsibility should transfer at the time of the adoption order
... You can have so many permutations – where the LA is the
placing agency, and then there is the LA where the adoptive
parents live, maybe a VAA providing some services and some
adopters live in a different GP area.*

Support services provided by the adoption teams

All the adoption teams provided a range of support services to adoptive families. Some services appeared to be universal, in that all the
adoption managers mentioned their provision, although not all were
provided in-house. There were also support services that had
developed in individual local authorities and were not widespread. All
the agencies were providing means-tested adoption allowances, but
only one manager mentioned that they encouraged adoptive parents
when appropriate to apply for Disability Living Allowance (DLA). She
reported that they had successfully supported adopters on appeal for
the higher band. Another LA employed specialist welfare rights
workers to complete financial assessments related to adoption financial support, and to support adopters to claim all appropriate welfare
benefits.

All the agencies ran occasional social events such as summer
picnics and Christmas parties. Most managers said that the events
were well attended: one manager giving an example of 150 people
attending the summer picnic. Newsletters were sent to all adopters (by
email or hard copy) providing news of training, events and activity
days, and enabling people to sign up.

All provided intensive telephone support, which was often appreciated, not only because of the opportunity to "offload", but because
parents were talking to somebody who understood adoption. Parents
sometimes liked coming into the office to discuss difficulties, as well as
having the opportunity for home visits from their adoption worker.

If adoptive families needed more support, a worker was allocated
and adoption social workers used their skills to work with parents.
One local authority employed adoption support staff who had been
family centre workers, but had specialised in working with adopters to

build attachments with newly placed children. They also provided "in the home" support and parenting strategies for any adoptive family with children under 12. Two adoption support teams had used the Bath and North East Somerset[65] "Locate model" to develop their support services, although they had not been able to provide the regular face-to-face follow-ups that were part of the original model. The Locate model originated from the idea that adopters need a psychologically-based service, as a matter of routine. It did not offer support on the "wait and see" approach, which depends on adoptive parents requesting professional help, but instead anticipated that there were likely to be difficulties. It aimed to deliver mental health services in a non-stigmatising way through routine follow up of adopted children. The Locate model was multi-disciplinary and offered consultation, training and direct therapeutic interventions to children and their parents. Regular consultation with adoptive parents was provided pre- and post-placement (Hudson, 2006). Ironically, although the service was highly regarded, Bath and North East Somerset lost the Locate service when CAMHS was recommissioned and the new provider did not have that skill set within its service. One authority had developed its own parenting support model of three sessions covering issues such as trauma, developmental delay and shame, to provide consistency.

Running support groups

Support groups for adoptive parents ran in all the local authority areas. Some were facilitated by LA post-adoption workers, others by VAA professionals (e.g. staff from the Post-Adoption Centre and After Adoption) and others were adopter-led. Some LAs also provided opportunities for support within adopters' monthly training seminars. There had been experimentation with the format of the support groups, as a few LAs had found that they were not well attended. One area had changed the usual format and for the first half of the meeting the leaders gave a 10-minute presentation on a specific theme (such as

---

65 Bath and North East Somerset was not one of the sample LAs.

the impact of social networking on adopted children), followed by discussion. It was too early to know whether this had been successful. Occasional workshops were also held for the relatives of adoptive families and one LA ran a support group for adoptive fathers.

There were also adoptive mother and toddler groups running in some areas. Managers stated that adopters spoke highly of the opportunity to meet with others in the same situation and they appreciated not having to manage difficult questions about very early development or their experiences of childbirth. An additional benefit was that networks could be established to support adoptive parents as the child developed.

Regular training events

There was variation in the way that training courses were delivered to adoptive parents. Some LAs had opened up all the foster carer training events to adopters and special guardians, and had a specific in-house programme for adopters. Other LAs commissioned individuals to run their regular training programme or commissioned a VAA to provide all the training. Some LAs thought that commissioning out training was very cost-effective and saved a great deal of expensive social work time. Examining cost-effectiveness of adoption support models was not part of this study but is an area that needs further research. Depending on the content of the training, it was delivered either in two-hour seminars, half and full-day events, or in a block of days. Training for adopters' extended family networks was offered in at least one authority. A partnership with libraries also allowed one authority to give adopters free access to a collection of relevant books on adoption issues. This authority also had DVDs made in-house to help adopters understand the perspectives of all parties to adoption, including those of adopted young people.

> ### Typical training courses available for local authority adoptive parents
>
> Caring for children who have experienced trauma, paediatric first aid, baby massage, attachment theory and its application, developing attachment through play and music, post-adoption contact, telling, life story work, working with conflict and angry children, internet safety, the power of music, managing difficult behaviour, safeguarding children, educational issues, Theraplay, sibling rivalry.

Some LAs also ran "big name" events where well-known psychologists provided a whole day's training. A few LAs commissioned Webster Stratton-based parenting programmes, or Safe Base, or a four-day therapeutic parenting programme (caring for children who have experienced trauma, originally developed by the National Child Traumatic Stress Network),[66] and two were piloting AdOpt.[67] Agencies were pleased with adopters' responses to the parenting programmes but also wanted the generic parenting programmes to pay more attention to attachment-related issues and PACE.[68]

The agency's website

All the agencies had a website but many were quite basic. Most of the managers recognised the need to improve their presence on the internet. One LA posted details on their website of all children needing placement so that adopters could be more proactive and not have to wait for their social worker to alert them. Another innovation in one LA was the use of Fronter[69] to enable adopters who were unable to

---

66 www.nctsnet.org/
67 http://adopttraining.org.uk/
68 PACE is an acronym used in Dan Hughes' work (2009) that stands for playfulness, acceptance, curiosity and empathy.
69 Fronter is a virtual learning environment used by many schools. See http:// uk.fronter.info

attend a training session or wanted more information to access resources, for example, on loss and grief, attachment and contact. The manager realised that there was far more Fronter could do to improve the interface between adoptive parents and support services and this was being developed.

Providing activities for children and young people

Most agencies provided some activities for young people. There was the same pattern, with some LAs providing activities in-house and others commissioning out to specialist organisations, and there was variation in the success of these activities. Some LAs had arranged for expensive activities only to find that take-up was poor, whereas others could not keep up with demand. Activities included arts and crafts, rock school, outdoor adventure activities, horse handling for those with special needs and disabilities, youth clubs for older children, groups for children aged 8–11years and under-fives play days (where parents could also meet for coffee).

A few agencies, recognising the need for adoptive parents to have some respite and for adopted children to meet others who were also adopted, were running residential weekends for older children, summer day camps (during the holidays) and activities on Saturdays and Sundays. These activities had proved very popular and were seen as a better way of providing respite than placing children with foster carers.

Respite and shared care

There was generally great reluctance to use foster carers to provide respite or shared care. Social workers did not want to disrupt attachments by placing the child in foster care. It was extremely difficult to ensure that a young person would be cared for by the same carer each time respite was needed and therefore children would experience multiple carers. To receive respite, most LAs also made the child a looked after child and this brought unnecessary bureaucracy and was unsettling for child and family. Only one LA had a more positive view of respite care and were able to use Section 17 in a flexible way to keep adopted children from having looked after status.

Other LAs used other services to give parents some respite. Some paid for daytime child-minding or holidays such as PGL activity holidays. Others were developing young people's activity weekends (see previous section) or mentoring schemes.

Involving adoptive parents in post-adoption support services

There were various ways in which adopters were involved in the delivery of services. Some LAs had involved adopters when post-adoption support services were first established, asking about the kinds of services they would like to see developed. One local authority used comments from evaluations completed by adopters at the end of a piece of work to inform future work. A few LAs also ran a buddy scheme for new adoptive parents. Following a recent consultant's report into recruitment, one LA was informed that adopters preferred learning from peers rather than from social work professionals. The agency was therefore introducing an adopter recruitment mentoring scheme, using adoptive parent volunteers who would be linked up to new applicants during the assessment process. This new scheme would complement the LA's own adopter buddy scheme, which is manned by trained "adopter buddies" who are linked to approved adopters requesting support. The trained adopter buddies are also involved in the preparation groups and one parent sits on the corporate parenting panel to present adopters' views in council meetings.

Another agency found that a series of workshops about parenting teenagers had developed into an adoption support group run by the adoptive parents but financed by the LA. The group was about to become a registered charity and had been actively lobbying MPs and suggesting changes to services.

Educational support

In some LAs, the links with virtual schools were already established and adopted children had always been within their remit. In other areas, these links were only just beginning. Where links were strong, dedicated adoption workers were within the virtual school to ensure that, where appropriate, children had a keyworker in school, a personal education plan and a transition plan. Schools were also encouraged to become more familiar with the principles of attachment theory and strategies within the classroom to use this approach, for example, by using the work of Louise Bomber (2011).

In other LA areas, educational psychologists played a key role. In two LAs, an educational psychologist provided termly one-hour slots for adopters, who could book in for a consultation. The educational psychologist provided advice verbally and in writing for the adoptive parents so that they would know what questions to ask of and from schools. They also provided workshops on educational matters for adoptive parents and contributed to preparation groups. In one area, educational psychologists also took referrals for video interactive guidance for adopted children as a means to improve and support attachments.[70] In the other LA, the educational psychologist also provided intensive case consultations if a child was at the point of exclusion, and occasionally chaired multi-professional meetings.

However, managers noted that not all schools have their own educational psychologist and buying in is expensive. Budget cuts have resulted in some children not being assessed by an educational psychologist until an application for a statement of special educational needs is made. Managers also spoke about the variation in schools, with some being more inclusive and keen not to damage children's self-esteem, while others used more detentions and exclusions.

A more unusual example of educational support was provided by one adoption support team, which had developed a partnership with adult community learning services and libraries. They had designed an event for adopted children in Key Stages 1 and 2 based in the library, with the aim of helping parents engage with young children through reading; this developed literacy skills but also improved relationships. This event was, however, designed to replace a residential event with the same partners for which there was no future budget.

---

70 For information on video interactive guidance, visit www.videointeraction guidance.net/

Child and Adolescent Mental Health Services (CAMHS)

The availability of appropriate CAMH services for looked after and adopted children provoked the most concern. While LA adoption services had become more therapeutic in response to the needs of adoptive families, managers stated that some local CAMHS did not have any clinicians who were trained in helping children with attachment difficulties. Managers mentioned that, in some areas of the country, CAMHS would not accept referrals from children with insecure attachments, stating that there was no evidence base for interventions. Other CAMHS refused to acknowledge developmental trauma. Adoptive parents in our interviews had also given examples of how they had been turned away in these circumstances and refused help.

Managers complained that, instead, children were provided with medication and an intervention based on the skill set within the mental health team – not necessarily the intervention that met the child's needs. Managers stated that CAMHS: 'doesn't work for us . . . The reality is unless we beat down the door we can't get services . . . CAMHS seems to run a parallel service.' Without a good CAMHS, LA adoption teams often had no alternative but to pay for private therapists or commission independent adoption support services. There was frustration and anger that health services were able to avoid their responsibilities and that children's services were left to pick up the bill. While there were examples given of very expensive long-term packages of therapeutic support paid for by the LA, most families could only be provided with six sessions. In response, one LA with poor local CAMHS had commissioned regular local clinics provided by independent post-adoption support services, but places were very limited while demand was described as massive.

Other managers spoke well of their local CAMHS but this seemed to be because one or two individuals within CAMHS had taken a particular interest in work with adopted and looked after children and had completed specific training in attachment therapies. Often the individual professional had a personal connection or was fascinated by adoption, as one manager explained:

That's why work with our children is so interesting for other professionals – because they can present so well because of the opportunities they have had, but once they disregulate they are acting out, their fury is unbounded.

However, even where local CAMHS provided good services, commitment to working with adopted children was not embedded or agreed at a senior level and concerns were expressed about what might happen if the individuals left or retired.

A more successful model of provision seemed to be when CAMHS had been jointly commissioned by the LA and health service and the service could receive direct referrals from the adoption team. Specialist or Tier 4 CAMHS were more attuned to the needs of looked after and adoptive families, had a highly skilled team, and had been created in a partnership between the agencies. The specialist CAMHS team had close working relationships with the social workers in the adoption teams and relationships were especially good when the teams were co-located in the same building. All these CAMHS teams had DDP-qualified therapists working within the service, as well as other types of therapy, such as family or art therapy. They also offered consultation time for members of the adoption teams. Sometimes the consultation might be about the suitability of a match or plan for adoption, as well as providing advice on supporting families. Some of the CAMHS teams were also involved in preparation groups, so that adopters had often met the therapists/psychologists before needing to ask for help. They were also able to offer individual work with families and/or children. This type of CAMHS was highly valued by adoptive parents.

It was noticeable that the specialist/Tier 4 CAMHS worked in a different way with adoptive families than was the norm for Tier 3 services. In local CAMHS, the therapist has a private relationship with the child and the work was not discussed with the parents. This can be a very unhelpful dynamic in adoptive families and can encourage splitting. The specialist services had a more inclusive model and were more likely to work through the adoptive parents, rather than directly with the child. However, there were also two LAs that had specialist CAMHS provision for looked after children, but adopted children were excluded from the service if a referral was made post-order and the service had not been previously involved.

Another LA was launching a dedicated CAMHS just for adopted children. Staffing was planned to include child psychotherapists, clinical psychologists, the adoption support manager and a senior practitioner. Unlike local CAMHS, referrals would come from the adoption team, thereby enabling a more appropriate response, as the manager explained:

> CAMHS are not an A&E service but we are often a crisis inter-vention service, and so we need robust interventions in a timely way. So when a family is desperate, we don't want to say, 'In three weeks' time on a Tuesday afternoon at 2pm you can have a consultation'. They need something now and in a more timely way.

The plans for the new service included a network meeting with the adoptive parents and professionals before work began to ensure that the family was involved from the start. It would also be possible for one therapist to see the parent and another to work with the child. It was intended that the two professionals would work together to form the professional hub.

One of the LAs had a Multi-Treatment Foster Care (MTFC) programme running and some of the most challenging adopted children and their families could transfer into the programme. This gave adopters extra support and gave them the same level of support as foster carers in the programme.

Post-adoption mentoring schemes and youth services

In two LAs, partnerships had developed with youth services with the intention of providing services for adopted teenagers. One had come about as adoptive parents had requested "heavy-duty babysitting", because they could not find anyone able or willing to care for their child so that they could have a break. Some of these adoptive parents had no family members who could help. In another LA, mentors for adopted young people had been found in the local community who could do ordinary activities with a young person such as take them fishing. Another LA had developed a PALS (Post Adoption Linking Scheme) mentoring service where a mentor worked with the young person. The service was said to be very highly regarded and valued by adoptive parents, as it provided respite without the need for the child becoming looked after. Examples given were of a worker visiting for three hours a week, or two workers if siblings needed time individually.

Mentors and PALS undertook a whole range of different activities, such as taking the child to activities to develop self-esteem, helping with school-based work, or developing independence skills. These workers could sometimes be the only people who could speak to the young person. An example given was of a young woman who was putting herself at risk with older men but refused to discuss her behaviour with anyone except the PALS worker, who was able to talk to her about her safety and sexual health.

A post-adoption team in partnership with youth services also ran eight activity days a year in one LA, four days for 8–12-year-olds, and four days for 13–19-year-olds. This was a long-term project developed from what young people had said about the value of being able to meet others who were adopted. Young people were involved in designing their own newsletter and specifying activities. Alongside the days was the possibility of a youth worker doing some individual work with a young person. The youth service also ran the LA participation groups; adopted young people had joined these and found speaking at children's councils and other events a powerful builder of self-esteem.

Partnerships with youth services were under-developed in other LAs, sometimes because the connections and partnerships had not been made, and sometimes because LA cuts had meant that youth services had virtually disappeared.

Overall, adoption managers emphasised the importance of relationships with other professionals, and when these were strong the team was more successful in engaging support services to keep children within their families. Good relationships were important at all levels of the organisation – between social workers and other professionals and between the senior managers of the different services. In some LAs, there were at least annual meetings of the senior managers from different services. One manager provided a vivid analogy of the child being the plant that needed to thrive and grow, the adoptive family being the soil and the growth medium, and the adoption support workers being the container holding everything in place.

Developing matching and support plans

Managers were asked about how support plans were developed. There was a consensus that plans began to be written at the same time as the child permanence report (CPR) and were developed during the match. Children's social workers often took the lead role but were helped by the adoption workers and by other professionals, such as the psychologists who were based in the teams. In two LAs, all adoptive parents were encouraged to talk or meet with the adoption medical adviser to help them reflect on what they had read in the CPR and how the child's history might affect their development. In another LA, all adopters received a detailed medical report that included a developmental assessment for the under-fives and had the opportunity to see one of the consultants. However, there were concerns that this service could not be sustained, as the detailed development assessment took a half-day to write up and the NHS was reluctant to fund the rising workload as the numbers being adopted increased.

A few managers emphasised the importance of planning and getting the pre-placement work right. Some LAs had skilled and experienced workers who ensured that every child had a life story book that the child and their adoptive parents would want to use. There were examples of very creative work with children, books written especially for individual children, calendars with pictures that had been made for children to help them understand the process of introductions, and ones for children already living in the family who might have a new brother or sister joining them.

All the adoption managers thought that adoption support plans needed to be improved. Managers commented that they were often tokenistic and vague, but that they recognised the problems and improvements were underway. There were several reasons given for support plans being too generic:

- First, the child's needs were not always apparent, especially if they were very young.
- Second, the child's social worker was focused on getting through the court processes and finding the child a family without delay, and not looking forward into the future. Many children's social workers had little experience of adoption work and were overly optimistic about the lack of impact of maltreatment on children's development.
- Third, some adoptive parents did not want to engage with support plans, as they wanted to normalise family life and stop all contact with social workers. All the managers stated that adopters were given a copy of the support plan.

Four managers did not mention any difficulty with the child's social workers writing the support plan. In these LAs, a permanence team operated that prepared children and birth families for adoption. The teams normally began work around the time of the court proceedings when permanency other than reunification was planned. Consequently, social workers in the permanency teams had a great deal of experience in adoption work and worked alongside the adoption team to prepare the support plans. Other LAs were setting up a similar model, as one manager explained:

We're trying to get more front-loaded ... get support built in from the start ... but it's often not identified. If you have a foster carer who is not looking forward either and the children are hitting all their milestones, it is difficult to get evidence for the support plan.

The BAAF support form (now updated) was not well liked, particularly because it did not easily fit within an attachment-based way of working. Complaints were that the form did not meet children's needs (e.g. disabled), that it was too lengthy and repetitive; most of the LAs had adapted the form. For example, one LA combined the matching, linking, family-finding and support reports into a single form.

Some LAs held a professionals' meeting specifically to examine support before the match went to panel. Another LA had plans to involve adoption support services at the time of the placement. It was intended that, in future, a worker from the adoption support service would attend the placement meeting to ensure that the elements of adoption support were considered and planned for beyond the adoption order, including contact arrangements, therapeutic interventions, education support, ongoing training, and support groups. It was hoped that engaging with adoption support staff in this way would help adoptive parents to feel more able to come back and ask for help at a later date.

A support plan is a statement of intent, and managers acknowledged that, even if there was nothing in the support plan, there was still a duty to provide help if the family asked. However, managers reported that some adopters were still reluctant to come forward until the situation was quite desperate.

Working with families in crisis

Managers were asked how adoptive families had made contact with them when they needed urgent help. All the managers agreed that it was quite straightforward for those who were receiving newsletters or were already in contact with the adoption team. The contact details of the adoption team were on all the literature and on the websites. However, not all the agencies had a helpline that was open every day, and some had all initial calls screened first by a contact centre, as they were finding taking calls too resource-intensive.

Where necessary, families could be seen within 24 hours, but usually managers described telephone counselling as holding the situation until a worker could be allocated. Packages of support could then be agreed. In some agencies, "team around the child" meetings were held to consider appropriate support if there was the possibility that the child might become looked after, while workers in other LAs presented the case to panels to ensure that everything possible had been done to divert from care.

Managers thought that adopters appreciated a speedy response from workers who were knowledgeable and where the response was of the right intensity. One manager explained that adoptive parents became frustrated if their crisis was at level 10 and the agency's response was much lower at three or four. It was important to match the response to the level of need. In one LA, families had their worker's email and work mobile number, and they could send an email knowing that they would get a response. The manager described it as *a more humane and immediate service*. The making of regular appointments also kept adoptive parents going, as they knew someone would be visiting soon.

Adopters who were trying to make contact with adoption support services sometimes came in at the "front door" – through duty and assessment or LA contact/customer support centres. The managers' view was that if the caller made any mention of adoption, their adoption team would be contacted and the referral passed over quickly. One manager described it as being like a "hot potato", with duty and assessment teams keen to leave it to adoption support. However, not all the managers were confident that they knew of all the referrals that involved an adopted child. For example, adoption teams were not always informed of referrals of older adopted young people who might present as homeless, or teenagers who were quickly put on a pathway to independence.

Safeguarding

Managers were asked how adopters, who had rung asking for help, ended up in Section 47 investigations. Managers said that often adopters rang in crisis and that the way they spoke about the child and their voicing of raw emotion could raise safeguarding concerns. Some of the situations that came in at the "front door" were bordering on child protection. One manager explained:

The adopters have borne the child's projections and trauma for so long that they themselves have become emotionally abusive or paralysed and passive victims from the child's violence.

The adoption team recognised the trauma that the adoptive parent was experiencing and that it had often been going on for years. On the other hand, the child's social worker could respond punitively, taking the view that they needed to rescue the child from such emotionally abusive parents. The child's social worker sometimes felt let down and angry that the adoptive parents had been assessed and trusted with the child, only to ask for the child to be taken away. One manager noted that if adopters were perceived as having failed, the department often judged them in a far harsher way than foster carers who had experienced a placement breakdown. On the other hand, adoptive parents might also ring and ask for the child to be "fixed" and be reluctant to want to change their own behaviours. Some parents also refused to have anything more to do with the child.

Some managers thought that, unless handled carefully, Section 47 investigations were not a good way to deal with the difficulties. Adopters were encouraged to be open and honest about the problems, but at the same time post-adoption support workers could not collude with adoptive parents and ignore evidence of abuse. Adoption support workers needed to keep the child as the focus, and they were mindful of recent cases in the media where adoptive parents had been abusive. As one manager said:

It's treading a fine line between buying into parental narratives of events to the detriment of keeping [child at home]. We are a service for children, we have to be, and although we parent the parents much of the time, it is always around the needs of the child.

Managers were able to give examples where there had been tensions between the child's social worker and the adoption support workers about the management of a situation. One manager explained:

The idea that adoption workers are not key workers is a big issue. It's not safe or helpful for us to be, and it needs a children's worker from the LAC team. It can feel like we're dumping the problem on others ... If you ask for a placement for a child [because the adoption is disrupting] the response can be quite punitive ... 'These people took this child on for life and we can't just accommodate every time the child has a tantrum'. There can be an unsympathetic approach to adopters without any real understanding. So our team are going around doing roadshows at team meetings and I'm linking with team managers, as well as offering a consultancy service to social workers.

Other managers were also trying to ensure that all such investigations would be undertaken jointly (the child's social worker and adoption support worker), as they knew of examples where the conduct of the investigation had resulted in the parents feeling devastated, with no acknowledgement of what they had experienced. The tensions in the work were clear:

The child's social worker's focus is solely the child and in cases where the child has made an allegation ... things have unfolded in a very unhelpful way and later been shown to be unproven. The child care team has felt we were colluding with the adopters whereas we were trying to say ... 'You have to understand the child in the context of their history' and it's important to understand that, while things have developed in a negative way, that's not where everybody started out and if you are going to move the situation on you need to be more attuned to the needs of the parents in the same way as we want them [the parents] to attune to the needs of their child. Sometimes children say, 'That wasn't true, what I said', but by that time, an awful lot of damage has happened.

Disruptions

If children became looked after, most of the LAs used the looked after children procedures, using care planning and reviews to plan for the child's future. Only two of the LAs held meetings that focused on the disruption. The role of post-adoption support workers is to support the family, and without the child in placement, they usually remained involved with the parents for only a short time. Once they pulled out, managers recognised that sometimes parents felt excluded from decision-making, as they were not always informed of reviews or meetings. Some managers also thought that adopted children could get lost in the system if they returned to care, and they had experience of adopted children having multiple failed foster placements before moving on to residential or secure accommodation. In their experience, it was often only at that point that the child's social worker recognised just how challenging it was to parent the child.

Managers were asked how disruptions could be avoided. They wanted more rigorous assessments, particularly of sibling groups and of those adopting for a second time, as the latter often did not realise how difficult it would be. There was also a demand for better and more life story work with children and young people who were struggling with a lack of information about their past and integrating their past with the present. Managers thought that there needed to be more focus on the early planning stages, allowing adoptive parents time to reflect on the possible match, as well as more accessible support services if difficulties emerged.

The future development of adoption support services

Adoption managers were asked how they would like to see adoption support services develop and where they identified gaps in services. All the managers wanted their teams to receive further training and the opportunities to develop skills to an advanced level. Some wanted more access to clinical supervision and a renewed focus on practice rather than process. Many of the teams were developing innovative approaches in adoption work.

In an ideal world, managers wanted adoption workers to be able to "check in" with adoptive parents once a year with a personalised letter or phone call. This would give the opportunity to problem-solve and troubleshoot, and offer age-appropriate services along the way. There was a recognition that services for older young people needed to develop and those running mentoring schemes wanted to see the service expanded.

Not all managers thought that adoption had a central place in the department. One manager's wish was that: 'Adoption needs to be owned by the wider department rather than tacked on at the end, and then adoption support tacked on the end of that, and finally birth relative support at the end of that. You just go on and on until no-one can see you.' Other managers wanted more joined-up services at a management level and much clearer lines of communication.

There was a general view that multi-disciplinary teams were the best way to provide services and that increasing the number of psychologists in the adoption team would be beneficial. An extended in-house psychology service would reduce waiting times and, importantly, routine appointments could be offered to adopters at the time of matching, again at placement and then follow-up appointments into the first year of placement. One team wanted all adopted children to have a comprehensive adoption transition package delivered by a multi-disciplinary adoption team. The package would comprise six sessions delivered by the team, which would prepare the foster carer on his/her own, include several sessions with the foster carer and adoptive parents together, and then involve sessions with just the adopters once the child had moved, including some Theraplay. Other managers wanted more family support workers to provide the bridge between foster care and adoption.

The focus of much adoption support is on improving the attunement of the parents to the child and working on parenting. It was thought that sometimes social workers failed to notice or work with an adoptive parent's own concerns, for example, an adoptive parent might be struggling with his or her own history or experiences of loss. The way in which services were currently structured meant that sometimes the fact that parents were feeling very negative about themselves was missed. A few managers wanted to have a counsellor in the team who could work with the adults' issues.

Some managers wanted to see changes to the financial regulations. There was a suggestion that all adoptive parents should receive an enhanced child benefit (not means-tested) and that this should be the adoption allowance. This would save local authorities a significant amount of money in administering the allowance and conducting annual reviews. Other managers wanted the financial regulations to change so that expectations were lowered, so that adopters did not presume that an enhanced allowance would be granted simply because a child was older or from a minority ethnic background.

Lack of good CAMHS dominated the comments on improving services. One manager said she wanted: 'A CAMHS that does not say looked after children are not a priority. I want a CAMHS that sticks to the rules – every CAMHS is different. I'd force them to provide a full service or have to buy in.' The unfairness and inequity of the partnerships between health and children's services was commented on by several managers. Another manager said: 'We do the assessments, we provide the services, and we plug the gaps, we plug lots of other people's gaps.'

Transfer between child and adult services was a weak area and one that needed much more work. Managers mentioned particular issues for children with a disability and the transfer between child and adult mental health services.

Summary

- Twelve adoption managers were interviewed about the adoption support services in their LAs. Five of the LAs had one adoption team providing all adoption services and seven had a separate team for post-adoption support.
- There were three different models of service provision. Model A was the most traditional model and was a team comprising qualified and unqualified social workers; Model B comprised a team mainly of social workers with a part-time psychologist or therapist;

and Model C was a multi-disciplinary team providing specialist CAMHS and social work services.

- Many of the social workers in the teams had been trained in DDP, play or filial therapy. They were working therapeutically in families, but social work supervision did not always support therapeutic practice.
- Placements out of area were of great concern, because access to and the type of interventions provided by CAMHS varied greatly across the country. Managers were concerned that CAMHS did not have to offer a comprehensive service and could turn children away because of rigid eligibility criteria or because they argued that it was a LA's responsibility to pay for therapy.
- There was a common "menu" of post-adoption services provided by the LAs. However, each LA had developed specific post-adoption services, often drawing on existing partnerships with education and community health services. There were many examples of innovative and creative support services. In most LAs, the links between post-adoption services and youth services were under-developed.
- Managers were beginning to develop services for those parenting teenagers and for adopted teenage children. Two LAs were able to use respite care in more flexible ways, utilising mentors, a PALS scheme, and weekend and holiday residential weekend breaks. One LA had begun and another was introducing a training programme in non-violent resistance for working with child to parent violence.
- Adopters who rang at the time of a crisis might have their calls answered by customer care centres, or by the duty and assessment team. The call could escalate to a Section 47 investigation and unless handled carefully and jointly-worked, managers acknowledged that it could be a very damaging experience for the family.
- Managers thought that post-adoption services were aware of most children who came back into care after an adoption disruption but older young people could slip through if they presented as homeless or were quickly put on a pathway to independence. The transfer of adopted young people from children's services to adult services was also an area of weakness.

- If children were not returning home quickly, the post-adoption service often passed over all responsibility to the child's social worker. It was recognised that parents could feel excluded as they were not always informed of meetings and reviews, and that adopted children could get "lost" in the system.
- Managers wanted to develop a multidisciplinary service to be able to deliver a better transition from foster to adoptive care and services that were more attuned to the needs of adoptive children and their families.

16 Summary, discussion and recommendations

This study used a mixed-methods approach to calculate the rate of adoption disruption in England and to understand from different perspectives why adoptive placements disrupt. The study comprised two distinct phases:

- In phase one, data on the number of disruptions were collected from adoption managers and combined with national data on looked after and adopted children.[71] The new combined dataset enabled the research team to calculate the disruption rate and to examine the factors that increased the risk of disruption. The dataset was the largest ever compiled in England, and provided the base for this first national study of adoption disruption. However, even with a large dataset, the number and types of variables it contained limited the analysis and, whilst providing important statistical information, a qualitative approach was needed to understand the process and impact of disruption on those most closely involved with the experience. Furthermore, the research team was concerned that, for the reasons outlined in Chapter 2 on methods, there may have been some under-reporting of disruptions by adoption agencies.

- In phase two, adoption disruption was examined using alternative approaches. A series of interviews was conducted with key people about the experience of adoption disruption and adoptions in difficulty. Thirteen local authorities participated in this second phase. On behalf of the research team, the LAs sent out surveys to adoptive parents who had adopted a child between 1 April 2002 and 31 March 2004. The survey asked parents whether their child still lived at home and how the adoption was faring. Surveys were returned by 210 adoptive parents (a 34 per cent response rate). The

---

71 National data are collected by the DfE each year from every local authority; the dataset is known as the SSDA903 return.

same survey was posted on the Adoption UK (AUK) website and was completed by 188 adoptive parents. It is important to note that the AUK survey was open to anyone who had adopted a looked after child, and there were differences between the survey responses in the length of time that children had been living with their adoptive parents. Only 31 per cent of the AUK member's children had been living in their adoptive home for more than eight years, compared with the LA sample, in which 87 per cent of the children had been with their adoptive families for eight or more years. In total, 390 adoptive parents who were caring for 689 adopted children responded to the survey.

From the survey responses, 35 families were selected where the child had left the adoptive home prematurely (under the age of 18 years). The adoptive parents in these families were interviewed, together with 35 parents whose child still lived at home, but where parents reported major difficulties in caring for them. Before the interviews, parents were asked to complete a questionnaire containing well-being measures. To provide a comparison and calibration of the measures, a further 35 parents who had responded to the LA survey stating that there were no or very few difficulties were also asked to complete the questionnaire. However, this "Going well" group was not interviewed due to resource limitations.

Furthermore, 12 young people who had experienced an adoption disruption were interviewed, as were 12 adoption managers who were asked about the post-adoption support services in their local authority. In total, interviews were held with 70 adoptive parents, 12 adopted young people and 12 adoption managers.

Prior to the study, there had been concerns about the adoption disruption rate. Some commentators had argued that disruption was a frequent event and that the stability of adoption was over-played when making decisions about which kind of permanent placement was suitable for children unable to return home. Questions had been asked in the House of Commons about the disruption rate, but with no national data on the number of children who returned to care after a disruption, answers were muted. To complicate matters, previous research had often not distinguished between adoptions that had broken down from matching to placement, or from placement to order, and those that disrupted post-order. To compare the disruption rates between different types of permanence, the same time point must be selected, and post-order is the most appropriate. In this study, we were able to compare the disruption rates of children on adoption, special guardianship and residence orders but were unable to make comparisons with long-term foster care. At present, it is impossible to identify children in the national dataset whose foster placements are intended to be permanent, but who have no legal order. The follow-up time for each type of order also differed, as special guardianship orders (SGOs) have only been available since December 2005, and data on residence orders (ROs) have been collected from April 2005, whilst adoption order data were available from 2000/01.

The database created for this study contained details of:

- 37,335 adoption orders, of which 525 were known to have disrupted;
- 5,921 special guardianship orders, of which 121 were known to have disrupted; and
- 5,771 residence orders, of which 415 were known to have disrupted.

Children on adoption, special guardianship and residence orders

An adoption order remains the most frequently used legal order for children who need a permanent substitute family. Our analysis found that, at the financial year ending 31 March 2013, about 14 per cent of looked after children who ceased to be looked after left care with an adoption order, 10 per cent left on a SGO and six per cent on a RO. The rapid rise in the number of SGOs since 2005 does not seem to have affected the use of other orders. We expected that with the introduction of SGOs, there would be a corresponding decline in ROs. Surprisingly, the number of ROs has also increased, as has the number of adoption orders. It might be argued that social work practice has improved – a greater number of children are provided with permanent placements and a greater number are leaving the care system than ever before into a placement secured by a legal order.

The characteristics of children on the three types of order differed. Compared with those on SGOs and ROs, adopted children tended to be younger at entry to care, and were more likely to have entered care under section 20 of the Children Act (1989). Sixty per cent of those on adoption orders were under four years old, whereas the same was true for only about 45 per cent of those on SGOs and ROs. Minority ethnic children were more likely to be on SGOs and ROs than adoption orders.

Adopted children had experienced a greater number of moves in foster care, compared to children on SGOs and ROs, and had waited longer from entry to care to final placement. Movement and delay create great instability and stress in children's lives and this has been shown (even when background factors are controlled) to be associated with an increase in behaviour problems (Rubin *et al*, 2004, 2007). Sustained stress for children is very harmful (Lupien *et al*, 2009). Children on SGOs and ROs had fewer moves, mainly because about half of those on SGOs and one-third on ROs were placed initially with a family or friends carer and did not move again – their first placement became their permanent placement. Children on ROs were, on average, the oldest at entry to care, had the most failed reunification attempts, and were the oldest at the time of the order.

Adoption disruption

The majority of adoption disruptions occurred more than five years after the order had been made and when children were teenagers; 61 per cent were aged between 11 and 16. The placements of children who were older at entry to care, who had had more moves whilst looked after, and who had waited longer to be placed with their adoptive families were more likely to disrupt. Three-quarters of children who experienced a disruption were more than four years old at placement with their adoptive family. Children who were four years old or older at placement were 13 times more likely to disrupt than those who were placed as infants. This much larger dataset highlights the impact of delay and the findings echo much of the previous research and support the Government's attempts to reduce delay in decision-making.

The child's gender and ethnicity were not associated with greater risk of disruption. This finding challenges the view that boys are more difficult to parent. The large dataset also allowed for a closer analysis of adoption orders made to previous foster carers. About 15 per cent of the children had been adopted by their previous foster carer. The proportion of children adopted by former foster carers has barely risen over the last 13 years; this is surprising, given the increase in the use of adoption and the policy and practice emphasis on reducing moves in care. Instead, the dataset shows that foster carers were using special guardianship and residence orders. Foster carers' preference for these orders may be entirely appropriate when there is frequent contact with the birth family. However, we also found that children who were adopted by their foster carers entered care at a similar age to those placed with stranger adopters. But whilst the mean age of children when placed with foster carers who went on to adopt them was two years, there was an average wait of a further two years before the adoption order was made. One-quarter of the foster families waited more than three years. Unlike previous studies, this study found that adoptions by foster carers were just as likely to disrupt compared with children placed with stranger adoptive parents, even when controlling for age. It is likely that, with such a large dataset covering a 12-year period, differences that appear in small datasets lose statistical significance.

The delays for children adopted by their foster carers may be for a number of reasons. For example, adoptive parents may not have been found and the foster carer may have stepped in to offer permanent care, or the foster carer may have wanted to adopt but not been supported by the LA, or support packages may have taken months to agree, or perhaps other delays occurred, caused by social work and legal practice. We undertook a similar analysis of adoption data in Wales and found the same long delays for children adopted by their foster carers (Wijedasa and Selwyn, 2014).

Many other studies have commented on the variation in practice in LAs and this was the case in this study too. The percentage of adoptions that had disrupted over the 12-year period varied from 0–7.4 per cent by LA. There is insufficient research to understand why there is such variation. It is not safe to assume that LAs with higher disruption rates have poorer practice; for example, it may be that the LAs with higher disruption rates take more risks and place older children who are more challenging.

Disruption rates

Disruption rates can be calculated using a simple calculation to establish the proportion, i.e. for adoption 525/37,335 x 100 = 1.5 per cent. However, this calculation takes no account of the length of time since the making of the adoption order. We knew that most adoptions disrupted during the teenage years and therefore some children would not have been with their families long enough for the placement to disrupt. Therefore, we used a method known as event history analysis that takes into account "time" in the analysis.

Over a 12-year period, using the information supplied by adoption managers, the rate of adoption disruption was calculated to be 3.2 per cent, which indicates that three in 100 adoptions would be likely to disrupt over the 12 years. Of course, this does not mean that this is the risk for any particular child, but 3.2 per cent was the rate across the whole sample. The most important factors that predicted disruption were the child's age, followed by older age at placement and a longer waiting time between placement and adoption order. *Teenagers were ten times more likely to have a disruption compared with young children.* This is a new and important finding, since adoption support has been focused on providing support services in the first few months and years of an adoptive placement. Whilst support at this initial time point is undoubtedly important, adoption services have been slow to develop for teenagers and for adopters who are parenting adolescents. The findings on support are discussed later in this chapter.

Special guardianship and residence order disruptions

Unlike adoption orders, about two-thirds of SGOs and ROs that disrupted, disrupted quickly. Most occurred within two years of the order being made and when children were under 11 years of age. The findings on the effects of age and movement were the same as those reported for adoption. Children who were older at entry to care and at the time of placement or those who had experienced more moves in care were at greater risk of disruption. The child's gender and ethnicity were not associated with greater risk of disruption. Unlike children on adoption or residence orders, whose placements were more likely to disrupt if they entered care because of abuse and neglect, those on SGOs were more likely to disrupt if they entered care for reasons other than maltreatment.

SGO and RO disruptions were less likely if the order was made to a kinship carer. Kinship care was very stable; children placed with unrelated guardians were three times more likely to experience a SGO disruption than those placed with kin.

Comparing adoption, SGO and RO disruptions

Before making the comparison, it is important to highlight that disruption rates for all three types of order were low, compared with the movement that is reported for those who are reunified with their birth parents (e.g. Wade *et al* (2011) found that about 65 per cent of reunified children returned to care at least once during a five-year follow-up) or for those who remain in the care system (Hannon *et al*, 2010). Of course, that may be because those who remain in care are the children with the most challenging behaviours, or because they enter care late as adolescents with entrenched difficulties (see Sinclair *et al* (2007) for a discussion of these issues).

Data were available for each type of order over different periods. To ensure a "like for like" comparison, the orders were compared over a five-year follow-up period using event history analyses. Over a five-year period:

- 147 in 1,000 ROs would have disrupted;
- 57 in 1,000 SGOs would have disrupted;
- 7 in 1,000 adoptions would have disrupted.

Adoption orders were the most stable, although we found that the very low rate of disruptions in the early years rose to 3.2 per cent after 12 years. SGO and RO disruptions occurred irrespective of the child's age since the making of the legal order. Most disrupted quickly and when children were younger than 11 years old. Unlike adoption disruptions, being a teenager had no statistical effect on the risks of a SGO or RO disruption. Of course, the adolescent years may pose additional risks for the SGO and RO placements that continue, but data are not yet available over such a long timespan. Adoptions were far more likely to disrupt during adolescence, which suggests that adoptive parents may have more difficulty negotiating the teenage years, and/or they remain committed to children for longer compared with guardians and carers. Certainly, there was evidence to support both hypotheses in the interview data, and the commitment and tenacity of adoptive parents was very evident in their narratives.

Survey responses

Surveys were completed by 390 adoptive parents who had adopted 689 children from 77 different LAs. Because of the sampling strategy, the children from the LA survey were older (average age 14 years) and had been living with their families for longer compared with the AUK members' children (average age 11 years). It was difficult to ascertain the representativeness of the survey sample because the response rate for the LA survey was 34 per cent (typical rate when trying to contact adopters from 10 years ago), and there are no national data collected on adoptions over time with which to make comparisons. It could be argued that those who respond to surveys are those who feel the strongest about the topic and that the "middle ground" is less likely to be represented. Indeed, the AUK survey was posted on a message thread titled "disruption". With those caveats in mind, the two surveys using different samples produced similar results.

Just over one-third of adoptive parents reported no or few difficulties, often describing family life as "brilliant". Where support had been requested, it usually had been provided and adopters were complimentary about service provision. For another 30 per cent of families, whilst family life was described as good, they faced some challenges stemming from the child's special needs and getting the right support in place.

About one-quarter of families described major challenges in parenting their child, who had multiple and overlapping difficulties, and the struggle to get appropriate support. Parents reported that they were physically and mentally exhausted and that there had been a negative impact on marital and family relationships. Some of the comments indicated that, after a tricky patch, good relationships had been re-established, while other parents were still battling to get the support that they needed, and other comments suggested that a disruption was close.

About nine per cent of the young people had left home under the age of 18. Most had been teenagers at the time of the disruption: average age 14–15 years old. Parents noted that the move from home had been triggered by a combination of challenging behaviour, inadequate support, and feeling blamed for the child's difficulties. Most parents were still active in the parenting role, although a few of the parents and/or young people were refusing to have contact with each other.

The two surveys corroborated the administrative data analysis in finding that the teenage years were the time of greatest risk of disruption. However, the proportion of disruptions reported was greater in the surveys in comparison with the disruption information supplied by adoption managers. Although it could be argued that the surveys may be more accurate, an alternative explanation is that those who experienced difficulties might have been more likely to respond to a research study on adoption disruption than those where all was going well.

It is probably safe to conclude that the proportion of adoptions that disrupt post-order lies between two and nine per cent.

Interviews with adoptive parents

From the survey responses, 35 parents whose child had left home prematurely (under the age of 18) and 35 parents whose child was still at home, but where parenting was challenging, were interviewed in-depth about their adoption experiences. The families were selected because they were having or had had great difficulty and they are not typical of adoptive families generally. However, given the consistency in the parents' accounts of the types of challenging behaviour and the response from agencies, we do think that the families are typical of those who are experiencing great difficulty. The two groups are referred to as the "Left home" and the "At home" groups, and some of the key findings are outlined below.

Only eight of the 70 children had not been abused and/or neglected by their birth parents before being placed with their adoptive families. However, even those eight children had experienced maltreatment through abandonment or rejection at birth, or had been born showing signs of drug withdrawal. There is now a strong evidence base (see, for example, Lazenbatt, 2010; Jones et al, 2011) that shows that the consequences of child maltreatment can be long-lasting. Long-term consequences include mental and/or physical disabilities resulting from the initial injuries; psychological problems related to experiencing trauma such as post-traumatic stress disorder; attention problems; hyperactivity; anxiety; depression; anger and aggression; and longer-term health problems such as diabetes and heart conditions (see www.acestudy.org). The negative impact of earlier abusive experiences does not simply disappear with adoption. The children in our samples were already carrying risks for poor outcomes as they entered care. Research generally finds better outcomes for children placed for adoption at earlier ages and with fewer moves in care. However, in this sample the risks of poor outcomes were increased, as most children were late-placed and had had several moves in care.

The transition of children from foster care to their adoptive family

We found that more than half of the adoptive parents (59%) knew that they had been linked (and some matched) with children, but a placement had not materialised. Most commonly, links had not been pursued because social workers had chosen other adopters. Adopters viewed this as a competitive and stressful process. We did not ask specifically about feelings relating to these failed links and matches, but some adopters commented that they had started to invest emotionally in children with whom they had been linked. We would assume that unsuccessful links had brought feelings of loss. Many parents come to adoption (in this study, 77 per cent of the interview sample) because of being unable to carry a baby full-term or because of infertility and/or failed treatments. They had already experienced many losses. There needs, therefore, to be greater consideration by social workers of the impact on prospective adopters of links and matches that do not proceed.

It is well known in practice that the first few weeks of an adoptive placement are extremely tiring in a practical sense, as parents must ensure that children have clothes, a school place, etc, and tiring emotionally in adjusting to life as a family. Many adopters describe the first few weeks as exhausting and like a whirlwind. Adopters in this study were no exception. Therefore, it is important that, pre-placement, adoptive parents are boosted and feel well supported and strengthened for what is to come. However, in this study we found that this was not the case for nearly one-third (30%) of parents, who described themselves as exhausted and battered even before the child had moved in. Poorly managed introductions and transitions were associated with disruption. Social workers need to be aware that, where introductions and/or transitions have not gone well, additional support should be made available at the start of the adoptive placement.

The foster carer's role in the transition

The support of the foster carer was key to a successful transition. The majority (61%) of adoptive parents described the foster carers as welcoming. Carers helped the parents understand the child's routines, prepared the child well for the move and held celebration parties and events to mark the transition. In contrast, 30 per cent of foster carers were obstructive, for reasons such as not approving of the parents chosen; wanting to keep the child themselves; wanting the child removed as quickly as possible; or struggling with their own feelings of loss and grief. Foster carers who prevented the adoptive parents visiting or caring for the child, who withheld important information, who set the timetable for introductions based on their own agenda and not the child's needs, or who made the move to the adoptive family fraught and highly charged emotionally created a highly stressed transition for both the child and adoptive parents.[72] Adoptive parents gave examples of foster carers who told them that the child was unlovable, or, at the other extreme, had clung to children sobbing, as the child left the foster home. Some children went into their adoptive placements without having been given "psychological permission" to move on and make new close relationships. Other children arrived in their adoptive families without personal possessions or toys, even though they had spent several years in care. Both situations are likely to leave children feeling insecure and without a sense of who they are.

Quality of foster care

Adoptive parents were also concerned about the poor quality of foster care. Worryingly, 41 per cent expressed concerns about the maltreatment of children whilst in foster placements, including the cold, clinical care shown by some foster carers who lacked emotional warmth. This study did not interview the foster carers and therefore we do not know what their views might have been. However, the findings raise questions about the fostering of children with plans for adoption. Where adoption is the plan, are foster carers more likely to be emotionally distant as they prepare for the inevitable move?

Although there has been recent interest in the grief and loss that

---

72 One would also assume that the transition would be stressful for the social worker, and would perhaps reduce their capacity to support the child and new parents.

foster carers experience when children move on (e.g. Hebert *et al*, 2012), there has been little research on the strategies that foster carers employ to protect themselves from their experiences of repeated losses. For example, how do foster carers who specialise in caring for infants provide love and stay attuned to the infant's needs, knowing that the infant will soon leave? Alternatively, it may be that foster carers *do not recognise* that the children need comfort. Studies in the UK (e.g. Hardy *et al*, 2013) and in the US and Europe (e.g. Dozier *et al*, 2009; Van Andel and Knorth, 2012) have all found that physical involvement of carers with infants and young children in their care is low – much less than the touch and comfort a parent would give their child. One explanation for lack of touch is that foster carers are fearful of allegations being made and/or they misunderstand the LA's safeguarding policy. Attachment theory has also been used to explain this finding, noting that young maltreated children have often not learnt to convey their needs and/or they reject the carer's attempts to comfort them. In response, the foster carer may describe the infant/child as easy to care for as they make few demands, and consequently a pattern of distant and avoidant relating becomes established. The difficulties in the child–parent relationship become noticeable only when the child moves into an adoptive family.

Adoptive parents commented on how their expectations of what family life should be like were different from the experiences that the children had in foster care, in particular, children found intimacy difficult. For example, one adoptive mother kissed her husband on his return from work in front of the child. The child's response was to ask curiously, 'Are you going to have sex now?' Being part of an adoptive family and being looked after in a foster placement were very different experiences for many children. It is important to remember that adopted children have often been neglected and have experienced more moves in foster care compared with children who have other types of legally secured permanent placements. The quality of foster care is therefore extremely important in helping children learn to trust that adults can meet their needs and that they can make meaningful relationships with them. The findings in this study raise important questions about the training of foster carers who are moving children on to adoptive families, the support available for carers to manage their own feelings of grief and loss, and the messages that some carers had taken to heart about "keeping their distance".

Social work support during introductions and the transition

Most parents thought that they had been well supported by their social worker during the introductions. In cases where professional support was absent, this was due to social workers being on leave, retiring or leaving their employment at the time of the introductions. However, adoptive parents also highlighted that they were very vulnerable at this point in the adoption process because of their own needs and desires, so it was difficult to remain grounded. Adoptive parents who felt that they had not been supported stated that they felt they were on a conveyor belt, with no time for reflection and no opportunity to say "Stop". Parents whose adopted children had left home were more likely to state that they had felt unsupported by social workers during the introduction and transition.

Information

Just fewer than half of the parents thought that important information had not been shared with them, and a greater number of parents thought that the significance of what they were given was not fully explained. Some adoption social workers advised parents to "read between the lines" and other adoption workers "translated" the social work jargon that had been used to describe the children in the various documents. Six parents stated that they would not have proceeded if they had had all the information, but other parents wanted the information so that they would have been better prepared. Importantly, parents wanted to know whether they could expect their child to be able to live independently as an adult, or whether they would always need some form of adult/social care.

Over one-third of the adopters (37%) had met one or both birth parents prior to the child moving in, and 19 per cent had met an extended family member. The majority of these meetings had been constructive and had allowed adoptive parents to see the birth mothers, in particular, in a positive light. In some LAs, the meeting took place with the adoptive parents' social worker present and this support was valued.

Challenging behaviour

For 80 per cent of the families, children's challenging behaviour started during the first few years of placement and escalated at adolescence. Twenty per cent of parents described an uneventful first few years, with challenging behaviours only emerging at puberty followed by a rapid escalation that parents found difficult to manage. There is a lack of knowledge and research on challenging behaviours that emerge in adolescence. It is known that 75 per cent of all adult mental health disorders begin in adolescence (Chief Medical Officer, 2013) and the adoptive parents may have been describing the onset of behaviours that might later become diagnosed as adult mental health problems.

Adopted young people in this sample were carrying many of the risks associated with the development of mental health problems. They had been maltreated, had parents who had mental health problems, had fathers who were often violent (75 per cent of the children had been exposed to domestic violence), had had many moves in care, and had been late-placed. It is likely that a combination of genetic, biological and environmental factors triggered the severe behaviours that the parents described. Puberty brings additional changes that adolescents often find stressful; it is a time of hormonal changes and is a period where there is a rapid brain spurt. There are also developmental tasks associated with adolescence, such as the development of identity, which is more complex for adopted young people. Adopted young people and their parents also reported bullying because of their adoptive status.

The behaviours that challenged families had been evident from very early on in the placements. Early sexualised behaviour had continued into adolescence, with girls in particular making themselves very vulnerable to sexual exploitation by running away and having fleeting sexual relationships, often with older men. Children who had self-harmed under the age of 10 years continued to self-harm. However, during adolescence the self-harm became life-threatening and young people needed to be hospitalised for their own safety. The most frequently described challenging behaviour was child to parent violence.

Child to parent violence

We had not expected child aggression and violence to feature so strongly in parental accounts of challenging behaviour. We had expected ADHD and attachment difficulties to feature as causes of disruption, and although parents described great difficulty in managing these behaviours on their own, they were not difficulties that broke families. However, it was violence to parents and to siblings that was the main reason that 80 per cent of young people had had to leave home. Parents gave many examples of being beaten, suddenly attacked, threatened, intimidated, and controlled. Some parents had been prevented from leaving their homes and had their support networks undermined. Many parents said that they lived in fear. Child to parent violence brought shame on the families; nor was it a topic that could be easily raised with social workers, friends or extended family members. Child and adolescent aggression and violence within the adoptive home raises important issues for post-adoption services and for children's services more generally.

The prevalence of child to parent violence in the general population is unknown and there are disputes about the extent of serious and persistent cases. Consequently, estimates vary widely, with studies showing that it occurs in 3–29 per cent of families (Gallagher, 2004; Holt, 2012). A recent UK analysis (Condry and Miles, 2014) of reports to the Metropolitan Police during 2009–10 found that of all the 2,336 reports involving adolescent to parent crime, 51 per cent were for violence. The research in this area is in its infancy and studies often do not differentiate between the kinds of violence and control that require parents to change their behaviour, and other types of aggressive behaviour. In one of the few studies that considered young people on the edge of care and who were receiving family support services,

Biehal (2012) found that 112 (54%) of a sample of 209 young people were reported as having been violent to their parents in the previous six months.

Some studies (e.g. Kernic *et al*, 2003; Walsh and Krienert, 2007; Kotch *et al*, 2008; English *et al*, 2009) have examined the factors that increase the risk of child aggression, such as exposure to domestic violence, paternal behaviours, neglect under the age of two years old, and exposure to alcohol in utero. All of these risk factors were evident in our sample. The majority (91%) of the young people who had left home had been exposed to domestic violence. However, the mechanisms by which these factors "cause" aggression remain unclear. Young people who misuse substances or who suffer from mental illnesses such as schizophrenia, bipolar disorder or depression can also be violent. Parents reported that mental health services were reluctant to "label" young people, although many had diagnoses of attachment disorders. Young people's behaviour was often disturbing to themselves and their parents.

What is clear is that early aggression is a persistent trait. Children who are aggressive at eight years old (and when this remains untreated) are likely to be aggressive at 30 years old and the trait is likely to continue across generations (Huesmann *et al*, 1984). They are also likely to take that aggression into their dating relationships (Laporte *et al*, 2009), be perpetrators of domestic violence, and to engage in serious antisocial behaviour and criminal activities. The majority of young people in this sample who were aggressive displayed the trait early in their placement and had done so in foster care but had not received any interventions.

Most previous research has focused on boys who are violent to their birth mothers. Boys make up about 70 per cent of the instigators in these studies, although there is a recognition that girls can be aggressive, and that fathers and siblings can also be attacked (Holt, 2012). The gender difference has been found across studies and countries and is similar to the gender divide of behaviour problems more generally. We too found that more boys were involved in child to parent violence and that the gender difference was statistically significant. However, it should be noted that 14 (44%) of the 32 girls were also violent and the type or severity of violence did not differ by gender.

In this study, several adoptive parents used the term "domestic violence" to describe the violence from the child to parent. However, there are many differences between domestic violence and child to parent violence. For example, in intimate partner violence, a woman may express guilt and self-blame but professionals would want to help the woman acknowledge that the responsibility lay with the abuser. In contrast, adoptive parents' self-blame was often reinforced by the professionals' responses, who assumed that the responsibility lay in the adopters' own poor parenting. From parents' accounts, those supporting the family did not seem to have understood *who* was doing *what* to *whom*. Child protection investigations seemed to have been started as a matter of course and to have involved little joint working with post-adoption social workers. Parents spoke about the lasting effect of investigations on their employment and mental health, and their feelings of betrayal and loss of trust in professionals.

Adoptive parents subjected to child to parent violence were offered the same parenting programmes or anger management workshops repeatedly; one young person had had 20 different anger management courses provided by six different agencies. The violent behaviour was not seen as an attempt to control others but as a problem with controlling temper and emotions. The poor service response is not limited to adoptive families, but has been reported in the police and children's service's response to child to parent violence in other types of families too (Holt and Retford, 2013).

There are a number of interventions designed to reduce/remove child to parent violence. Some have been evaluated (see, for example, programmes run by Oxleas CAMHS, and the development of the Non Violent Resistance (NVR) programmes (Omer 2004; Omer *et al*, 2008)). Two of the sample LAs in this study had recently introduced or were about to introduce NVR as an intervention for families experiencing child to parent violence. It would be useful if these interventions were evaluated with adopted and fostered young people.

Support and interventions

Most (60%) of the adoptive parents had not kept in touch with the agency that had approved them or placed their child. When parents tried to get help and advice, they were faced with a number of hurdles and barriers to accessing services, such as: not knowing which services were available; not being able to get through the "front door" as the child's difficulties did not meet agency criteria; services not being delivered following assessments; disputes over the funding of interventions; and inappropriate services being offered. Each of these barriers to accessing services deserves further exploration, but here we consider eligibility criteria and interventions that did not match the child's needs.

Eligibility criteria

It was surprising to find that behaviours on the autistic spectrum were not deemed a disability in some LAs and therefore the services of the disability team could not be utilised. The new special education needs regulations and code of practice (introduced in September 2014) should prevent this happening in future. Children who had been diagnosed with a condition on the autistic spectrum were also turned away by some local CAMHS teams, as they stated that the children would not benefit from therapy. This left parents very much alone and trying to cope with some extremely challenging behaviour. Other adoptive parents found that they could not access CAMHS because the latter's priorities were looked after children and not those adopted. There was enormous variation across the country in the response from agencies, particularly from CAMHS.

There also seemed to be confusions about diagnosis and the overlap between attachment difficulties, autistic spectrum disorders, and foetal alcohol spectrum disorders. Consequently, children often puzzled professionals, who described them as "conundrums". We would suspect that part of the confusion was that the family life and experiences that had been provided in the adoptive home had given many children good social skills that did not fit the expected diagnostic profile. There was a great reluctance to refer on to more specialised services.

There were also children who had had interventions from a number of services and where there had been no noticeable improvement and who were out of control. They were very vulnerable young people who put their own lives and sometimes those of others in danger. Yet, for these adoptive families respite was almost impossible to arrange, except when it was provided as a last-ditch attempt to keep the family together. Even then, the child had to become looked after again and be allocated a children's social worker before respite could be arranged. The use of residential care to stabilise the situation was only considered in a handful of situations. It was unclear how many of the children's situations had reached the joint panels that are held in local authorities to make decisions about residential care. Parents were not informed of these and many did not know about the existence of therapeutic schools such as The Mulberry. Since the 35 young people had left home, 10 of the young people had been placed in residential care or in a secure establishment. Most of the young people who had left home had had multiple failed foster placements.

Service-led interventions

Many adoptive parents complained that the only interventions that could be provided by the LA and their local CAMHS were those that were "off the shelf". It was shocking to hear from two families that because their daughters had disclosed sexual abuse, the local CAMHS would not work with them, as they had had no training in dealing with sexual abuse. A 12-year-old child had been kept in police cells overnight and another young person admitted to a general hospital ward because there was no mental health provision available. Some adopters were lucky to find social workers or psychologists working in the local service who understood attachment difficulties and the problems of maltreated children, and they received a good service. Far more frequently, parents were offered medication, parenting courses or cognitive behavioural therapy (CBT) from CAMHS; and from children's services, parenting courses, life story work and sticker charts. While parents appreciated the parenting courses in the early years, they did not begin to meet their needs during their child's adolescence. The type of intervention seemed to be determined by the skill set of who was in post rather than by the needs of the child. Some parents and children had the same intervention on multiple occasions with little effect. Scarce resources were wasted and ineffectively targeted.

There were examples of good practice where LA post-adoption teams and CAMHS had commissioned specific therapists or referred children on to specialist Tier 4 CAMHS or adoption support agencies. These services were rated highly by adoptive parents. A few LAs were able to provide specialist CAMHS in-house because of joint funding arrangements. Again, adopters reported that they provided a very good service. One-quarter of all the adoptive parents rated the support they had received from the social work post-adoption services as the most useful support they had received, and nine parents (13%) rated similarly the support from CAMHS.

The managers of post-adoption services who were interviewed and who had Tier 4 CAMHS within their service thought that the model provided the best way of getting the right kinds of intervention of the right intensity, to the families in a timely way.

One of the first interventions often offered to families was life story work with the child or young person. Accounts of how this work was undertaken raise concerns about the skill levels of the staff involved and the quality of the supervision that they were receiving. Parents gave examples of direct work that had distressed children and in some cases was thought to have brought about the escalation of difficulties.

Social work supervision

Working directly with children and young people and with adoptive families raises issues about the supervision of work that has a therapeutic element. Social work supervision has become dominated by a casework approach and the process of reflecting and considering the family dynamics and impact on the worker and the child or family has reduced or disappeared. Research has highlighted the importance of social work supervision that contains a reflective element and its association with greater job satisfaction, higher staff retention rates, reduced levels of stress, and improved practice (Carpenter *et al*, 2013).[73] However, efforts to improve social work supervision have focused on the management of newly qualified social workers and those working in child protection.

Social workers in post-adoption services have a complex role, but this role differs from that of children's social workers. Usually, they do not have the authority or responsibilities of a children's social worker, but are often working with families in crisis, where emotions are running high and where they may be providing support over a much longer period than would be expected of a children's social worker. Ambivalence, projection, transference and counter-transference need to be understood in therapeutic work.

Many of the adoption social workers in our sample of 13 LAs were highly skilled and were working therapeutically with adoptive families. They had undertaken further training in play and filial therapy and in dyadic developmental psychotherapy. Yet adoption services have been omitted from developments to improve the supervision of practice. The complexities of adoption work deserve a re-examination of the best models of supervision for this type of work.

Comparison of the "At home" and "Left home" groups

The analysis of the questionnaire measures of children's well-being completed by adoptive parents (the SDQ and ACA) highlighted the extraordinary level of difficulties in both groups of children. Unlike general population studies, where boys usually have more behavioural difficulties than girls, in this study the gender profiles of challenging behaviour on the standardised measures were very similar. It should

---

73 A core objective of the newly qualified social worker programme was to enable employers to provide structured, reflective supervision, and its provision was highly praised by senior managers in the participating LAs.

be noted that none of the measures we used focused on violence. Noticeable were the much higher rates of:

a) statements of special educational needs: 37 per cent of children in the sample, in comparison with three per cent in the general population and 28.5 per cent of looked after children (DfE, 2013b).
b) diagnosis on the autistic spectrum: 23 per cent in the sample in comparison with about one per cent in the UK child population (Office for National Statistics, 2005).

Using information from the adoptive parents, Table 16.1 highlights the factors that were associated with disrupted adoptive placements.

The young people who had left their adoptive families had had a worse start in life compared with those who remained "At home", and that seemed to set in motion a chain of events that ultimately led to an adoption disruption. However, there were points along the journey when perhaps that pathway could have been changed. Pre-adoption work with children and foster carers, better preparation of children, remedial action when transitions had not gone well, and early targeted interventions when difficulties first emerged seem to have been the points where a knowledgeable, non-judgemental and skilled social worker could have made a difference.

At the start of the adoptive placements, many parents also wanted to keep children at home for longer before sending them to school. This presents some difficulties for social workers. It is often very difficult to gain consent from the education authority for a delayed start and there are other concerns that children will be out of step with their peers and fall further behind in their learning. However, in some circumstances, social workers might need to make a stronger "case" for a delayed start. Strategies need to be in place to reduce sibling jealousy and rivalry in sibling placements if one child is staying at home with their mother and the other has to go to school within a few days of arriving.

Table 16.1
Significant differences between the "Left home" and "At home" groups

	Left home	At home
Child's pre-care experiences		
Neglect	*	
Sexual abuse	*	
Sexual exploitation	*	
Domestic violence	**	
Longer exposure to adversity	**	
Older at entry to care	**	
Adoption journey		
Number of moves in care	**	
Adopters not feeling prepared	**	
Introductions handled badly	**	
Foster carer supported the transition		*
Adopters' feeling that the child did not fit in from the start	**	
Adopters' belief that the child started school too soon after joining the family	**	
Difficulties emerged quickly	**	
Partner less concerned about challenging behaviours		*
Adopters feeling blamed by social workers	**	
Adopters' daily activities limited by the child's behaviours	**	
Adopters did not blame or regard the child as having responsibility for challenging behaviours		*
Child behaviours		
Relationship difficulties mainly with adoptive mother	**	
ACA measure clinical range of attachment difficulties	*	
Child did not ask questions about birth mother	*	
Child to parent violence taking place	**	
Intense sibling conflict	**	
Siblings thought by parents to be equally responsible for arguments and conflict		*
Running away (reported to police as a missing person)	**	
Serious criminal offences	**	
Drug misuse	*	

** Significant at the 0.01 level; * Significant at the 0.05 level

Young people who had experienced a disruption

Twelve young people were interviewed about their experiences of adoption disruption. Only five of the young people's parents had also been interviewed as part of the study. The young people's accounts emphasised how they felt that their voices had not been heard: some had not wanted to be adopted; others thought that they should have been removed from their adoptive families much sooner, or that they should have been allowed to make direct contact with birth family members. A few acknowledged that their behaviour had been violent and many thought that they and their adoptive families had needed support. Young people wanted to have their own independent worker, as they felt that there was a conflict of interest if the same worker was also supporting their adoptive parents.

Many of the young people acknowledged that their behavioural difficulties stemmed from their early experiences. Some young people were able to voice how attempts to "mother" them made them feel angry "like volcanoes", and left them wanting to inflict pain on their adoptive mothers. One young person had been abused by her adoptive family and it was clear that the adoptive parents had mental health issues of their own. Yet it was surprising how few young people blamed their adoptive parents for the disruption. Only three of the young people thought that they should have remained with their adoptive family and that, no matter what they had done, their adoptive parents should have stuck by them. These three young people viewed the disruption as a rejection.

Some young people complained that the boundaries imposed by their adoptive parents had been too strict and rigid and that they had kicked up against these. The young people thought that they had had to "grow up quick" because of early neglect and that they had needed a looser rein. This is an interesting area because some research has associated firm boundaries with adolescent aggression, but adoptive parents are often advised to maintain firm boundaries to make young people feel secure and keep them safe.

The lure of the birth family and the possibilities of what life might be like with another family led five of the 12 young people to trace their birth families. Renewed contact was not successful and resulted in disappointment and further rejection. Nevertheless, young people thought that it had had to be done. The psychological presence of the birth family was apparent in the interviews with young people and their adoptive parents. Some young people wanted to understand why they had been adopted and wanted much more detailed knowledge of their birth family and events. There was no obvious place for them to go, particularly as most young people found it difficult to talk to their adoptive parents. It was surprising that a "contact and questions" service was not more easily available for adolescents, and this is something that adopted teenagers would like to see developed by post-adoption services.

Adoption disruption was a time of great vulnerability and risk for the young people. Most had had a series of moves through foster and residential care, with three young people prosecuted whilst in residential care for the damage that they had done to the property or for assaulting staff. The offences were affecting their future life chances. Others had been "befriended" by adults/gangs who groomed them for their own illegal purposes.

The use of hostels and independent living for such vulnerable young people should be questioned. Young people who left their adoptive family aged 15 years or older found it very difficult to access children's services and were signposted towards housing or benefit advice. They had no entitlement to leaving care services and were financially poor, lonely and vulnerable to further abuse. The young people had received little support to continue with their education.

Social workers need to be aware that young people are especially vulnerable at the time of a disruption and that more searching questions need to be asked if young people are befriended by adults who offer accommodation. It is unacceptable for a young person who has lived in a family to be placed in a hostel at the time of a disruption.

At the time of the interview, only one of the young people had no contact with their adoptive family. Four of the young people had re-established good relationships with their adoptive parents and their future relationships looked more positive. The remainder of the young people had tenuous links, with most hoping that relationships would improve. Most wanted to re-establish relationships but not live *in* the family. Young people talked about moving to live close to their adoptive parents. Four young people wanted to return to their adoptive home but from their perspective, reunification had not and was not being planned and some of the young people said that the social workers openly blamed their adoptive parents for the disruption. From both the adoptive parents' and the young people's perspective, too little social work attention was paid to improving parent–child relationships. Disruption was viewed as the end of the adoption, although for most of the young people their adoptive parents were their best chance of having adult help and support in the future.

Interviews with managers of local authority adoption teams

Twelve managers were interviewed about the adoption support services provided by their local authority and their plans for developing the service. The structure of services differed by local authority, with some providing services in-house and others commissioning out. There were many examples in the LAs of innovative and creative support services that remained unknown outside the consortium or the LA.

Most managers already had or were hoping to develop a multi-disciplinary service, with social workers working alongside clinical and educational psychologists, occupational therapists and nurses. Some of the local authorities had developed an in-house CAMHS service for looked after and adopted children. In-house services were able to provide therapeutic interventions based on attachment theory. Teams were often co-located and CAMHS worked closely with the social work team. Dyadic developmental psychotherapy was the most popular type of training for adoption support workers and those working within the specialist CAMHS. Multi-disciplinary teams were highly rated by adoptive parents and by those who worked in them.

Managers who only had access to local CAMHS (Tier 3) reported the same kind of access and delivery problems as those reported by adoptive parents. Managers were frustrated that CAMHS did not have to provide a full service and that children's services was left to plug the gaps. The provision of therapy was particularly contentious, with health services arguing that it was a children's services funding responsibility, and children's services arguing the opposite.

Two LAs were able to provide flexible respite care using, for example, mentoring schemes and residential weekends away for young people. This area of service was under-developed in most LAs. Managers were focusing on improving websites, the quality of support plans, the transition from foster care to the adoptive family, and increasing the range of services for adolescents.

Managers complained that, although the notifications had improved, some LAs were still failing to notify when an adopted child moved into another LA area. Only one of the 13 LAs was proactive and notified other LAs when their three-year responsibility ended. Yet in one of the sample LAs, about half of the children on the caseload of the post-adoption support team were those placed into that LA by other LAs. Most managers thought that it was often children placed into their area or families who had moved into the area who had the most difficulties. It should be noted that adoptive families new to an area often have no named contact and perhaps more effort needs to be made to engage with them.

Conclusion

We began this study knowing very little about adoption disruption. To our knowledge, there had never been a funded study in the UK which focused on disruptions post-order. The disruption rate was lower than we expected, and the reasons for that became obvious when we met the families. The commitment and tenacity of adoptive parents was remarkable. Most parents, even those whose children had left home, still saw themselves as the child's parents and were supporting their children from a distance. An adoption manager, who was interviewed for this study, suggested that perhaps a revolving door approach was needed for some adopted adolescents, whereby they could spend time away from their families without it being seen as a failure. Instead, most of the families we interviewed spoke of an "all or nothing" social work approach that blamed and judged parents when relationships were just not working, and parents needed respite or young people wanted to leave. A key value[74] of social work in professional practice is compassion and respect for individuals. It is probably easier to practice if there is a clear duality of victim and abuser. Who was the victim and who was the abuser was not assessed in families where there was child to parent violence. Splits and conflicts between children's social workers and post-adoption social workers then emerged. It left adoptive parents feeling blamed, demoralised and unsupported. It was apparent that many parents had lost faith in professionals of all kinds and felt betrayed.

With more maltreated children being adopted out of care and resources pumped in to reduce delay and recruit more adopters, the support needs are easily forgotten, as they are mainly required some way down the line and services, especially for adolescents, are under-developed. Although disruption rates are low (and could be lower with better support), each one of the parents and young people who were interviewed had a story of personal tragedy and pain. It is important not to forget the hundreds of families who are "At home" managing very challenging children. The survey results estimate this group at about one-quarter of adoptive families who are parenting adolescents, and even one in five of the "Going well" group had teenage children whose SDQ scores indicated probable mental health problems. Children's histories of abuse and neglect left them with a legacy that affected their relationships as they were growing up and which the young people told us continued to affect their intimate relationships.

Adoption offers tremendous advantages and opportunities for maltreated children who cannot return home and the adoption re-forms have rightly given that opportunity to more children. Adoption

---

74 College of Social Work code of ethics – see www.tcsw.org.uk.

provides the opportunity for developmental recovery and many children do recover. There is a strong evidence base for the benefits of adoption (e.g. Donaldson Adoption Institute, 2013). However, given what we now know of the challenges and impact on adoptive parents and the pain and distress of young people who struggle to live *in* a family, the spotlight now has to be shone onto post-adoption support. Within a local authority, adoption services are usually a small service and adoption support is usually the smallest element within that. Support services are at the end of the line when resources are allocated nationally and locally. Yet the adoption reform agenda needs to consider the whole adoption journey and ensure that support services receive the same level of interest and investment as services at the front end.

RECOMMENDATIONS

Our recommendations for policy, practice and further research flow from our findings, and are set out below.

Recommendations for central government

- Draw attention to the existing guidance on the responsibility of the placing LA to notify the receiving LA when an adopted child moves to another area.
- Require receiving local authorities to send a letter to families moving into their area, introducing their adoption service, and provide regular newsletters containing contact details and information on support services.
- Support the development of an online national database of adoption support services and evidence-based practices to support adoptive families. Adoptive parents and professionals found it very difficult to know what adoption support services were available.
- Require adoption agencies to demonstrate that adopted children, as well as their adoptive parents, know about and have access to support services.
- Develop best practice guidelines in relation to life story books and later-life letters.

- Encourage the development of interventions that focus on the child–parent relationship and whole family interventions.
- Support the evaluation of the effectiveness of the youth justice system's interventions to address child to parent violence (CPV) for adoptive families in which there is CPV. Such interventions include Non Violent Resistance (NVR) and Break4Change.[75]
- Examine legislation and guidance to ensure that respite care can be provided without making the child "looked after".
- Entitle young people leaving adoptive families to leaving care services, especially support for further education.
- Promote more effectively good practice and innovation in post-adoption services, and support implementation. This could be done through established organisations such as BAAF, Research in Practice and C4EO (www.C4EO.org.uk). We saw and heard about many examples of good practice in individual local authorities, but they were not widely known.
- Require CAMHS to provide a *comprehensive* mental health service for children and adolescents. Children should not be turned away because they have symptoms that the particular local service cannot manage. If services are unable to be provided in a local CAMHS (Tiers 1–3), there should be a duty to refer in a timely way to a more specialist service or to commission the service. Tiers 1–3 have an important role to play in prevention and early intervention. Responsibilities of agencies need to be clarified, particularly when therapy is the identified need.
- Increase the coverage and availability of Tier 4 CAMHS (with an adoption specialism).

Recommendations for team and service managers

- Improve training, supervision and support needs for foster carers and family placement workers in relation to the carer's and professional's role and responsibilities for children who move from

---

75 The subject of an EU project comparing NVR and Break4Change. The UK evaluation is being led by Dr Paula Wilcox, University of Brighton.

foster care to an adoptive family. More attention needs to be paid to issues of grief and loss.

- Promote the use of evidenced interventions (e.g. Leve *et al*, 2012) designed to improve foster carer and child relationships.
- Improve training on how to identify and work with children who are avoidant and resistant to their carer's attempts to comfort them.
- Improve linking and matching practice to remove the sense of "winners" and "losers" in the process, and discourage the stretching of adoptive parents' preferences. Matching a child with adoptive parents whose expressed preferences are different to those of the child increases the risk of disruption.
- Improve support for adopted children in schools. Teachers need to be better informed about adoption and the risks of bullying, and to be more aware of the impact of activities that focus on the family and the possible impact of specific teaching on subjects such as maltreatment and attachment theory.
- Raise professional awareness of child to parent violence (CPV) in adoptive families. Social workers and other professionals working with adoptive families need training on this issue. CPV was the main reason that adoptions disrupted.
- Provide children with the opportunity to express their own views and opinions to a person independent of the worker supporting their parents when they are in conflict with their adoptive parents.
- Provide needs-led rather than service-led interventions. Too often, parents and children received what was available in-house and not what was needed.
- Ensure that there are appropriate services for children whose difficulties are on the autistic spectrum.
- Develop specialist services to be delivered by multidisciplinary teams offering a range of interventions matched to children's needs. Such services are required by the small proportion of adopted children who have very challenging behaviour and high support needs.

- Develop post-adoption services for adolescents and those parenting teenagers. High quality life story and direct work are needed for adolescents who wish to revisit the events that led up to their adoption. There is also a need for a "supported mediated contact service" for adolescents who wish to re-establish contact or simply need questions answering.

- Provide respite care in packages that meet the needs of families and without young people having to become looked after to receive the service. Suitable services might be delivered by more joint working with youth services or by commissioning services from activity-based organisations. Innovative ways of providing respite (such as the PALS and mentoring schemes offered by some of the LAs) should be promoted and extended.

- Clarify the role of the post-adoption support service. There should be an expectation that they are *always* notified of any adopted child coming to the attention of children's social workers, leaving care teams, or those working with young people in hostels or towards semi-independent living.

- It should be expected and seen as good practice that there would be joint working (post-adoption workers and children's social workers) in cases where allegations are made against adoptive family members or where child protection investigations are begun.

- Increase social workers' awareness of the vulnerabilities and risks to adopted young people at the point of disruption. Social workers need to ask more questions and be more inquisitive about motives when young people move in with unrelated adults in an unplanned way. Structures and procedures when there are concerns of sexual exploitation should be used.

- Implement the guidance (DCSF and CLG, 2010) on the provision of accommodation to homeless 16- and 17-year-old young people. This includes completing an assessment of need and providing access to independent advocacy.

Recommendations for social workers

- Identify young children who are aggressive in foster care and intervene to address the aggression. The message from research on aggression in general population samples is that most children will not "grow out of it".
- Be aware of the development and capacity of individual children with adoption plans. Social workers need to work with children's ambivalence, ensure that children understand why they cannot live with their parent, and prepare them for placement. Adoption is a process, not an outcome, and children need to be helped to understand what is happening in their life. Children stated that they did not understand what was happening to them or why they could not live with their families at the time at which they were placed for adoption.
- Provide comprehensive and explicit information to adoptive parents with truthful information about the child. Adoptive parents need to be helped to understand the information they are given, and the current *and* potential implications for them and their child in the future.
- Plan introductions and transitions around social workers' availability to support the family and when both adoptive parents can be present. Avoidable stressors should be mitigated to help promote a smooth transition. If the transition has not gone well, additional support should be planned for the parents and for the child at the start of the placement.
- Include questions about CPV in *all* assessments for post-adoption support services. Information may not be volunteered because of the shame and the stigma felt by families.
- Complete assessments of need for all families who are in difficulty. Regulations require the provision of services to prevent disruption. If the assessment of need is at the time of a disruption, the needs of the parents, other children in the household, and the young person who is leaving should be considered.
- Consider residential care when children are out of control and are a

danger to themselves and to others. There is sometimes a need to stabilise young people before therapeutic work can begin.

- Continue to work on improving child and parent relationships after a disruption. Reunification with the adoptive family should not be discounted. Even when young people are on a pathway to independence, they would benefit if a way could be found for their parents to support them, although this may be at a distance.

Recommendations for research

There are five main areas for future research:

- *Improving the quality of foster care for infants and young children.* Research on: understanding the motivations of foster carers who foster infants; their parenting styles; strategies for dealing with loss; and the impact on children's development of those strategies. Investigate the factors that lead to some foster carers having very limited physical contact with infants. Some children in this sample were removed at birth but had very poor outcomes. We therefore need to understand much more about how poor quality care may interact with genetic vulnerabilities.
- *Preparation of children for adoption.* Research is needed on understanding the stress response of children in foster care and how abnormal levels could be reduced to ensure better transitions between foster care and adoptive homes. Was the child odour that adoptive parents identified related to stress hormones or other causes?
- *Identification of aggression and child to parent violence and effective interventions.* Examine the best ways of early identification of aggression. It should be noted that neither the SDQ or ACA-SF measures measured the aggression in this sample. Evaluate the effectiveness of CPV interventions with adoptive families.
- *Cost–benefit/effectiveness analysis of different adoption support models.* Research on understanding the benefits, effectiveness and risks of commissioning external services or of providing services in-house.

- *Adoption support services for adolescents and young adults.* Research and develop practice guidance on contact services for young people who wish to renew contact or get answers to questions that trouble them. Investigate the longer-term outcomes for young adopted people as they make the transition to adulthood. Look especially at the needs of those who are not going to be able to live independently as adults; there has been little work on the needs of these young people, their families, and their transition to adult services.

References

Adoption and Foster Care Analysis and Reporting System (AFCARS) (2013) *Preliminary Estimates for FY 2012*, available at: www.acf.hhs.gov/program/cb

Barth R., Berry M., Yoshikami R., Goodfield R. and Carson M. (1988) 'Predicting adoption disruption', *Social Work*, 33, pp 227–233

Beckett C., Pinchen I. and McKeigue B. (2013) 'Permanence and "permanence": outcomes of family placements', *British Journal of Social Work*, advance access 1–18 doi 10.1093/bjsw/bsc206

Berry M. and Barth R. (1990) 'A study of disrupted adoptive placements of adolescents', *Child Welfare*, 69:3, pp 209–225

Biehal N. (2012) 'Parent abuse by young people on the edge of care: a child welfare perspective', *Social Policy and Society*, 11:2, pp 251–263

Biehal N., Ellison S., Baker C. and Sinclair I. (2010) *Belonging and Permanence: Outcomes in long-term foster care and adoption*, London: BAAF

Bjelland I., Dahl A., Taug H. and Necklemann D. (2002) 'The validity of the Hospital Anxiety and Depression Scale: an updated literature review', *Journal of Psychosomatic Research*, 52:2, pp 69–77

Bomber L. (2011) *What about Me? Inclusive strategies to support pupils with attachment difficulties make it through the school day*, Duffield: Worth Publishing

Boyne J., Denby L., Dettenring J. and Wheller W. (1984) *The Shadow of Success: A statistical analysis of outcomes of adoption of hard to place children*, Westfield, NJ: Spaulding for Children

Brodzinsky D. (2005) 'Reconceptualising openness in adoption: implications for theory, research, and practice', in Brodzinsky D. and Palacios J. (eds) *Psychological Issues in Adoption: Research and practice*, Westport, CT: Praeger, pp 145–166

Brodzinsky D. (2006) 'Family structural openness and communication openness as predictors in the adjustment of adopted children', *Adoption Quarterly*, 9, pp 1–18

Brodzinsky D. (2011) 'Children's understanding of adoption: developmental and clinical implications', *Professional Psychology: Research and practice*, 42:2, pp 200–207

Brown G. (1983) 'Accounts, meaning and causality', in Gilbert G. and Abell P. (eds) *Accounts and Action*, Aldershot: Gower

Cann A., Calhoun L., Tedeschi R., Taku K., Vishnevsky T., Triplett K. and Danhauer S. (2010) 'A short form of the Posttraumatic Growth Inventory', *Anxiety, Stress and Coping*, 23:2, pp 127–137

Carpenter J., Webb C. and Bostock L. (2013) 'The surprisingly weak evidence base for supervision: findings from a systematic review of research in child welfare practice 2000–2012', *Children and Youth Services Review*, 35, pp 1843–1853

Chief Medical Officer (2013) *Annual Report of the Chief Medical Officer 2012: Our Children Deserve Better: Prevention pays*, available at: www.gov.uk/government/uploads/system/uploads/attachment_datafile/255237/2901304_CMO_complete_low_res_accessible.pdf

Child Welfare Information Gateway (2012) *Adoption Disruption and Dissolution*, Washington, DC: US Department of Health and Human Services, Children's Bureau, available at: www.childwelfare.gov/pubs/s_disrup.cfm

Coakley J. (2005) *Finalised Adoption Disruption: A family perspective*, Doctoral dissertation, Berkeley: University of California, Berkeley

Coakley J. and Berrick J. (2008) 'Research review: in a rush to permanency: preventing adoption disruption', *Child and Family Social Work*, 13, pp 101–112

Condrey R. and Miles C. (2014) 'Adolescent to parent violence: framing and mapping a hidden problem', *Criminology and Criminal Justice*, 14:3, pp 257–275

Crawford J., Henry J., Crombie C. and Taylor E. (2001) 'Normative data for the HADS from a large non-clinical sample', *British Journal of Clinical Psychology*, 40, pp 429–434

Dance C., Ouwejan D., Beecham J. and Farmer E. (2010) *Linking and Matching: A survey of adoption agency practice in England and Wales*, London: BAAF

Department for Children, Schools and Families, and Communities and Local Government (2010) *Provision of Accommodation for 16- and 17-year-old young people who may be homeless and/or require accommodation*, London: DCSF and Communities and Local Government

Department for Education (2013a) *Children Looked After in England (Including Adoption and Care Leavers) Year Ending 31 March 2013*, statistical first release SFR 36/2013, available at: www.gov.uk

Department for Education (2013b) *Outcomes for Children Looked After by Local Authorities in England, as at 31 March 2013*, London: DfE

Department of Health (1998) LAC 98 (20) *Achieving the Right Balance*, London: Department of Health

Diener E., Emmon R., Larsen R. and Griffin S. (1985) 'The satisfaction with life scale', *Journal of Personality Assessment*, 49:1, pp 71–75

Diener E., Suh E., Lucas R. and Smith H. (1999) 'Subjective well-being: three decades of progress', *Psychological Bulletin*, 125, pp 276–302

Donaldson Adoption Institute (2013) *A Family for Life*, available at: www.adoptioninstitute.org/wordpress/wp-content/uploads/2014/01/2013_04_FamilyForLife.pdf

Dozier M., Lindhiem O., Lewis E., Bick J., Bernard K. and Peloso E. (2009) 'Effects of a foster parent training program on young children's attachment behaviours: preliminary evidence from a randomised clinical trial', *Child and Adolescent Social Work Journal*, 26, pp 321–332

English D., Graham J., Newton R., Lewis T., Thompson R., Kotch J.B. and Weisbart C. (2009) 'At-risk and maltreated children exposed to intimate partner aggression/violence: what the conflict looks like and its relationship to child outcomes', *Child Maltreatment*, 14, pp 157–171

Evan B Donaldson Adoption Institute (2004) *What's Working for Children: A policy study of adoption stability and termination*, available at: www.adoptioninstitute.org/old/publications/Disruption_Report.pdf

Evan B Donaldson Adoption Institute (2008) *Adoptive Parent Preparation Project: Meeting the mental health needs of adolescent children*, available at: www.adoptioninstitute.org/old/publications/2008_02_Parent_Preparation.pdf

Evan B Donaldson Adoption Institute (2010) *Keeping the Promise*, available at: www.adoptioninstitute.org/publications/2010_10_20_KeepingThePromise.pdf

Festinger T. (1986) *Necessary Risk: A study of adoptions and disrupted adoptive placements*, Washington, DC: Child Welfare League of America

Festinger T. (1990) 'Adoption disruption: rates and correlates', in Brodzinsky D. and Schechter M. (eds) *The Psychology of Adoption*, New York, NY: Oxford University Press, pp 201–218

Festinger T. (2002) 'After adoption: dissolution or permanence?', *Child Welfare*, 81:3, pp 515–533

Festinger T. (2014) 'Adoption disruption: rates, correlates, and service needs', in Mallon G. and Hess P. (eds) *Child Welfare for the 21st Century: A handbook of practices, policies, and programs* (2nd ed), New York, NY: Columbia University Press

Festinger T. and Maza P. (2009) 'Displacement or post-adoption placement? A research note', *Journal of Public Child Welfare*, 3, pp 275–286

Ford T., Votaries P., Meltzer H. and Goodman R. (2007) 'Psychiatric disorder among British children looked after by local authorities: comparison with children living in private households', *British Journal of Psychiatry*, 190, pp 319–325

Fratter J., Rowe J., Sapsford D. and Thoburn J. (1991) *Permanent Family Placement: A decade of experience*, London: BAAF

Gallagher E. (2004) 'Parents victimised by their children', *Australian and New Zealand Journal of Family Therapy (ANZJFT)*, 25:1, pp 1–12

Gibaud-Wallston J. (1978) 'Self-esteem and situational stress: factors related to a sense of competence in new parents', *Dissertation Abstracts International*, 39, 1-B

Gilmore L. and Cuskelly M. (2008) 'Factor structure of the parenting sense of competence scale using a normative sample', *Child: Care, Health, and Development*, 35:1, pp 48–55

Glidden L. (2000) 'Adopting children with developmental disabilities: a long-term perspective', *Family Relations*, 49:4, pp 397–405

Goerge R., Howard E., Yu D. and Radomsky S. (1997) *Adoption, Disruption, and Displacement in the Child Welfare System, 1976–94*, Chicago, IL: University of Chicago, Chapin Hall Center for Children

Goodman A. and Goodman R. (2011) 'Population mean scores predict child mental disorder rates: validating SDQ prevalence estimators in Britain', *Journal of Child Psychology and Psychiatry*, 52:9, pp 100–108

Goodman A. and Goodman R. (2012) 'Strengths and Difficulties Question-naire scores and mental health in looked after children', *British Journal of Psychiatry*, 200:5, pp 426–42

Goodman R. (1997) 'The Strengths and Difficulties Questionnaire: a research note', *Journal of Child Psychology and Psychiatry*, 38, pp 581–586

Groze V. (1996) *Successful Adoptive Families: A longitudinal study of special needs adoption*, Westport, CT: Praeger Publishers

Grusec J., Hastings R. and Mammone N. (1994) 'Parenting cognitions and relationship schemas', in Smetana J. (ed) *Beliefs about Parenting: Origins and developmental implications*, San Francisco, CA: Jossey-Bass, pp 5–19

Hannon C., Wood C. and Bazalgette L. (2010) *In Loco Parentis*, London: Demos, available at: www.demos.co.uk/files/In_Loco_Parentis_-_web.pdf? 1277484312

Hardy C., Hackett E., Murphy E., Cooper B., Ford T. and Conroy S. (2013) 'Mental health screening and early intervention: clinical research study for under 5-year-old children in care in an inner London borough', *Clinical Child Psychology Psychiatry*, doi: 10.1177/1359104513514066

Hawkins A., Beckett C., Rutter M., Castle J., Groothues C., Kreppner J., Stevens S. and Sonuga-Barke E. (2008) 'Communicative openness about adoption and interest in contact in a sample of domestic and intercountry adolescent adoptees', *Adoption Quarterly*, 10, pp 131–156

Hebert C., Kulkin H. and McClean M. (2012) 'Grief and foster parents: how do foster parents feel when a foster child leaves their home?', *Adoption & Fostering*, 37:3, pp 253–267

Holloway J. (1997) 'Outcome in placements for adoption or long-term fostering', *Archives of Disease in Childhood*, 76, pp 227–230

Holt A. (2012) 'Research in parent abuse: a critical review of methods', *Social Policy and Society*, 11, pp 298–298

Holt A. and Retford S. (2013) 'Practitioner accounts of responding to parent abuse – a case study in ad hoc delivery, perverse outcomes and a policy silence', *Child and Family Social Work*, 18, pp 365–374

Hopkins J. (2006) 'Individual psychotherapy for late adopted children: how one new attachment can facilitate another', in Kenrick J., Lindsey C. and Tollemache L. (eds) *Creating New Families: Therapeutic approaches to fostering, adoption and kinship care*, Tavistock Clinic Series, London: Karnac Book, pp 95–106

Howard J., Smith S., Zosky D. and Woodman K. (2006) 'A comparison of subsidised guardianship and child welfare adoptive families served by the Illinois adoption and guardianship preservation program', *Journal of Social Service Research*, 32:3, pp 123–134

Howe D. (1996) 'Adopters' relationships with their adopted children from adolescence to early adulthood', *Adoption & Fostering*, 20:3, pp 35–43

Howe D. (1997) 'Parent-reported problems in 211 adopted children: some risk and protective factors', *Journal of Child Psychology and Psychiatry*, 38, pp 401–412

Hudson J. (2006) 'Being adopted: psychological service for adopting families', in Golding K., Dent H., Nissim R. and Stott L. (eds) *Thinking Psychologically about Children who are Looked After and Adopted*, Chichester: Wiley, pp 222–254

Huesmann M., Lefkowitz M. and Eron L. (1984) 'Stability of aggression over time and generations', *Developmental Psychology*, 20:6, pp 1120–1134

Hughes D. (2009) *Attachment-Focused Parenting: Effective strategies to care for children*, New York, NY: Norton and Co

Hunt J. and Waterhouse S. (2012) *Understanding Family and Friends Care: The relationship between need, support and legal status*, London: Family Rights Group and Oxford University Centre for Family Law and Policy, available at: www.frg.org.uk/

Ivaldi G. (2000) *Surveying Adoption: A comprehensive analysis of local authority adoptions 1998–1999 (England)*, London: BAAF

Johnston C. and Marsh E. (1989) 'A measure of parenting satisfaction and efficacy', *Journal of Clinical Child Psychology*, 18:2, pp 167–175

Jones R., Everson-Hock E., Papaioannou D., Guillaume L., Goyder E., Chilcott J., Cooke J., Payne N., Duenas A., Sheppard L. and Swann C. (2011) 'Factors associated with outcomes for looked after children and young people: a correlates review of the literature', *Child: Care, Health and Development*, 37, pp 613–622

Joseph S. and Butler L. (2010) *Positive Change Following Adversity*, PTSD Research Quarterly, 21:3, available at: www.ptsd.va.gov

Keller A. (2009) 'Odour memories: the first sniff counts', *Current Biology*, 19, pp 21–25

Kernic M., Wolf M., Holt V., McKnight B., Huebner C. and Rivara F. (2003) 'Behavioural problems among children whose mothers are abused by an intimate partner', *Child Abuse Neglect*, 27:11, pp 1231–46

Kirk D. (1964) *Shared Fate*, London: Free Press of Glencoe, The Macmillan Company

Kohler J., Grotevant H. and McRoy R. (2002) 'Adopted adolescents' pre-occupation with adoption: impact of adoptive family dynamics', *Journal of Marriage and the Family*, 64, pp 93–104

Kotch J., Lewis T., Hussey J., English D., Thompson R., Litrownik A.J., Runyan D.K., Bangdiwala S.I, Margolis B. and Dubowitz H. (2008) 'The importance of early neglect for childhood aggression', *Pediatrics*, 121, pp 725–731

Krusemark E., Novak L., Gitelman D. and Li W. (2013) 'When the sense of smell meets emotion: anxiety-state-dependent olfactory processing and neural circuitry adaptation', *Journal of Neuroscience*, 33:39, pp 15324–15332

Laporte L., Jiang D., Pepler D. and Chamberland C. (2009) 'The relationship between adolescents' experience of family violence and dating violence', *Youth and Society*, 43:1, pp 3–27

Lazenbatt A. (2010) *The Impact of Abuse and Neglect on the Health and Mental Health of Children and Young People NSPCC Inform*, available at: www.nspcc.org.uk/Inform/research/briefings/impact_of_abuse_on_health_pdf_wdf73369.pdf

Leve L., Harold G., Chamberlain P., Landsverk J., Fisher P.A. and Vostanis P. (2012) 'Practitioner review: children in foster care – vulnerabilities and evidence-based interventions that promote resilience processes', *Journal of Child Psychology and Psychiatry*, 53, pp 1197–1211

Livingstone Smith S. (2006) 'Where are we now? A post ASFA examination of adoption disruption', *Adoption Quarterly*, 9:4, pp19–44

Lowe N., Murch M., Borkowski M., Weaver A., Beckford V. and Thomas C. (1999) *Supporting Adoption*, London: BAAF

Lupien S., McEwen B., Gunnar M. and Heim C. (2009) 'Effects of stress throughout the lifespan on the brain, behaviour and cognition', *Nature Review Neuroscience*, 10, pp 434–445

Maniadaki K., Sonuga-Burke E., and Kakouros E. (2005) 'Parents' causal attributions about attention deficit/hyperactivity disorder: the effects of child and parent sex', *Child: Care, Health, and Development*, 31, pp 331–340

Mash E. and Johnston C. (1983) 'The prediction of mothers' behaviour with their hyperactive children during play and task situations', *Child and Family Behaviour Therapy*, 5, pp 1–14

Masson J., Bailey-Harris R. and Probert R. (2008) *Principles of Family Law*, London: Sweet and Maxwell, 8, paragraph 22–009

McDonald T., Propp J. and Murphy K. (2001) 'The post-adoption experience: child, parent, and family predictors of family adjustment to adoption', *Child Welfare*, 80:1, pp 71–94

McRoy, R.G., Grotevant, H.D. and Zurcher, L.A. (1988) *Emotional Disturbance in Adopted Adolescents: Origins and development*, New York, NY: Praeger

Meltzer H., Gatward R., Corbin T., Goodman R. and Ford T. (2003) *The Mental Health of Young People Looked After by Local Authorities in England*, London: Stationery Office

Meltzer H., Gatwood R., Goodman R. and Ford T. (2000) *The Mental Health of Children and Adolescents in Great Britain*, London: Stationery Office

Minnis H., Pelosi A., Knapp M. and Dunn J. (2001) 'Mental health and foster care training,' *Archives of Disease in Childhood*, 84, pp 302–306

Neil E. (2004) 'The "Contact after adoption" Study: indirect contact and adoptive parents' communication about adoption', in Neil E. and Howe D. (eds) *Contact in Adoption and Permanent Foster Care: Research, theory and practice*, London: BAAF, pp 46–64

Office for National Statistics (2005) *The Mental Health of Children and Young People in Great Britain*, London: Palgrave Macmillan

Office of the Deputy Prime Minister (2004) *The English Indices of Deprivation 2004* (revised), available at: www.communities.gov.uk/documents/communities/pdf/131209.pdf

Omer H. (2004) *Nonviolent Resistance: A new approach to violent and self-destructive children*, Cambridge: Cambridge University Press

Omer H., Schorr-Sapir I. and Weinblatt U. (2008) 'Non-violent resistance and violence against siblings', *Journal of Family Therapy*, 30, pp 450–464

Paterson R., Luntz H., Perlesz A. and Cotton S. (2002) 'Adolescent violence towards parents: maintaining family connections when the going gets tough', *Australian and New Zealand Journal of Family Therapy*, 23:2, pp 90–100

Pavor W. and Diener E. (1993) 'Review of the satisfaction with life scale', *Journal of Personality Assessment*, 49:1, pp 71–75

Quinton D. (2012) *Rethinking Matching in Adoptions from Care: A conceptual and research review*, London: BAAF

Quinton D., Rushton A., Dance C. and Mayes D. (1998) *Joining New Families: A study of adoption and fostering in middle childhood*, Chichester: Wiley

Quinton D. and Rutter M. (1988) *Parenting Breakdown: The making and breaking of intergenerational links*, Aldershot: Avebury

Quinton D. and Selwyn J. (2007) 'Adoption: research, policy and practice', *Child and Family Law Quarterly*, 18:4, pp 459–477

Randall J. (2013) 'Failing to settle: a decade of disruptions in a voluntary adoption agency in placements made between 2001–2011', *Adoption & Fostering*, 37:2, pp 88–199

Rosenthal J. (1993) 'Outcomes of adoption of children with special needs', *The Future of Children*, 3:1, pp 77–88

Rubin D., Alessandrini E., Mandell D., Localio A. and Hadley T. (2004) 'Placement stability and mental health costs for children in foster care', *Pediatrics*, 113:5, pp 1336–1341

Rubin D., O'Reilly A., Luan X. and Localio A. (2007) 'The impact of placement stability on behavioural well-being for children in foster care', *Pediatrics*, 119:2, pp 336–344

Rushton A. (1999) *Adoption as a Placement Choice: Argument and evidence*, London: The Maudsley Hospital

Rushton A. (2003) *The Adoption of Looked After Children: A scoping review of research*, London: Social Care Institute for Excellence

Rushton A. (2004) 'A scoping and scanning review of research on the adoption of children placed from public care', *Clinical Child Psychology and Psychiatry*, 9:1, pp 89–106

Rushton A. and Dance C. (2004) 'The outcomes of later permanent placements: the adolescent years', *Adoption & Fostering*, 28:1, pp 49–58

Rushton A. and Dance C. (2006) 'The adoption of children from public care: a prospective study of outcome in adolescence', *Journal of the American Academy of Child and Adolescent Psychiatry*, 45:7, pp 878–883

Rushton A., Dance C., Quinton D. and Mayes D. (2001) *Siblings in Late Permanent Placements*, London: BAAF

Rushton A., Monck E., Upright H. and Davidson M. (2006) 'Enhancing adoptive parenting: devising promising interventions', *Child and Adolescent Mental Health*, 11:1, pp 25–31

Rustin M. (2006) 'Where do I belong?', in Kenrick J., Lindsey C. and Tollemache L. (eds) *Creating New Families*, Tavistock Clinic Series, London: Karnac Books, pp 95–106

Schmid M., Petermann F. and Fegert J. (2013) 'Trauma disorder: pros and cons of including formal criteria in the psychiatric diagnostic systems', *BMC Psychiatry*, 13:3, doi: 10.1186/1471-244X-13-3

Sellick I. and Thoburn J. (1996) *What Works in Child and Family Placement*, London: BAAF, p 67

Selwyn J., Farmer E., Meakings S. and Vaisey P. (2013) *The Poor Relations? Children and informal kinship carers speak out*, Bristol: University of Bristol, available at: www.bristol.ac.uk/hadley

Selwyn J., Frazer L. and Quinton D. (2006b) 'Paved with good intentions: the pathway to adoption and the costs of delay', *British Journal of Social Work*, 36:4, pp 561–576

Selwyn J., Frazer L. and Wrighton P. (2006c) 'More than just a letter: service user perspectives on one local authority's adoption postbox service', *Adoption & Fostering*, 30, pp 6–17

Selwyn J., Quinton D., Harris P., Nawaz S., Wijedasa D. and Wood M. (2010) *Pathways to Permanence for Minority Ethnic Children*, London: BAAF

Selwyn J., Sturgess W., Quinton D. and Baxter C. (2006a) *Costs and Outcomes of Non-Infant Adoptions*, London: BAAF

Sinclair I., Baker C., Lee J. and Gibbs I. (2007) *The Pursuit of Permanence*, London: Jessica Kingsley Publishers

Smith S., Howard J., Garnier P. and Ryan S. (2006) 'Where are we now? A post-ASFA examination of disruption', *Adoption Quarterly*, 9:4, pp 19–44

Stager S., Chassin L. and Young R. (1983) 'Determinants of self-esteem among labelled adolescents', *Social Psychology Quarterly*, 46, pp 3–10

Stoiber K. and Houghton T. (1993) 'The relationships of adolescent mothers' expectations, knowledge, and beliefs to their young children's coping behaviour', *Infant Mental Health Journal*, 14, pp 61–79

Tarren-Sweeney M. (2007) 'The Assessment Checklist for Children – ACC: a behavioural rating scale for children in foster, kinship and residential care', *Children & Youth Services Review*, 29, pp 672–691, available at: www.child psych.org.uk

Tarren-Sweeney M. (2013) 'The Assessment Checklist for Adolescents – ACA: a scale for measuring the mental health of young people in foster, kinship, residential and adoptive care,' *Children and Youth Services Review*, 35, pp 384–393

Tarren-Sweeney M. (2014) *Clinician's Guide to The Assessment Checklist Series: Specialised mental health measures for children in care*, London and New York: Routledge

Tedeschi R. and Calhoun L. (1996) 'Posttraumatic growth inventory: measuring the positive legacy of trauma', *Journal of Traumatic Stress*, 9:3, pp 455–471

Tedeschi R. and Calhoun L. (2004) 'Posttraumatic growth: a new perspective on psychotraumatology', *Psychiatric Times*, 21:4, pp 1–4

Teti D. and Gelfand D. (1991) 'Behavioural competence among mothers of infants in the first year: the mediational role of maternal self-efficacy', *Child Development*, 62, pp 918–929

Thoburn J., Norford L. and Rashid S. (2000) *Permanent Family Placement for Children of Minority Ethnic Origin*, London: Jessica Kingsley Publishers

Treacher A. and Katz I. (eds) (2000) *The Dynamics of Adoption: Social and personal perspectives*, London: Jessica Kingsley Publishers

Triseliotis J. (2002) 'Long-term foster care or adoption? The evidence examined', *Child and Family Social Work*, 7, pp 23–33

Van Andel H. and Knorth E. (2012) 'Foster Carer–Foster Child Intervention (FFI): an intervention designed to reduce stress in young children placed in a foster family', *Adoption & Fostering*, 36:2, pp 19–28

Wade J., Biehal N., Farrelly N. and Sinclair I. (2011) *Caring for Abused and Neglected Children: Making the right decisions for reunification or long-term care*, London: Jessica Kingsley Publishers

Walsh J. and Krienert J. (2007) 'Child–parent violence: an empirical analysis of offender, victim, and event characteristics in a national sample of reported incidents', *Journal of Family Violence*, 22, pp 563–574

Weiss D. and Marmar C. (1997) 'The Impact of Event Scale – revised', in Wilson J. and Keane T. (eds) *Assessing Psychological Trauma and PTSD*, New York, NY: Guilford Press, pp 399–411

Wijedasa D. and Selwyn J. (2014) *Beyond the Adoption Order An investigation of adoption disruption in Wales*, report to the Welsh Government, available at: www.wales.gov.uk/topics/health/publications/socialcare/reports/adoption/?lang=en

Wright J. (2009) 'The princess has to die: representing rupture and grief in the narrative of adoption', *Psychoanalytic Study of the Child*, 64, pp 74–91

Wrobel G., Kohler J., Grotevant H. and McRoy R. (1998) 'Factors related to patterns of information exchange between adoptive parents and children in mediated adoptions', *Journal of Applied Developmental Psychology*, 19:4, pp 641–657

Zigmond A. and Snaith R. (1983) 'The hospital anxiety and depression scale', *Acta Psychiatrica Scandinavica*, 67:6, pp 361–370

Appendix A

UK studies that report adoption disruption rates 1990–2013

+–	Country	Sample size	Method	Length of exposure to disruption (follow-up period)	Disruption definition	Pre-order disruption rate	Post-order disruption rate
Fratter et al, 1991	England	1,165	Special needs adoptions made by 24 VAAs 1980–1984. Age of children less than 3 yrs–2+ years. Survey.	18 months –6.6 years	Irrevocable breakdown before or after order.		21%
Holloway, 1997	England	129	All children wth a permanence plan in one LA 1986–1990. Review of administrative data and case records.	3–5 years	Any termination of the placement, except leaving the family after the child's 18th birthday or moving to independent living aged 16+.		2%
Quinton et al, 1998	England	61 families	Late-placed children 5–9 yrs old. Interviews with parents and social workers, measures, direct assessment of child completed by parents and teachers. Assessment one month after joining new family, at six months and one year later.	1 year	No longer living in the adoptive home.		5%

+-	Country	Sample size	Method	Length of exposure to disruption (follow-up period)	Disruption definition	Pre-order disruption rate	Post-order disruption rate
Lowe et al, 1999	UK	72% of adoption agencies	Postal survey of managers in 1994. 138 disruptions reported.		Returned to care.		6% of the 138
Thoburn et al, 2000	UK	210 special needs children placed by a VAA	Minority ethnic adopted children from the Fratter et al, 1991 sample. Case file and interviews with 38 families and 28 young people, use of standardised measures.	10–15 years		24%	
Rushton et al, 2001	England	72 families	72 families parenting 133 children. Sibling study. Face-to-face interviews with parents, social workers at three months and 12 months post-placement.	1 year	Child no longer living with adoptive family.	10%	

+-	Country	Sample size	Method	Length of exposure to disruption (follow-up period)	Disruption definition	Pre-order disruption rate	Post-order disruption rate
Selwyn et al, 2006a	England	97	97 older children (4–12 yrs) placed for adoption 1991–1996 from one LA. Case file review, measures completed by parents and teachers, and interviews with adoptive parents.	5–10 years	Child no longer living with adoptive family.	11%	6%
Rushton and Dance, 2006	England	99	Children 5–11 years old at placement. Adopters interviewed at placement, one year, and six years later.	On average six years later	Child no longer living in the adoptive home.	23%	
Biehal et al, 2010	England	97	Follow-up children aged 7–18 years. Postal survey.	7.6 years since entering care	Child no longer living in the adoptive home.	13%	
Dance et al, 2010	England	131 children	Case file review. Interviews with sub-sample of adopters and social workers.	Six months	Child no longer living with adoptive family.	5%	

+-	Country	Sample size	Method	Length of exposure to disruption (follow-up period)	Disruption definition	Pre-order disruption rate	Post-order disruption rate
Randall, 2013	England	328 children	All placements made by one VAA 2001–2011. Case file analysis of risk factors and support provided.	2–12 years	Child no longer with adoptive family.	38%	3.7%
Beckett et al, 2013	England	22 children adopted by non-relatives	Follow-up of a complete cohort of 59 children involved in care proceedings in 2004–2005 in one LA, 22 of whom were adopted. Case file study.	3–5 years	Complete termination of placement intended to be child's permanent home.	14%	

US studies that report adoption disruption rates 1990–2006

Authors	Sample size	Method	Follow-up period	Disruption definition	Pre-order disruption rate	Post-order dissolution rate
Berry and Barth, 1990	1,155 children	Out of care children aged over three years placed 1980–84. 99 children aged over 12 years. Review of case records.	7 years	Placements that end and where the family returns the child to care or ceases to assume reponsibility for the child.	24.2%	
McDonald et al, 2001	159 parents	Survey of adopted children in Kansas City.	18 months–24 months	Child not living in the home following legal finalisation.		3%
Festinger, 2002	497 children	Random sample of children adopted out of care in New York in 1996. Review of case records and telephone interviews.	4 years	Children removed from their adoptive home after legal finalisation of adoption and spent time in foster, group or other placement.		3.3%
Coakley, 2005	1,131	Children adopted through California DSS. Survey.	0–16 years	Child not living in the adoptive home following legal finalisation.		7.1%
Livingstone Smith, 2006	15,947	Children placed for adoption by Illinois 1995–2000.	7–13 years	Children who were either not living in the adoptive home or where the placement had been re-designated as a foster home. First disruption considered.	9.5%	

Appendix B

Measures

Assessment Checklist for Adolescents short form (Tarren-Sweeney 2007, 2014). www.childpsych.org.uk The ACA was designed to measure a range of mental health difficulties observed among children in care and for those subsequently adopted from care that are not adequately measured by standard rating instruments, such as the Child Behaviour Checklist (CBCL), the Strengths and Difficulties Questionnaire (SDQ) and the Conners scales. These difficulties consist of a number of attachment-related difficulties (indiscriminate, non-reciprocal and pseudo-mature types), insecure relating, trauma-related anxiety, abnormal responses to pain, over-eating and related food maintenance behaviours, sexual behaviour problems, self-injury and suicidal behaviours. The short form (37 items) used in this study excludes items related to self-esteem and suicidal behaviours. The following description of the ACA is adapted from Tarren-Sweeney, 2014.

Sub-scale I: Non-reciprocal behaviours covers emotionally withdrawn, avoidant, and non-reciprocal social behaviours, with high scores being suggestive of a severely avoidant–insecure attachment style and/or the inhibited form of reactive attachment disorder. *The items are: does not show affection; hides feelings; refuses to talk; resists being comforted when hurt; seems alone in the world (not connected to people or places); withdrawn.*

Sub-scale II: Social instability covers a combination of unstable, attachment-associated difficulties in social relatedness and behavioural disregulation, including pseudo-mature and indiscriminate social

Measures used in the study

Three groups of adoptive parents: 1) Going well with no major difficulties; 2) Challenging at home; 3) Left home and disrupted.

Adult completed measures

Construct	Name of measure	Author	Focus	Adopter group
Happiness and subjective well-being	Satisfaction with life scale	Diener et al, 1985	Broad satisfaction with five areas of life	ALL
Health	Hospital anxiety and depression scale (HADS)	Zigmond and Snaith, 1983	Screen for depression and anxiety	ALL
	Impact of event scale – revised	Weiss and Marmar, 1997	Screening tool for PTSD	3 only
	Post-traumatic growth scale	Tedeschi and Calhoun, 2004	Positive change following adversity	3 only
	Parenting sense of competence	Gibaud-Wallston, 1978	Parenting self-efficacy and satisfaction	ALL
Children's emotional and behavioural difficulties – parent completed	Strengths and Difficulties Questionnaire (SDQ)	Goodman, 1997	Screening: emotional, conduct, hyperactivity, peer problems and pro-social behaviours.	ALL
	ACA short form (4–17 years)	Tarren-Sweeney, 2014	Difficulties more associated with care populations, e.g. dissociation/ trauma symptoms, food maintenance behaviour, sexual behaviour.	ALL

relating. *The items are: craves affection; impulsive (acts rashly, without thinking); precocious (talks or behaves like an adult); prefers to be with adults rather than peers; prefers to mix with older youths; relates to strangers as if they were family; too friendly with strangers; tries too hard to please other young people.*

Sub-scale III: Emotional disregulation/distorted social cognition covers a pattern of highly dysregulated emotion and affective instability, coupled with distorted social cognition (negative attributions, paranoid beliefs). *The items are: says friends are against him/her; starts easily ("jumpy"); can't get scary thoughts or images out of his/her head (not due to watching a scary movie); extreme reactions to losing a friend, or being excluded; intense reaction to criticism; says his/her life is not worth living; uncontrollable rage.*

Sub-scale IV: Dissociation/trauma symptoms measures a pattern of trauma-related dissociation and anxiety symptoms. *The items are: appears dazed, "spaced out" (like in a trance); can't tell if an experience is real or a dream; feels like things, people or events aren't real; has panic attacks; has periods of amnesia (e.g. has no memory of what happened in the last hour); hits head, head-banging.*

Sub-scale V: Food maintenance syndrome measures a pattern of excessive eating and food acquisition that appears to be primarily triggered by acute stress. *The items are: eats secretly (e.g. in the middle of the night); eats too much; gorges food; hides or stores food; steals food.*

Sub-scale VI: Sexual behaviour measures age-inappropriate sexual behaviour. *The items are: forces or pressures other youth or children into sexual acts; inappropriately shows genitals to others (in person or through video or photo); seems overly preoccupied with sex (e.g. crude sexual talk, inappropriate sexual comments); sexual behaviour not appropriate for age; tries to involve others in sexual behaviour.*

Hospital Anxiety and Depression Scale (HADS) (Zigmond and Snaith, 1983): 14 items. The HADS is an adult measure with 14 items that ask a person to reflect on their mood in the past week. Seven items assess depression, five of which are markers for anhedonia (an inability to experience pleasure), and two concern appearance and feelings of slowing down. Seven items assess anxiety, of which two assess autonomic anxiety (panic and butterflies in the stomach), and the remaining five assess tension and restlessness. Bjelland and colleagues' review (2002) reported that 8/9 for both anxiety and depression scales represented the optimal cutting point and 11/12 indicates severe. A major attraction of the HADS is that it was designed for use with clinical populations, so it excludes items that might reflect physical illness.

Impact of event scale–revised (IES-R) (Weiss and Marmar, 1997): 22 items. The IES-R is an adult self-report measure of current subjective distress in response to a specific traumatic event. The 22-item scale is comprised of three sub-scales representative of the major symptom clusters of post-traumatic stress: intrusion, avoidance, and hyper-arousal. The intrusion sub-scale includes eight items related to intrusive thoughts, nightmares, intrusive feelings, and imagery associated with the traumatic event. The avoidance sub-scale includes eight items related to avoidance of feelings, situations and ideas. The hyper-arousal sub-scale includes six items related to difficulty concentrating, anger, and irritability, psychophysiological arousal upon exposure to reminders, and hyper-vigilance.

Parenting sense of competence (Gibaud-Wallston, 1978): 17 items. The PSOC was developed to measure two aspects of competence in parents of infants: skill/knowledge and value/comforting. Johnston and Marsh (1989) translated the scale for parents of children ages four to nine years and validated it using a normative sample of mothers and fathers, renaming the two factors of competence as Efficacy and Satisfaction. Gilmore and Cuskelly (2008) have provided further evidence of validity and an additional factor of "Interest" using a larger normative sample with parents of infants and children under the age of 18 years. The measure was used by Rushton and colleagues

(2006) in their RCT of enhancing adoptive parenting and is currently used by the Post-Adoption Centre in London in the initial assessment of families they work with.

Revised post-traumatic growth inventory short form (Tedeschi and Calhoun, 2004): 10 items. Post-traumatic growth is a wide-ranging concept, still in development; but to date, three broad domains of positive change have been noted throughout the literature. First, relationships are enhanced in some way, e.g. people describe that they come to value their friends and family more and feel an increased sense of compassion for others and a longing for more intimate relationships. Second, people change their views of themselves in some way, e.g. that they have a greater sense of personal resilience, wisdom and strength, perhaps coupled with a greater acceptance of their vulnerabilities and limitations. Third, people describe changes in their life philosophy, e.g. finding a fresh appreciation for each new day and re-evaluating their understanding of what really matters in life. Post-traumatic growth occurs in the context of suffering and significant psychological struggle. For most people, post-traumatic growth and distress will coexist, and the growth emerges from the struggle with coping, not from the trauma itself. Second, trauma is not necessary for growth. Individuals can mature and develop in meaningful ways without experiencing tragedy or trauma. Although a majority of individuals experiencing a wide array of highly challenging life circumstances experience post-traumatic growth, there are also a significant number of people who experience little or no growth in their struggle with trauma. The most widely used measure is the Post-Traumatic Growth Inventory (PTGI), and to reduce the burden on adopters, we selected the short form of the measure (Cann *et al*, 2010).

Satisfaction With Life Scale (SWLS) (Diener *et al*, 1985): five items (http://internal.psychology.illinois.edu/~ediener/SWLS.html) The SWLS is a short five-item instrument designed to measure global cognitive judgements of satisfaction with one's life. It is one of the most widely used instruments for assessing life satisfaction in both research and clinical settings (Pavor and Diener, 1993). A version is available for children aged 10 years and over.

The Strengths and Difficulties Questionnaire (Goodman, 1997): 25 items. The SDQ is a brief behavioural screening questionnaire about 3–17-year-olds. It has 25 items divided into five scales: 1) emotions; 2) conduct; 3) hyperactivity/inattention; 4) peer relationship problems; and 5) pro-social behaviour. Further information can be found at www.sdqinfo.com.

Index

adopters on 223–7
shortcomings 171–80
structure 307–13
websites 316–17
Locate model, for support 314
looked after children (LAC) 11–12,
20–9
loss
adopted children on 6
adopters on 83, 236–8, 345
in disruption 212, 231
foster carers on 90–1, 346–7
illness and death 134–5
love for the children 228–9
low mood
of adopters 235
in PTSD 264, 265
young children 117–18
loyalty, difficulties 277

major difficulties group 62–5
managers of adoption teams
disruption identification 12
interviews 18, 336, 361–2
on support 307–34
surveys 30
manipulative behaviour 102, 104,
115–16, 131–2
sibling relationships 143–5
marital relationships 146–8
marital status, of adopters 71–2
matching
process 83–4
recommendations 366
support plans 324–6
medical information
in matching 324
missing 96–7
medical professionals
support from 191–2
see also Child and Adolescent
Mental Health Service
(CAMHS); Great Ormond
Street Hospital

memories
of birth families 156–7, 161
odour in 106
memory books 90
mental health
adopted children 60–1, 62–4
abused children 344
in adolescence 349–50
disruption precipitation 198,
199
SDQ findings 248, 249–50
support lack 171–3
adoptive parents 234–6, 276
birth mothers 80
birth parents 349
mental health services 182–7
see also Child and Adolescent
Mental Health Service
(CAMHS)
mentoring schemes 318, 322–4, 331
minority ethnic adopters 71
minority ethnic children 3, 22
mood, low
see low mood
motivation, of adopters 72–5
multi-disciplinary service, for
support 361–2

neglected children 23, 80–1, 351
non-reciprocal behaviours, ACA
scores 253, 254, 255, 388
Non-Violent Resistance (NVR) 310,
352
nursery, settling into 107–8

odour, of children 105–7
operational recommendations
365–7
oppositional behaviour 127–9, 199,
280
out of area placements 171–2,
311–13

parental responsibility 9–10